Understanding race and crime

CRIME AND JUSTICE
Series editor: Mike Maguire
Cardiff University

Crime and Justice is a series of short introductory texts on central topics in criminology. The books in this series are written for students by internationally renowned authors. Each book tackles a key area within criminology, providing a concise and up-to-date overview of the principal concepts, theories, methods and findings relating to the area. Taken as a whole, the *Crime and Justice* series will cover all the core components of an undergraduate criminology course.

Understanding race and crime

Colin Webster

Open University Press

Open University Press
McGraw-Hill Education
McGraw-Hill House
Shoppenhangers Road
Maidenhead
Berkshire
England
SL6 2QL

email: enquiries@openup.co.uk
world wide web: www.openup.co.uk

and Two Penn Plaza, New York, NY 10121-2289, USA

First published 2007

A catalogue record of this book is available from the British Library

ISBN-10 0 335 20477 5 (pb) 0 335 20478 3 (hb)
ISBN-13 978 0 335 20477 9 (pb) 978 0 335 20478 6 (hb)

Library of Congress Cataloging-in-Publication Data
CIP data applied for

Typeset by RefineCatch Limited, Bungay, Suffolk
Printed in Poland by OZ Graf S.A.
www.polskabook.pl

The **McGraw·Hill** Companies

Contents

Series editor's foreword

Colin Webster's book, the latest in Open University Press' *Crime and Justice* series, tackles the complex and sensitive subject of 'race and crime' in a clear, forthright manner. His book admirably reflects the aim of the series, which has been to produce short but intellectually challenging introductory texts in key areas of criminological debate, in order to give undergraduates and graduates both a solid grounding in the relevant area and a taste to explore it further. Although aimed primarily at students new to the field, and written as far as possible in plain language, the books are not oversimplified. On the contrary, the authors set out to 'stretch' readers and to encourage them to approach criminological knowledge and theory in a critical and questioning frame of mind.

Webster's book discusses core aspects of the 'race and crime' debate, which has emerged in criminology in a variety of guises over the years. A central focus is on gaining a sociological understanding of the dual processes of 'criminalisation' and 'racialisation' and the relationships between them – in other words, social processes which construct and label certain groups and assign them negative attributes such as 'criminality' or 'inferiority'. The two processes can easily become intertwined in what are essentially racist discourses, he argues, to the extent that even without the explicit use of a crime-related term, phrases such as 'black youth' are used to signify 'criminality', and vice versa terms like 'crime' and 'riot' become racially loaded. The early chapters explore relevant discourses both in a historical context (especially in relation to the 'scientific' racism found in early criminological writing) and in relation to current concerns about insecurity and 'fear of crime', which are often overtly or implicitly racialised.

A further key element of Webster's argument is that, while it is important to analyse statistical patterns of both crime and victimization in terms of ethnicity, key debates about, for example, the apparently disproportionate involvement of young black men in crime, cannot hope to be resolved without a close examination and understanding of the very different and highly specific *contexts* in which various kinds of incident occur. This requires not just statistical analysis, but careful qualitative research and in-depth case studies, aimed at understanding how human choices and actions in particular situations are shaped by, on the one hand, broad social structural and cultural constraints (including racial discrimination and social injustice in the wider society, and cultural reactions to it) and, on the other, features of the immediate context. He illustrates this through a number of case studies, including one on street robbery. Later in the book, his focus widens to major socio-cultural issues and their relationship to crime, including the development of cultures among marginalised groups in which various forms of 'masculinity' become highly valued, as well as the continuing heated debates in the United States about the claimed existence of a separate, largely African-American 'underclass' inhabiting black urban 'ghettos'.

Another significant proportion of the book is devoted to debates about race and the criminal justice system, especially questions and evidence relating to whether visible minorities are treated differently by the police and courts. This includes a case study of the Stephen Lawrence murder and investigation. Finally, there is an important chapter on racist state crime, and specifically genocide, a topic which has been surprisingly (and unjustifiably) neglected by criminologists.

Despite the ambitious scope of the book, the author has managed to tackle all the major topics without grossly over-simplifying arguments or 'skating over' key evidence. He has also, in my view, successfully achieved the difficult balance between the standard 'textbook' approach of summarizing previous literature in a way helpful to readers new to the subject, and conveying his own strongly held views and distinctive approach.

Other books previously published in the *Crime and Justice* series – all of whose titles begin with the word 'Understanding' – have covered criminological theory (Sandra Walklate), justice and penal theory (Barbara Hudson), crime data and statistics (Clive Coleman and Jenny Moynihan), youth and crime (Sheila Brown), crime prevention (Gordon Hughes), violent crime (Stephen Jones), community penalties (Peter Raynor and Maurice Vanstone), white collar crime (Hazel Croall), risk in criminal justice (Hazel Kemshall), social control (Martin Innes), psychology and crime (James McGuire), victims and restorative justice (James Dignan), drugs, alcohol and crime (Trevor Bennett and Katy Holloway), public attitudes to criminal justice (Julian Roberts and Mike Hough), desistance from crime (Stephen Farrell and Adam Calverley), prisons (Andrew Coyle) and political violence (Vincenzo Ruggiero). One (Walklate) is already in its third edition, four are in second editions, and other second editions are in preparation. Other new books in the pipeline include texts on modernization and criminal justice, criminological research methods, 'cybercrime', and policing. All are topics which are either already widely taught or are growing in prominence in university degree courses on crime and criminal justice, and each book should make an ideal foundation text for a relevant module. As an aid to understanding, clear summaries are provided at regular intervals. In addition, to help students expand their knowledge, recommendations for further reading are given at the end of each chapter.

Mike Maguire
February 2007

Acknowledgements

I dedicate this book to the memory of my late father Bill Webster and those of his generation who helped defeat Nazism. I thank Ena Faal for her belief and support over the years. Yusuf Ahmad and Karim Murji were influential in me being commissioned to write this book. Fabbeh Husein's partner Teresa tolerated our endless conversations about 'race'. Les Johnston and then Mark Simpson as heads of criminology at the University of Teesside offered unfailing support, mostly by not asking whether I'd finished the book. I'm indebted to Rob MacDonald at Teesside University whose professional and intellectual encouragement, mentorship and friendship gave me the confidence to 'keep it real'. Another debt is owed to Ben Bowling who helped instigate my belated academic career and has generously supported my race and crime interests since. The University of Teesside and its School of Social Sciences provided some sabbaticals in which I read and thought a great deal and wrote little. Between the Pina Colada and other seemingly more pressing research tasks, the writing of this book got squeezed out. This is where I thank my Open University Press editors Justin Vaughn then Chris Cudmore for their infinite patience in supporting this long overdue book. My series editor Mike Maguire has been a true gentleman and scholar. Finally, I acknowledge my relatively recently gained criminology colleagues at Leeds Metropolitan University who had no truck with the notion of me not delivering a book I said I would when they employed me.

chapter one

Conceptualising 'race' and crime: racialisation and criminalisation

Biological and cultural racism
Race and ethnicity
Criminalisation and racialisation
The problem of 'racism'
Race relations and situational racism
Focusing on white ethnicity and perpetrators
The importance of context
Structure, themes and purposes of the book
Further reading

Biological and cultural racism

The terms 'race' and 'crime' probably already sit quite easily (or uneasily) together in the reader's mind, if not as a natural association, then at least as an understandable one. This book is about the different ways in which this association has prevailed in some of the thinking, attitudes and activities found in modern societies towards the problem of crime and the issue of race. Talking about race and crime in the same breath invites a number of pitfalls. The most glaring of these is that the notion of 'race' does not have any scientific validity. Classifying or distinguishing humans by the races to which they are said to belong is completely arbitrary because all human groups have a common biological ancestry (Cavalli-Sforza 2001; Olson 2002). It is not possible to argue on current evidence that the distinctive behaviours of a group have a biological origin. Most of the groups to which we belong have nothing to do with biology and everything to do with culture (Rose *et al.* 1984; Montagu 1997; Diamond 1999; Jones 2000; Lewontin 2000). Of course, groups are distinctive in appearance and these distinguishing features are used socially to sort people into categories according to the colour of their skin or the shape of their eyes. Any propensity to interpret these differences in biological terms and draw conclusions about their ancestry is the root of racism. Further, not only are these physical categories deemed to constitute different races, they are often said to be of a different 'quality' from one another, so that some are inferior while others are superior. The immense consequences that ensue from this social activity are described in this book.

Some writers argue that there has been a shift in the ways people think about race, from the belief that race is grounded in biology to the belief that race is based in cultural difference or descent. For example, some people believe that it is 'natural' that people will want to live among 'their own kind' (Barker 1981; Goldberg 1993; Solomos and Back 1996). Cultural or 'new racism' is distinctive to the contemporary period in which 'manifestations of race are coded in a language which aims to circumvent accusations of racism. In the case of new racism, race is coded as culture' (Solomos and Back 1996: 19). Whether racial groups are taken to be constituted through biology or culture, what is common to racism is that it promotes persistent exclusion or actually excludes people from entitlements by virtue of their being deemed members of different racial groups. In ascribing supposed racial characteristics to individuals said to belong to a group different from their own, racists 'explain' racial differences as natural, inevitable and therefore unchangeable. These characteristics are then evaluated negatively to justify unequal treatment of the defined group (Goldberg 1993; Cashmore 1996). Such beliefs can become embodied in social practices and institutions, including those that are concerned with the problem of crime.

Race and ethnicity

Just as race is often confused with culture, so it is often confused with ethnicity, so that race, culture and ethnicity are used interchangeably. In its benign sense 'ethnicity' refers to a group possessing some degree of coherence and solidarity based on an awareness of common origins and interests. However, ethnic groups can be seen by their members or by others as homogeneous, self-perpetuating, defensive and unchanging, and many groups who organise themselves, or are described by others, as an ethnic group are often regarded as a 'race' (Cashmore 1996). Similar to cultural difference, ethnic difference can become a coded way of talking and thinking about race.

Whether coded or not, some people continue to believe in the existence of races, while the explicit promotion of racism in public speech and actions is usually considered socially unacceptable and as promoting racial hatred, and in some jurisdictions is illegal. Because of such censure racists aim to circumvent accusations of racism, usually through declaring themselves 'victims' of the presence of vilified groups. As Chapter 5 shows, violent racists rationalise their behaviour by inverting the meaning of racism so as to accuse their real victims of racism, thus enabling themselves to be seen as the victims. Most racists believe that they have been victimised in some way, as can be observed at different points in this book.

Criminalisation and racialisation

The key conceptual framework that informs much of this book relies on an understanding of processes of 'criminalisation' and 'racialisation' and their relationship. Criminalisation refers to the process whereby some groups receive more attention from, and are more likely to come into contact with, the police and the criminal justice system because of some imputed or ascribed characteristic of criminality. Racialisation refers to those instances where social relations between people have been structured by attributing meaning to biological and/or cultural characteristics, as a result of which individuals may be assigned to a social group – a general category of persons – which is said to reproduce itself biologically and/or culturally (Miles and Brown 2003). This process defines and then confines and constructs different groups, usually through assigning negatively evaluated attributes such as 'criminality' or 'inferiority'. For example, when criminalisation and racialisation work together, 'the couplet *Black youth* can be employed in racist discourse to signify *criminality*' (Keith 1993: 234), and then terms like 'crime' and 'riot' become racially loaded. Racialisation and criminalisation are socially constructed through processes of interaction between groups and can be embodied in institutional practices.

The problem of 'racism'

The term 'racism' is often used in discussions of crime and criminal justice to refer to different and discriminatory treatment of individuals and groups by the police and criminal justice system on grounds of their supposed racial background. The term will appear many times in this book, but a note of caution needs to be sounded from the beginning about how racism is understood. Some writers have used the concept of racism to refer to all beliefs, actions and institutional processes that discriminate against and subordinate 'black' or 'Asian' people. There are a number of well-known problems with this all-encompassing unitary definition. According to Miles and Brown (2003), this concept of racism can ignore social class and gender divisions and conflict within both the 'white' and 'black' populations;

it *assumes* what should be demonstrated in every particular instance (white racism); it ignores intentional or explicit expressions of racism as indicators of the presence or absence of racism, which is a particular problem when allegations of racism in institutions are made; it limits the range of historical instances of racism, for example, racism against Jewish, Irish, Gypsies and other racialised groups such as the 'unfit' and 'criminals'; it suggests that racism is the prerogative of 'white' people, seen as a homogeneous and totally dominant group, and as a necessary consequence of what white people do to black people and those from other minority ethnic groups; it obscures the complexities and distinctions between belief and action, the intended and unintended consequences of action. For example, police officers may hold racist views but this does not necessarily mean that they will act on those beliefs in their operational duties. Finally, it implies that 'white' people lack the capacity to understand, analyse and explain racism. Overall, as Miles and Brown (2003: 80) argue,

> systematic comparative analysis is essential: it is necessary to demonstrate that 'black' people collectively are treated in a certain manner or experience a particular disadvantage, and that the same treatment and disadvantage are not experienced by any other group.

The book follows this injunction as far as is possible.

Having sounded this note of caution, racism can and does promote exclusion or actually exclude people from material and other resources, from public space and from justice, by marking out, creating and maintaining different distinct bounded groups. The expression of racism is a response to varying material and cultural circumstances over time and in different contexts. It has many dimensions and is historically and spatially specific. Racism in its 'pure', omnipresent and isolated form is relatively rare and usually involves territorial exclusion, 'ethnic cleansing' or even extermination (Bauman 1989). Those who express racism and those who are its victims are located in and interact with wider social relations and ideologies such as existing economic and political relations. For example, race and racism as ideologies can mask other forms of power such as social class. The problem of racism requires the simultaneous explanation of a particular instance of exclusion and its relationship with a multiplicity of other forms of exclusion. For example, studies, whether of disproportionate offending and victimisation or of discrimination by the police and criminal justice system, invariably compare white and black and minority ethnic groups to discover differences in treatment, but this in itself tells us very little unless we take into account other factors such as social class, demography, area, gender, family, school and employment processes. In many cases these other factors may override or cancel out the influence of race or ethnicity. In other instances the influence of race or ethnicity may be present among all these other factors. This book does not begin from the position of an *a priori* theory of racism which then seeks instances of racism to support the theory. Neither does it rule out the possibility that racism is likely to be an important influence on some social, including criminal and justice, processes.

Race relations and situational racism

This book employs two different conceptual approaches to understanding race and crime (see Rex and Mason 1986; Gilroy 1987; Miles 1993; Banton 1997; Back and Solomos 2000). The race or ethnic relations approach explores group consciousness of difference and group conflict, whereas the racism approach explores racism and racialisation as an ideology masking social exclusion and having many instances and causes. There are few reasons why these two approaches should not be combined. Although race or ethnic relations usually involve behaviour that is at least in part racially or ethnically motivated, the approach does not presume from the outset that racism is *necessarily* present. To be sure, when individuals define someone as belonging in a racial or ethnic category other than their own, this usually involves regarding that person as having rights and obligations different from those of a person belonging to the same racial or ethnic category as themselves, to discriminate against and exclude them. A key and often ignored dimension of race or ethnic relations, however, emphasised in this book, is that this relationship changes and is dynamic. Whenever individuals or groups define others as belonging to a different race or ethnicity from themselves, they implicitly or explicitly define themselves as belonging to a race or ethnicity also. Each group becomes dependent on the other for its identity, and changes in the situation, power or status of one group influence the position of the other. Often this giving and taking of identity is denied when majority groups define minority groups as belonging to races or ethnicities.

Deploying these approaches, understanding race and crime requires attention to the changing interaction and conflict between minority and majority communities in areas such as family, schooling, employment, housing and other social contexts, as well as policing, crime and criminal justice, the implication being to study factors that influence, usually negatively, this interaction – in particular, certain structural conditions encouraging race relations situations and problems; frontier or boundary situations of conflict over scarce resources; occupational and residential segregation; different access to power and prestige; cultural diversity and limited group interaction; and migrant or minority groups as an underclass fulfilling low-waged roles in urban labour markets.

Solomos and Back (1996) have added a third integrated approach, which they call a 'situational model of racism'. This model attempts to account for processes which involve the attribution of specific meanings to racial situations, contextualises racism within the specific conditions and instances of its enunciation, and connects these local manifestations of racism with wider or national public discourses and policies. In particular, the authors argue (1996: 20–1) that 'The local context has important effects resulting in complex outcomes where particular racisms may be muted while others flourish'.

Focusing on white ethnicity and perpetrators

In focusing on sole scrutiny of minority victims, perpetrators and communities, studies of race and crime have tended to ignore white communities and 'whiteness' as an ethnicity (Phillips and Bowling 2003). As already mentioned, it cannot be assumed that all racism and discrimination is perpetrated by whites on blacks or other minorities. Neither is the existence of some significant minority crime a myth, although the belief that a lot of crime is perpetrated by minorities on whites is a myth. Racisms involve social relationships that impact on the 'white majority' too, and the ways in which 'whiteness' and white racism come to be constructed are as important as the construction of minority identity in understanding race, crime and culture (see, for example, Dyer 1997; Taylor 2005).

Understanding white as well as minority perspectives on race and the racialised situations groups construct and are victimised by, brings in factors such as class and gender as complicating factors influencing these situations, crime, victimisation and criminal justice. For example, the expression of different sorts of racism is often rooted in different class experiences, levels and positions – found in the 'subordinate racism' or 'rough racism' of the street in contrast with 'respectable' or institutional racism (Cohen 1988).

The importance of context

The distinct perspective and argument of this book is that contexts of racialisation and criminalisation processes have for too long been ignored or have remained unknown. A quantitative survey approach has tended to dominate the race and crime debate in ways that can hide rather than reveal social processes, at the expense of drawing on closer-up, qualitative studies of actual groups and situations. The dominance of this approach may in part explain the inconsistent and contradictory findings and difficulty of drawing final conclusions from this kind of data. The debate has been further hindered by relying solely on somewhat parochial national data and debate rather than a more international perspective, and this perspective is a thread throughout the book.

The importance of context can be illustrated in a number of ways. Offenders are sometimes treated equally, but other times they are not, according to context. Race, crime and criminal justice outcomes may be influenced by the intersection of the type of crime and the place of its commission, the age, gender and 'race' of the offender, and the 'race' of the victim (Spohn 2000). These interaction effects between different factors may cancel out any direct or even indirect effects of race because these other factors or characteristics may be more important in actions and decisions. According to Walker *et al.* (2004), blacks as a group do not receive harsher sentences than whites, but those blacks who are unemployed and living in Chicago receive longer sentences than their white counterparts, as do unemployed Hispanics. If generally applied, this points to indirect rather than direct discrimination in the sentencing process because African-Americans as a group are disproportionately working-class, unemployed and living in hypersegregated areas making them less able to raise bail money or mount a defence – differences that result from economic or social disparities that attach to race (Smith and Natalier 2005).

Structure, themes and purposes of the book

Having dispensed with the preliminaries of conceptualising race and crime, the discussion now turns to the substantive areas covered in this book. Some of these areas have conventionally (and inexplicably) been neglected or ignored by the criminological literature about race and crime. For example, extralegal and extrajudicial killing and lynching as ways of terrorising and controlling African-Americans, as well as forming the historical basis of contemporary judicial executions, have mostly been ignored in discussions of racist violence and in the formation of the popular punitiveness of the American justice system. The book attempts to fill in other gaps such as the perpetration of racist state crime, which, like state crimes in general, has hardly been addressed within criminology (but see Morrison 2006).

In following a sociological as well as criminological approach (see Holdaway 1997) it is hoped to capture complex relationships between the respective roles of individual agency, intention and choice on the one hand, and cultural and social structural constraints on social action on the other, while recognising that human choices and constraints on these vary according to situations and context (see Hopkins Burke 2005). In freeing up and wanting to widen understanding of race and crime, this requires identifying not only, for example, injustices of racial discrimination in the criminal justice system, but also that these injustices are linked to wider social injustice. Indeed, as Cook (2006) argues, criminal justice is a 'two-way street' in which criminal and social justice are closely linked – that you cannot have one without the other.

Race and criminality are first associated in the founding work of criminology itself in the nineteenth and early twentieth centuries, as Chapter 2 shows. Early criminology both informed and was informed by a thinly veiled ideology of 'scientific' racism, which argued that some individuals and populations were biologically inferior. This methodological legacy – shorn of its more racist connotations – remains today in continued attempts to measure and compare the physical, psychological and cultural attributes of criminal and non-criminal populations so as to identify a distinct 'criminal type'. These origins of applied criminology directly resulted in the compulsory sterilisation and detention – and in the case of Nazi Germany, the mass elimination and murder – of the 'unfit' and the 'criminal', for the purpose of improving the 'racial qualities' of future generations.

Chapter 3 provides a context to the fear of crime, a fear that can be exacerbated in socially constructed 'racial situations'. This is illustrated across a contrasting range of places. Essentially, this chapter argues that general social anxieties and insecurities, and growing ethnic diversity arising from social, economic and cultural change, are often interpreted through the misty lens of neighbourhood-based nostalgic narratives of decline that induce among residents specifically racialised fears of crime.

Chapter 4 describes contrasting majority and minority crime and victim patterns across a range of societies, but focusing on Britain and the United States. Consistent with the book's argument that studies lack context, the chapter reviews an in-depth case study of street robbery to evaluate the claim that young black men are disproportionately involved in such crimes, as well as the thesis that among some minorities crime rates increase across generations. Finally, the chapter tackles the issue of why some visible minority ethnic groups appear to suffer disproportionate rates of crime as victims and offenders compared to their numbers in the population, and other minority groups do not.

Chapter 5 begins with a case study of the racist murder of Stephen Lawrence and the inquiry into the failed police handling of the murder investigation. This inquiry changed the ways in which racist violence was policed and dealt with by the law, with considerable consequences for patterns and trends in racist violence. How we might understand the underlying reasons for violence found in changing race relations in local and national contexts is explored alongside the motivations of perpetrators and relationships between perpetrator and victim groups.

Alleged different contact, conflict and treatment between the police and some visible minority groups are considered in the context of a more general adversarial policing of powerless and marginalised groups. Chapter 6 addresses the debate between those who argue that visible minorities are given inferior treatment by the police and those who argue that the existence of extensive police racism is exaggerated and that police racism and stereotyping have little impact in terms of the way in which officers go about their duties. Still others argue that disproportionate police attention devoted to some minority (and other) groups simply reflects their higher rate of offending. The chapter also focuses on one of the police's core functions, to maintain public order, and the particular resonance this has had in situations involving minority–police relations and disorders.

Chapter 7 examines whether different outcomes for visible minorities in the criminal justice process are the result of different types and rates of offending between ethnic groups or racial discrimination in the criminal justice system. Some writers have argued that once the different offending characteristics of individuals are taken into account, any different treatment on grounds of racial characteristics alone disappears and that all are equal before the law. Other studies have remained agnostic on whether different treatment on grounds of race or ethnicity is present or not because of the difficulty of measuring or modelling criminal justice processes and decision-making in the 'real' world, while yet other studies have argued that a residue of racial bias against minority defendants is present at all stages of the criminal justice process, from prosecution, conviction, sentence and remand to type of court disposal. It is argued that the life contexts of those brought before the criminal justice system are the most important explanation of criminal justice processes and outcomes, rather than these processes and outcomes in themselves.

Chapter 8 takes this argument further by examining the wider sociological issues that underpin processes of criminalisation and racialisation, and the encouragement or discouragement of delinquency and criminality. By focusing on working-class and minority youth transitions and social exclusion in family, care, neighbourhood, schooling and training, leisure and employment contexts, and the influence such transitions may have in generating risks of offending, this chapter also asks whether the development of certain sorts of masculinity encourage or mute anti-social and offending behaviour among marginalised groups.

The discussion in Chapter 9 questions the claimed existence of a separate crime-ridden African-American underclass inhabiting American black urban ghettos, long characterised as responsible for a catastrophic explosion of crime, joblessness, single-parent families and welfare dependency in inner-city areas. Accused of being disconnected from and culturally and behaviourally different from mainstream American society and values, the isolated and segregated African-American underclass is shown to be far more integrated into mainstream American values than previous studies allowed. Indeed, it is the pursuit of such values embodied in the 'American Dream' that can drive criminality and create hostility and resentment towards the African-American underclass.

Following on from earlier comments that criminology has mostly ignored state crimes in general, and racist state crimes in particular, Chapter 10, through focusing on the crime of genocide, redresses this omission in criminological research and discussion. The description and analysis of the historical, social and political processes, eventually leading to genocide in Nazi Germany and Rwanda, emphasise the different roles, motivations and relationships of perpetrators, victims and bystanders in mass murder. Contrary to popular belief, the pattern, logic and act of genocide are not the expression of incomprehensible, abhorrent irrationality on the part of perpetrators but can be understood as a conscious, evolving, political policy and strategy promoted by political elites to create a 'purified' racial utopia.

Further reading

Instead of tackling the race and crime debate directly, as is more usual in other accounts, the first three chapters of this book first furnish a conceptual, historical and contextual framework in which the debate might be more fruitfully begun. Consistently critical and interesting work on the concept of 'racism' is provided by Miles and Brown (2003). This somewhat structural and analytical approach can be balanced with the work of Solomos and Back (1996), who argue that racism should be understood as more specific and contingent in terms of conditions that give rise to racist expression, thought and action. Because racism is relational – it defines the self-identity of racists as well as the 'other' – attention should be paid to the ethnicity and ideology of 'whiteness'. Taylor (2005) offers a history of the formation of 'whiteness' as an ideology. A good example of how racialisation and criminalisation processes work together is Keith's (1993) work on race, policing and disorder. Finally, and consistent with the ethos of the book, Cook's (2006) marrying of criminal justice concerns with concerns about social exclusion and social justice provides a good indirect grounding for understanding race and crime.

chapter two

Origins: criminology, eugenics and 'the criminal type'

A transformation in how 'race' is thought about?

If, as Gilroy (2000: 11) observes, we are living through a 'profound transformation' in the way the idea of 'race' is understood and acted upon – how racial differences are seen and prompt identities – then we need to discover the historical legacy from where this transformation took place. Precisely because a long-term historic decline in race thinking, racial hierarchies and racial subordination has occurred, we might expect to see the continuation of race thinking in more unexpected ways. Gilroy (2000: 22) cites the examples of the apparently benign use of racial types in consumer advertising to represent 'exotic' style, or a transgressive stance, or the ideal of physical prowess, or even prestige, while the historic associations of race with crime 'remain undisturbed'. Meanwhile we have already seen how the emergence of a contemporary emphasis on cultural difference and the ethnic assigning of culture, so that 'ethnicity' supersedes crude appeals to 'race', has undermined the credibility of the idea of race. If, as Gilroy (2000) claims, the certainties of 'race' have receded in the contemporary period, then why, despite this apparent discrediting of the idea, does the association of race with crime linger on in all its residual, discriminatory and different forms? The answer may, at least in part, lie in popular and criminological legacies of how we think about 'criminals' and 'criminal populations'. These legacies assumed that social deviants in general, and criminals in particular, were biologically and culturally inferior to 'normal' populations, and that their inferiority was *visible* in their physical appearance. Arguably, although perhaps less explicitly than in the past, comportment, body shape, dress and physical looks continue to have popular salience in stigmatising groups, especially the poor and the criminal 'underclass', often in racialised ways (*Economist* 2006).

This chapter retraces and recaptures the sort of race thinking found in the linked intellectual traditions of scientific racism, criminal anthropology, biological criminology and eugenics. These ideas reached the zenith of their popularity from 1900 to 1930, were implemented through 'welfare', population and penal policies in a number of countries, most radically in National Socialist Germany between 1933 and 1945, and lingered into the 1970s in Scandinavia. Although mostly discredited today, these ideas, it is suggested, continue to insinuate themselves into popular and occasionally academic thinking about crime and criminality. For example, such ideas saw a popular resurgence in the 1990s, particularly in America (see Herrnstein and Murray 1994), which is a stark reminder of the continued popularity of biological thinking about human behaviour displaced into concerns about criminality. Starting with criminal anthropology, the chapter shows how the study of crime and criminality mapped race onto criminality from its beginnings. Criminality was seen as inherited and immutable and the 'born' criminal was an inferior biological type to 'normal' populations. The emergence of eugenics as a biosocial population policy insinuated itself into crime and penal policy as well as targeting social deviants, the 'unfit' and the mentally ill.

The beginnings of race and crime thinking in criminal anthropology

The early 'scientific' study of crime is exemplified in the writings of one of criminology's founders, Cesare Lombroso (1835–1909). Building on concepts widely held by nineteenth-century scientists, Lombroso's was the first seemingly coherent criminological theory based on empirical data and was subsequently highly influential, particularly on American criminology and the American eugenics movement (Rafter 1997; Gibson 2002; Black 2003; Becker and Wetzell 2006). In *Criminal Man* (first published in 1876) and *Criminal Woman* (1893), Lombroso argued that races could be hierarchically ranked and that inferior races are marked by their asymmetrical physical features and inferior intellect, but Lombroso's innovation was to equate white criminals with non-white races (see Lombroso 2004, 2006). On this account criminals were primitive throwbacks on the evolutionary scale and European criminals exhibited physical and psychological features that he believed were anomalies for the white race but normal for lower, less civilised races. He was the first criminologist to extend physical measurement to the criminal's entire body to distinguish normality from deviancy in the belief that external physical features – of skull, nose and ear shape, among a litany of physical 'anomalies' and 'stigmata' – reflected internal moral states and moral worth (Lombroso and Ferrero 2004). According to Lombroso, criminals were destined to crime by bad biological heredity. This theory of the born criminal attempted to demonstrate that criminals inherited physical imperfections and abnormalities – the 'stigmata of degeneration' that both signify and prove their primitive natures. Drawing on popular conceptions that character could be read from facial (and racial) features, these conceptions were rendered scientifically respectable, and laid the foundations for the idea that individuals and populations are criminal in their looks, including their 'racial' looks. Here 'race' and criminality are confused in the notion of criminals as 'a race apart'.

The criminal type

Although the physical study of the criminal, popular among early twentieth-century criminologists, sought psychological, cultural and social, as well as physical criteria to distinguish normality from deviancy, the non-criminal from the criminal, this effort was analogous to attempts by scientific racism to distinguish 'races' because the 'criminal type' was determined by hereditary and physiological circumstances. Organic or physical abnormalities were complemented by social abnormalities. An early nineteenth-century statistician of crime patterns, Quetelet, juxtaposed the 'typical criminal' (young, male, poor, and with little education) and the 'average man' (law-abiding, with rational and temperate habits, more regulated passions, having foresight, in good physical and psychological health, standing for the mainstream of civilisation, and representing the type of the nation in which he was found) (Morrison 1995). This accruing of moral statistics about the poor, the deviant and the dubious, their moral classification, was to go hand in hand with new forms of governance and control of these populations (Corrigan and Sayer 1985).

The British eugenicist Francis Galton (1822–1911) developed these ideas by arguing that hereditary qualities such as 'intelligence' could be specified across the whole population and followed the law of normal distribution, represented graphically by a bell-shaped curve, so that the majority of the population clustered around the 'average' or 'norm' for any particular quality or characteristic and the two tails, containing fewer individuals, represented the extremes (deviations from the norm). In this schema the lower classes, criminals, paupers and the unemployed held a social position that by and large reflected their natural attributes (in this case low intelligence).

Emergence of eugenic ideas in Britain

Galton defined eugenics as 'the science of improving stock'. Eugenics posed the problem of racial decline, which it saw as due to different rates of reproduction achieved by different sectors of the population, specifically contrasting the abundant fertility of the 'unfit' (criminals, alcoholics, imbeciles, etc.) with a lower birth rate of the better classes. In wanting to improve the physical and mental 'racial qualities' of future generations, eugenicists argued for a policy of intervention in the process of population reproduction – forced sterilisation – which in effect targeted and aimed at reducing the fertility of the lower classes, the physically and mentally 'unfit', the criminal, the degenerate and a whole panoply of individuals and populations considered socially undesirable (Garland 1985). Criminological theories linked a rag-bag amalgam of categories of the 'unfit' and 'defective' through chains of inference and reasoning by analogy, arguing that all could be commonly treated in ways that criminality could be treated. These 'included mental, moral and physical defectives . . . the criminal, the pauper, the idiot and the imbecile, the lunatic, the drunkard, the deformed and the diseased . . . [all of whom] are prolific and transmit their fatal taints' (Chapple 1904, cited in Garland 1985: 147–8). Or again, Rentoul (1903: 17–18, cited in Garland 1985: 148) proposed sterilising those suffering from 'leprosy, cancer, epilepsy, idiots, imbeciles, cretins, weak-minded under restraint, lunatics . . . prostitutes . . . mental degenerates . . . the sexual degenerate . . . confirmed tramps and vagrants, characters well known to workhouse officials and to the police . . . confirmed criminals'. The essence of degeneracy was almost always known by its outward taint or blemish – its physical manifestation. As Garland (1985) observed, criminological texts at the turn of the last century, in linking disparate themes and categories of the 'unfit', most commonly drew together criminality, degeneracy, the nation and 'the race' in an open appeal to the concerns about racial deterioration which were widespread in Edwardian Britain. Arguably, the underlying agenda was political as well as racial. For many commentators at the time, especially eugenicists, the threat and social crisis posed by the recent enfranchisement of working-class men (and later, women), and the problem of order which this enfranchisement was supposed to address but which could trigger 'disorder' (demands for socialism), were seen as a crisis of racial deterioration.

In general, commentaries at the time referred to the problem of 'increasingly disproportionate progeny' of the 'unfit', who threatened to 'swamp our civilisation', reduce 'national intelligence', national efficiency and the survival of the Empire and its imperial race. In particular, commentators railed against 'degenerate families', the abundant 'fertility of the unfit', their lack of sexual inhibition and social responsibility, and the 'racial productivity' of the habitual criminal. This overlapping of criminology and eugenics in their shared view of criminality and degeneracy as an innate essence manifested by physicalism, created overlapping target populations – the habitual criminal, the inebriate, the feeble-minded and the defective – and the 'unfit' were equated with the progeny of the criminal. For some eugenicists, the penal system was itself a eugenic apparatus to prevent reproduction. Finally, Garland (1985: 178) argues that both criminology and penal policy opened up respectable 'routes of advance for the eugenic programme'. Despite various attempts, however, to insinuate negative eugenics (forced sterilisation, as opposed to 'positive eugenics' or the 'selection of successes for breeding') into English legislation such as the 1914 Mental Deficiency Act and the new Poor Law, these met with little success. Even criminological studies of 'degenerate and criminal families' found less favour in Britain than in the United States. Eugenics was consistently opposed by Conservatives, who resisted many forms of state intervention, and by Catholics on moral grounds asserting the sanctity of life, and eugenicist programmes were rarely acceptable when presented in explicit terms. As a consequence, forced sterilisation was never introduced in Britain (Jones 1980; Barkan 1992; King 1999). The English campaign to legalize sterilisation continued until 1934 before petering out, by which time the Nazis had implemented their own eugenic sterilisation regime. In this sense it is important to realise that the eugenics movement was more a 'campaign' which ebbed and flowed than a fully fledged, state-endorsed, social and biological programme. Throughout the period of its ascendancy, and even when implemented, it was surrounded by controversy and opposition. Also, it is important to remember that not all eugenicists believed in the existence of 'races' as biological groups. Some eugenicists saw biological inheritance as an individual 'handicap' within families. In this sense there are grounds for arguing that eugenics, at least in its more benign forms, was the precursor to modern genetics (Black 2003).

Applied eugenics in America

Eugenic ideas may have originated in Britain (with Galton) but applied eugenics began in America, and Americanised eugenics influenced the emerging programmes in other countries, including Britain. Indeed, it was the British eugenicist Rentoul who most explicitly fixed on the notion of 'race suicide' in the context of America's supposed 'race problem', by arguing that the 'solution' to America's sacrificing of its 'high mental qualities' was to 'sterilize the negro' (cited by Black 2003: 208–9). But American eugenics had a much broader view, even though the conditions that favoured the successful implementation of negative eugenics were probably that America was a much more racialised society than Britain at the time (Kuhl 1994). It was in America that most eugenicist ideas first coalesced – from the use of IQ tests to justify incarceration of the so-called 'feeble-minded' to the enactment of mandatory sterilization laws in at least 30 states (Bruinius 2006). Ultimately, well over 65,000 Americans were coercively sterilised, and eventually America's eugenic movement spread to Germany, where it was said that 'National Socialism is nothing but applied biology' (Kuhl 1994; Black 2003; Bruinius 2006). If Indiana implemented the first sterilisation law in 1907, in the next two decades the United States became the pioneer in state-sanctioned programmes to rid society of the 'unfit', and became the model for laws in Canada, Norway, Sweden, Denmark, Finland, France and Germany. In 1933, one of the first acts of the newly elected National Socialist Party was to enact a comprehensive sterilisation law modelled consciously on American legislation.

This story of applied eugenics, then, is not uniquely American, but it began there, as in Britain, with statistical warnings about the growing numbers of paupers and criminals said to pose a grave threat within society; in the United States concern was expressed also about the growing numbers of 'unfit' foreign immigrant races that were said to threaten civilisation from without. In effect, the American eugenics movement created a large 'eugenic underclass', simply labelled 'the unfit', which was to be 'cleansed', and of course the category 'the unfit' always included criminal behaviour and most of the forcibly sterilised were ill-educated and poor. As scientists struggled to trace and then eradicate the supposed gene pool that caused what they referred to as 'the three Ds' – dependency, delinquency, and (mental) deficiency – in America eugenics began to go out of fashion by the late 1930s, and in England, as already mentioned, no sterilisation laws were enacted. Finally, as knowledge emerged after 1945 about the Nazi eugenics programme, American eugenics virtually ceased as a respectable or plausible idea. Although the idea was to resurface from time to time, attention shifted to the long-standing concern with miscegenation – a eugenic concern spoken of using a less explicit eugenicist language. After all, eugenicists believed that society must take control of human reproduction and ethnic intermingling.

The overlap between eugenics and criminology seen in Britain was greater in America, and lasted longer. Eugenic ideas spawned criminological research into 'criminal insanity' and 'genetic criminality', perhaps best exemplified by studies of the descendants of supposedly criminal families. Early examples of these studies were 'The tribe of Ishmael: a study in social degeneration' (McCulloch 1988, cited in Black 2003), *The Jukes* (Dugdale 1910) and *The Kallikak Family: A Study in the Heredity of Feeblemindedness* (Goddard 1927), all claiming to have discovered family lineages of congenitally nomadic criminals, vagabonds, prostitutes and paupers (Vold *et al.* 2002; Hopkins Burke 2005). These studies purported to show that criminality was passed down through inherited genes, 'proving' that criminal families tended to produce criminal children, and that criminals were born, not made. In Britain, Goring's famous study of male prisoners in London arrived at similar conclusions using a different method (Goring 1913, cited by Muncie 2004: 87). Other studies were to follow from the 1930s to the 1950s. Although less explicitly racist and conceding some intergenerational environmental influences on continued criminality within families, these studies were still concerned to identify and isolate the key physiological and hereditary characteristics of known criminals (see Muncie 2004; Vold *et al.* 2002). More recent studies in this tradition are assessed towards the end of this chapter.

Eugenics in National Socialist Germany

The scale, viciousness and virulence of the National Socialist state's eugenics programme implemented from 1933 to 1945 was incomparably worse than that of any other country and is still popularly much less known about than the Nazi extermination of the Jews. But as writers such as Burleigh (1994) and Friedlander (1995) have shown, Nazi Germany's eugenics and 'euthanasia' programmes laid the foundations of rationale, method, experience and practice for the subsequent Nazi genocide of the Jews and other 'racial enemies'.

According to Burleigh (2000), the Nazi state sterilised about 400,000 people in a decade, and deliberately murdered about 200,000 people in the wartime 'euthanasia' programme. By the time the Third Reich was over, the total number compulsorily sterilised had reached over 360,000, almost all of them before the outbreak of war in September 1939 (Evans 2005: 508). One of the first things the National Socialist government did on winning power was introduce the Law for the Prevention of Hereditarily Diseased Progeny [Offspring], by prescribed compulsory sterilisation, in July 1933. The Law against Compulsive Criminality was passed in November 1933, enabling preventive detention without trial and castration for habitual criminals. Again, eugenics was seen to overlap with criminology and penal policy in Nazi thinking about their target populations. Interior Minister Wilhelm Frick announced that the new regime was going to concentrate public spending on 'racially sound and healthy people', and reduce expenditure on 'inferior and asocial individuals, the sick, the mentally deficient, the insane, cripples and criminals' (cited in Evans 2005: 507). In 1934 alone, the first year of operation of the Diseased Progeny Law, the new Hereditary Health Courts, consisting of a judge, a public health doctor and another medical 'expert', acting on referrals from public health officers, care institutions and social workers, received over 84,500 applications for sterilisation (Evans 2005: 508). Under the sterilisation law, patients in institutions constituted 30–40 per cent of those sterilised, and the 'feeble-minded' (of supposedly very low IQ) in the wider community made up 60 per cent of those sterilised. Other categories beyond the asylums, ranging from those deemed to have hereditary illnesses to the asocial and criminals, were hunted down by official criminal and health records, medical officials, social workers and the police. The reasons given for sterilisation were frequently concerned more with social deviance than with any demonstrably hereditary condition. Proctor (1988: 205) noted the role of medical experts and the implications of the eugenics programme:

> By the late 1930s, German medical science had constructed an elaborate world view equating mental infirmity, moral depravity, criminality, and racial impurity. This complex of identifications was then used to justify the destruction of the Jews on medical, moral, criminological, and anthropological grounds. To be Jewish was to be both sick and criminal; Nazi medical science and policy united to help 'solve' this problem.

Indeed, the battle against the unfit and deviant began to reach its nadir in 'medicalised mass murder', begun in 1939. The overall trend was 'to remove entire groups of people, from the protection normally afforded by the rule of law, with the asylums following the concentration camps into an extra-legal limbo' (Burleigh 2000: 398). An operation, known by its codename 'Action T4', to decimate the adult asylum population began at the same time as the children's 'euthanasia' programme. Up to 6000 children were killed and, having reached their projected target of 70,000 adult victims, the T4 perpetrators were told by Hitler to halt the mass gassing of mental patients and to change the killing method to more concealed, discrete approaches – starvation and lethal medication – as there was 'popular disquiet' (Burleigh 2000: 402).

This fateful step from forced sterilisation to so-called 'euthanasia' was presaged from the beginning of National Socialist rule in 1933 when virtually all Nazi commentators drew a distinction between preventing the future creation of 'life unworthy of living' through sterilisation and the deliberate destruction of existing lives through 'euthanasia'. The latter was simply too controversial to be attempted in peacetime and, like the genocide, was later conducted in secret under the cover of war. These so-called 'mercy killings' never enjoyed legal sanction and constituted mass murder even in terms of the laws of the Third Reich. These murderous ideas, however, were not restricted to the coming of the Third Reich in Germany as earlier soundings had been aired about reducing welfare costs in the care of 'cripples and idiots'. Eugenic or racial hygiene policy under the Nazis (in its guise of 'euthanasia') was predicated on the idea – discussed long before the Nazi rise to power – of the destruction of 'lives not worth living', and of 'useless eaters'. Since the 1890s racial hygienists (eugenicists) had been campaigning to put the 'improvement of the race' at the centre of social policy concerns and targeted those whom they identified as 'weak, idle, criminal, degenerate and insane for elimination from the chain of heredity' (Evans 2005: 506). These and similar ideas were internationally influential just as German racial hygienists looked to the United States for their ideas.

As in other countries, the ideological foundations were already laid by the 1920s, in concerns about population growth for maintaining national strength and the links between 'racial fitness' and national efficiency (Proctor 1988). In Germany, however, the eugenics movement overlapped with the 'Nordic supremacy' movement, which was explicitly racist and nationalist, and it was this right wing of the racial hygiene movement that was ultimately incorporated into the Nazi medical apparatus (Proctor 1988). Here the nationalist and utopian roots of the movement were wanting somehow to restore Germany to 'racial purity' by removing the 'weakest' to increase its strength, and retrieve all ethnic Germans into a new Greater Germany, ultimately by means of an expulsionist population policy and war (Weindling 1989; Aly 1999; Burleigh 2000; Kershaw 2000a; Evans 2003). These racist political peculiarities, however, were complimented by the central place of biology in Nazi ideology, arguing that the genetics or 'acquired characteristics' of particular individuals, races and race mixtures were inherited and immutable. Hereditary or 'race' was transmitted from generation to generation uninfluenced by the environment or socialisation. Although this claimed primacy of race and biology over class, culture and economy remained contentious throughout the period of Nazi rule, German biomedical scientists, academics and doctors largely supported racial hygienic ideas and policies.

The role of criminology and penal policy in Nazi eugenics programmes and policies can be seen in a number of ways. First, despite the rhetoric or rationalisation provided by terms like 'applied biology', in reality, much forced sterilisation was targeted at social groups, and not, as the Nazis claimed, 'biological' categories having supposed serious hereditary illness. Sterilisation appeared principally as a punishment or a measure of social control of members of 'the underclass, beggars, prostitutes, vagrants, people who did not want to work, graduates of orphanages and reform schools, the slum and the street' (Evans 2005: 510) as well as 'habitual criminals'. Of course, sterilisation did nothing to correct the behaviour of existing 'anti-social' families, and there were many local and regional 'initiatives' against the 'anti-social' as a group. Debates were had over who were to be included in the list of those to be sterilised, on grounds that it was difficult to separate hereditarily determined criminality from ordinary environmentally conditioned deviance. In the event it was somewhat academic because 'habitual criminals' were now under the new rules: they were to be incarcerated for life and therefore could not reproduce. By 1938, Himmler's police apparatus launched a series of massive nationwide raids against the 'anti-social', resulting in the 'preventative arrest and detention' (without legal process) in concentration camps (previously reserved for political opponents and career criminals) of 10,000 individuals, again eliding the 'anti-social' with the 'criminal'.

Second, the public had to be persuaded through eugenicist propaganda which contrasted the deviant offspring of alcoholics and prostitutes with the norms expected of 'decent national comrades' (Johnson 1999; Gellately 2001). And what better way of persuading the public of the rightness of Nazi welfare and penal policy than to criminalise 'race' and racialise 'crime'? Films persistently elided the sick with the criminal; in the latter case sex offenders, murderers and racial caricatures of 'Jews' invariably featured heavily. Indeed, criminal biology was to forge a link in the medical solution to 'the Jewish question' (Proctor 1988: 202–5).

Third, legislators and administrators, influenced by criminal biology, began to assign so-called Gypsies (Romany, Sinti, Lalleri) to the criminal classes. Increasingly subject to police harassment and the increasingly close set of regulations governing them, the majority of Gypsies had criminal records 'which simply confirmed law enforcement agencies in their view that they were hereditarily disposed to criminality' (Lewy 2000; Evans 2005: 525). If there was a certain ambiguity in Nazi circles before 1938 about the racial and criminal providence of 'Gypsies' there was none about African-Germans – the so-called 'Rhineland bastards', and the children were sterilised in 1937, almost certainly on the basis of Hitler's authority alone. Next on the list of 'racial minorities' were homosexual men, 50,000 of whom were arrested, two-thirds of whom were convicted and sent to prison (although homosexuality was criminalised in many other countries as well).

Fourth, one of the leading research efforts of Germany's racial hygiene institutes was twin studies (for example, studies of identical twins raised apart) and the heritability of criminality (Wetzell 2000). Criminal biology was given a new urgency under the Nazis to discover early signs in the detection of criminal behaviour before the actual onset of the criminal career (although Lombroso was rarely cited by Nazi criminal biologists, probably because of his Jewish ancestry). Concerns on the part of criminal biologists were close in many ways to those of racial hygienists because the former argued that crime is both genetically determined and racially specific, and criminals were said to be reproducing at a faster rate than the non-criminal population. This was reflected in an accelerated interest in criminal biology throughout the Nazi period, which contributed to the belief that Jews were racially disposed to commit certain forms of crime. Nazi medical authorities followed this lead and conspired in the 'solution of the Jewish question' by arguing that if Jews were racially disposed to commit crime, they were so disposed to suffer from a host of other 'diseases'. Under the Nuremberg Laws of 1935, however, the Jews in particular came to occupy a special place in Nazi ideology, not as merely social ballast to be removed by imprisonment, or by removal from the chain of heredity, but as *racial enemies*. The regime was about to enter an altogether different phase of its racial policies. The discussion of this phase begins in Chapter 10.

The legacy of biological criminology and eugenics

In critically assessing the legacy described above, care is needed not to fall into the trap of condemning all subsequent and continuing biological criminology tradition after 1945 simply through 'guilt by association' with racism and Nazism. For example, twin and adoption studies continue, aimed at isolating 'a genetic factor' in criminality, but they must be judged on a scientific basis in their own terms. Just because twin studies were a major research interest under Nazi scientific racism, this does not mean that post-war and recent studies are implicated in or motivated by racism. For example, one of the best recent studies (Mednick *et al.* 1987, cited in Muncie 2004) concluded that certain factors *are* transmitted by convicted parents to increase the likelihood that their children – even after adoption – will be convicted for criminal offences. Exactly *what* is inherited remains unknown. There is not the space here to examine the detailed problems of such studies, but they are not ones of racism, and with these and other sorts of biological criminology studies mostly lay elsewhere (see Muncie 2004). Instead I will focus on traditions and studies that might be considered to belong to a racist criminological framework – surprisingly so, given the legacy described above. It is also noted here that although we live in more subtle times, the tendency to believe that outward appearance reveals inner characteristics continues in many forms of popular culture, and can become racialised (Dyer 1997).

Whatever the efficacy of studies that purport to show the extent to which biological differences explain differences in human behaviour, and particularly in criminal behaviour (from theories which suggest that criminals are imbalanced in their diet, chromosomes, neurotransmitters, hormones or nervous system to those which emphasise inherited general intelligence) – and this author for one is extremely sceptical – importantly these studies are about *individual* level differences. Very few studies claim that biological inheritance and/or biochemical effects that might determine, influence or predict human behaviour are the property of social or racial *groups*. In some cases though, biocriminology, even in overtly racist forms, continues today, where the 'born criminal' is often code for the defiant, the poor, and the black. For example, the best-selling social science book of the 1990s, Herrnstein and Murray's (1994) *The Bell Curve*, claimed that American blacks and Latinos inherit low intelligence, that intelligence differs by racial group, and that low intelligence predicts criminality. Meanwhile, criminal anthropological work continues in Canada and the United States, notably in Rushton's (1997) study *Race, Evolution, and Behavior*. Again, these claims are unusual in that studies of a correlation between low IQ and delinquency unusually refer to differences in 'intelligence' between individuals *within* groups, not *between* groups. This is particularly puzzling when in a different context Wilson and Herrnstein (1985) in their book *Crime and Human Nature*, for example, argued that biology should be considered as one element within explanations that should otherwise rely on many factors. Some people carry with them the potential to be violent or anti-social and that environmental conditions can sometimes trigger anti-social responses. Sociobiologists view biology, environment and learning as mutually interacting and dependent factors. Overall, most studies that evoke biological factors that may generate a predisposition towards making criminal decisions, argue that this occurs only when they interact with certain other psychological, social or environmental factors.

Herrnstein and Murray (1994), however, argued that differences in average intelligence are found between racial and class groups and that IQ predicts criminality between these race and class groups. This gives rise to the intergenerational transmission of a 'culture of poverty' based on the inheritance of innate ability which is different between blacks and other groups. Conceding some environmental influences on poor blacks, and some convergence between a new black middle class and whites in terms of their cognitive abilities, poverty and its associated problems, including crime, are explained primarily in terms of the lower cognitive ability of the poor compared to other groups. In particular, inherited intelligence is on average lower among blacks than whites and other ethnic groups, with clear implications for different rates of criminality between blacks and whites. These views about innate racial or ethnic differences are clearly aimed at the African-American underclass. The authors go on to argue that high-IQ people are shrinking as a proportion of the population as low-IQ people have more children and have them at younger ages. The result is that American society is both 'dumbing down' and becoming polarised into two very different groups. In conceding that environmental factors may influence behaviour, they go on to recommend some policy prescriptions such as reconstituting the traditional family, an end to 'state-subsidised' births that inadvertently encourage inappropriate births, especially among poor women, and the adoption of children out of a bad environment into a good one at birth to raise IQ (Herrnstein and Murray 1994: 410–13, 415–16). These claims are assessed in the next section.

Criticisms of biological criminology and eugenics

Biological criminology began as an attempt to morally judge and classify different populations as 'good', 'bad' and 'ugly' based on popular conceptions that criminals not only act differently but also look different from the 'normal population'. Biological and anthropological criminology's theoretical and methodological errors are legion (see Gould 1996). First, whether physique, appearance or intelligence is being measured, these studies find statistical associations (correlations) of factors, not that any one factor causes another. Second, measures around the average hide wide variation within and overlap across populations, and may not be true of individuals. Therefore, it is arbitrary to use these average values to distinguish between populations. This is the basis of Herrnstein and Murray's (1994) fallacy in asserting that average differences in IQ between American whites and blacks are largely inherited. Human populations are highly variable for all behaviours. Third, biologically inheritability is an individual phenomenon, not a group one. In any case, why should the violent behaviour of some desperate and discouraged individuals point to a specific disorder of their biology, brain or inheritance? Fourth, body type is influenced by social factors, including the adequacy and type of nutrition, extent of manual labour and social class position. Fifth, to posit the hereditability of criminality is to forget that such a specific behaviour as criminality cannot be genetically transmitted because it is a legally and socially defined construct. Sixth, we do not inherit behaviour, height or intelligence as such, as *fixed* capacities at birth; rather, we do inherit a *capacity* for interaction with particular environments, so that *any* biochemical preparedness for *some* behaviour may or may not be triggered. In any case, it is practically impossible to control for environmental and social influences and thus to be able to measure precisely the exact influence of a genetic effect. We certainly do not know when and how external environmental effects on the body trigger genes. Finally, studies that compare criminals and non-criminals are misleading because the former are only representative of a highly selected subset of those apprehended, charged and convicted. Biology has virtually nothing to tell us, so far, other than in very minor ways, about human consciousness or what it is to be human, never mind criminal!

Much of Herrnstein and Murray's (1994) argument rests on a belief that IQ actually measures intelligence using a single measure or number rather than what is culturally and linguistically learnt; that intelligence can be hierarchically ranked; and that it is genetically based and effectively immutable. These general claims and premises in effect reward learnt knowledge about the language and mores of the dominant culture and penalise subordinate cultures for their lack of experience or knowledge of the dominant culture. Moreover, there is plentiful evidence that these premises do not hold. For example, Thurston's (1947) discovery of multiple intelligences concluded that we are better at some things than others. Similarly, Gardner (1993: 4–8) argued that the ways in which different competencies and abilities are judged are highly culturally variable, and that there exist several relatively autonomous and irreducible human intellectual competences. The crucial fallacy, however, as already mentioned, consists in assuming that if heredity explains variation among individuals within a group (white Americans), it must also explain variation in average IQ between groups (whites and blacks). But group and individual differences are entirely separate phenomena. One result offers no basis to speculate about the other. Even if IQ were highly inheritable within groups, the average difference between whites and blacks in America might still only record the environmental disadvantage of blacks (see Fischer *et al.* 1996; Devlin *et al.* 1997).

Understanding the origins of race and crime in criminology and eugenics

Much of the discussion in this chapter points to the question whether the modern discipline of criminology is 'still in the grip of positivist vision' (Morrison 2006: 48). Starting in the nineteenth century, criminology became engrossed in two complimentary and convergent traditions – the statistical analysis of populations brought to bear upon crime and criminal justice, and the emergence of a positivist, specialist 'science of the criminal'. Garland (2002: 16) has argued that criminology was structured around these two basic projects – 'the governmental and Lombrosian', the former an 'administrative task', the latter a 'theoretical project' – and that they were mutually supportive. Concerns with the 'social question' and the 'problem' of the poor (fears of disorder) merged with the 'racial question' and the 'problem' of racial decline through fears about the fecundity and progeny of the poor and the criminal. Complimenting these concerns was (Garland 2002: 21):

> Another line of inquiry which flourished in this period, and whose advocates would later be seen as progenitors of criminology, centred not upon the population and its governance by a well-ordered state, but instead upon individuals and their ability (or lack of ability) to govern themselves.

All these elements congealed into the very stuff of criminology's concerns, and 'the underlying theme animating all of these studies was a concern with governance and the use of empirical data and scientific methods to improve government's grip on the population' (Garland 2002: 24). The idea of a specialist, independent, distinctive criminological science emerged centred on the figure of the 'criminal type'. Eventually, this pseudo-scientific movement applied its ideas by targeting certain individuals and groups – racially defined – for the prevention, treatment and elimination of the 'unfit' and criminal. At odds with the classicist 'egalitarian' legal principles which had previously underpinned criminal justice processes, the conception of the hereditary criminal type chimed with deep-rooted cultural and racist prejudices of the time and offered scientific respectability to middle-class perceptions of the 'criminal classes' (Garland 2002: 27). Criminology's origin and legacy in race thinking and its influence on race policy should remind us that knowledge about criminality and the ongoing attempts today to identify and differentiate criminals from non-criminals should carry with them a warning from history about the dangers of binary thinking – 'us' and 'them'.

Further reading

The historical development and influence of criminology have often been greatest when it reflected and reinforced popular prejudice and government interests. Garland (2002) has demonstrated this for Britain, and Becker and Wetzell's (2006) collection does it from an international perspective. The role that biological criminology played – with all its implicit and explicit racism – can be discerned from Gibson's (2002) work on Lombroso and Black's (2003) work on the history of American eugenics.

chapter three

Context: race, place and fear of crime

Although race relations situations may have as their ultimate cause rapid global social change, they are manifested locally at a smaller rather than at a larger scale. Accordingly, racial situations first have to be described and understood at the neighbourhood level. Different neighbourhoods are differently placed to cope with urban social, demographic and economic change. A locality's capacity (or lack of capacity) to adapt to change may be seen in fears and anxieties directed towards those who may be most immediately linked (however fallaciously) with change. As this and subsequent chapters show, not only can criminogenic factors coalesce, concentrate and become entrenched in certain neighbourhoods, so also can fear of crime. This chapter links fear of urban crime to particular changing neighbourhood economies and broader urban labour, housing and other markets (McGahey 1986) so as 'to integrate the study of individual differences and life histories with the study of the effects of communities and broader social context' (Smith and McVie 2003: 171). The essential argument, though, of this chapter is that 'race' and 'racial situations' can become repositories for 'fear of crime'.

Conceptualising fear of crime: the racialisation of fear

The concept of 'fear of crime' has a wider reach than responses to questions about crime and victimisation and their measurement in crime surveys. As Goodey (2005: 66) argues, such responses may more accurately display more general and amorphous feelings of 'vulnerability', 'insecurity', 'concern', 'anxiety' and 'anger'. In race relations or 'racial situations' these anxieties – although often 'coded' as 'fear of crime' – may take on wider meanings in which fear of crime emerges as an aspect of wider fears of social change. Using qualitative case studies, this chapter explores the ways in which real or imagined forces of change are associated with the co-presence or proximity of different ethnic groups and how this influences perceptions and fears about race and crime. Chapter 9 pursues this theme by focusing on the alleged existence of an isolated and feared African-American 'underclass'.

The presence or proximity of black and minority ethnic people can exacerbate white fear of crime and lead to the belief among whites that they face a higher risk of becoming a victim of crime and that the perpetrator is likely to be of a different ethnicity. In Britain, Australia and the United States perceived high levels of urban crime are often believed to be synonymous with the presence of minorities (Webster 1997, 2003; Collins *et al.* 2000; Bowling and Phillips 2002; Poynting *et al.* 2004; Walker *et al.* 2004). These fears are based on a mixture of mythical and real beliefs about who is a 'typical' offender or victim, while ignoring the broader picture (Goodey 2005). Fears can be projected onto groups, as people come to believe that crime is mostly inter-racial, even though most people are more likely to be criminally victimised by younger members of their own ethnic group, and young people generally are more likely to be victimised because of where they live or where they go (Bowling and Phillips 2002; Phillips and Bowling 2002; Walker *et al.* 2004, 2006; Bureau of Justice Statistics 2005; Nicholas *et al.* 2005).

Fear of crime: prevalence

Both the British Crime Survey (BCS) and the National Crime Victimization Survey (NCVS) in the United States show consistently high levels of fear of crime (Walker *et al.* 2004, 2006; Wood 2004; Bureau of Justice Statistics 2005; Nicholas *et al.* 2005). Despite levels of crime and the risk of becoming a victim of crime having fallen substantially since peaking in the early to mid-1990s in both the USA and the UK, comparatively high proportions of people still believe the crime rate to have risen. Despite the BCS 2004/5 recording the lowest level of risk of becoming a victim of crime since the BCS started in 1981, 63 per cent of people thought that crime in the country as a whole had increased. However, worry about burglary, car crime and violent crime has fallen by one-third since 2000. Also, people have relatively more positive perceptions of crime in their own area than nationally, with 42 per cent thinking that crime in their local area had increased. The proportion of people perceiving high levels of anti-social behaviour – from speeding cars, graffiti and rubbish to 'kids hanging around in the streets' – in their local area, after increases over the last decade, stabilised and recently fell significantly. Over a third said that anti-social behaviour was a 'very big' problem in their area. There is considerable variation between places and between social groups in fear of crime and in the levels and types of crime and anti-social behaviour perceived. Area characteristics are the strongest predictors of perceiving high levels of crime and anti-social behaviour. Those living in poor areas were four times more likely to perceive high levels than those in wealthy areas (Wood 2004; Nicholas *et al.* 2005; Walker *et al.* 2006). Pantazis (2006) has shown that crime risks, psychological criminal harm, insecurity, and perceptions of 'disorder' are much greater in poorer and socially excluded places than in affluent places.

The following contrasting studies draw out different themes associated with fear of crime in local racial situations. As can be seen, patterns diverge and converge across different localities, although the predominant themes that emerge are identified at the end.

Youngstown, Ohio: American deindustrialisation, class and race

Youngstown, Ohio, has been widely seen as a place of lost industry – the epitome of a deindustrialised town – or, more recently, of corruption and criminality. Deindustrialisation emerges as a key motor of change and decline influencing urban areas in several of the case studies reviewed here and elsewhere that heightens racial and class inequalities (Johnston *et al.* 2000; Webster *et al.* 2004; MacDonald and Marsh 2005). For example, Linkon and Russo's (2002) study of Youngstown strongly implicates loss of work with class and ethnic conflict, anxiety and segregation, and the emergence of a 'new underclass'. Rapid social and economic change became popularly represented by the media through the lens of fear of crime so that, over the period studied, Youngstown's epithet 'Steeltown U.S.A.' changed to 'Crime Town U.S.A.', and finally 'Murdertown'. In Youngstown, as elsewhere, the largely African-American South Side was worse affected by deindustrialisation and was least able to adapt to change.

The first arrival and rapid growth of African-American immigration from the Southern states between 1900 and 1930 saw the rise of local racism and the Ku Klux Klan. Through chain migration newcomers boarded with other recent migrants, creating separate, segregated neighbourhoods, reinforced by the assignment of steel company workers' housing, while workplace segregation was reinforced through the practice of hiring by personal connections – newcomers followed earlier migrants of their own ethnic group into similar levels and types of jobs. Thus while white workers dominated the skilled jobs, nearly all African-American workers were found in the unskilled, dirty and dangerous jobs in the coke plants and blast furnaces. This mirroring of residential and workplace segregation is found in many multiethnic manufacturing places in the United States and Britain (Fevre 1984; Kalra 2000). In-migration reached its peak in the early 1930s just as the Depression hit the steel industry, with Youngstown the hardest hit of America's industrial cities (with Denver), with unemployment at 23 per cent.

An upturn in fortunes during the Second World War led to very significant improvements in pay and conditions among steel workers during the 1950s as a result of strike action. But these post-war gains affected workers differently. While whites were able to move to the suburbs – helped by racially discriminatory home loans and higher wages – African-Americans, meanwhile, could only buy homes in the city. As whites moved out of the city, more African-Americans moved in, helped by new public housing developments. Escalation of this trend in the 1960s towards racially based suburbanisation (encouraged by changes in transportation patterns) saw a continuation of racially based hiring practices and workplace segregation, enforced by labour and company agreements, and an 'underlying solidarity around whiteness' (Linkon and Russo 2002: 42). White flight to the suburbs broke down more ethnically mixed working-class neighbourhoods, and lending and real estate practices prevented black home buyers from moving to the suburbs. Work, leisure and residential places became more ethnically divided, and the suburbs became more class divided, while at the same time residents and businesses moved away from the city centre, causing the downtown area to decline. Already we can observe the emerging classic twentieth-century American urban pattern of race relations which links ethnically based changed fortunes, residential and workplace segregation, white flight and suburbanisation.

As Youngstown stagnated economically in the 1950s, local organised crime and political corruption flourished. From 1974, as whites sought other employment in the emerging automobile industry and warehousing, new legislation and white flight from steel jobs improved wages and conditions for non-white workers. Nevertheless, because African-Americans were less likely to have savings or significant home equity, and were more dependent on the steel industry, they were disproportionately vulnerable when the mills closed. From 1977 a series of steel works were again closed and unemployment reached 25 per cent in 1983, hastening the abandonment of the city core, and workers either sought other kinds of work that often paid less or left the area. Many lost their homes, property values fell 'precipitously', and houses and city blocks were left empty. Most of the abandoned property was in the city, in neighbourhoods that had been populated mostly by African-Americans. Linkon and Russo (2002) argue that the longer-term consequence of this vulnerability was an intensification of racial divisions in the Youngstown area, which by the 1990s was among the most segregated communities in the country. Between 1980 and 2000, Youngstown often had the highest per capita murder rate in the country, and white crime fears largely focused on drug-related crime largely in black neighbourhoods. However, organised crime and an extensive pattern of bribery and corruption among the city's political leaders were more significant. African-American perceptions of the crime problem attributed the disproportionate impact of the mill closures on black families and the lack of economic opportunity for urban youth as the main causes. These perceptions further split the city and its suburbs and neighbourhoods within the city along lines of class and race.

The study found that class and race conflicts rooted in the steel industry were linked to the city's high crime rate, and from early on local organised crime had protected the interests of immigrants against white racism. Linkon and Russo (2002: 244) concluded their study by suggesting that a severe loss of population, a rising minority population, increasing concentrations of poor black residents and rising poverty rates in the city can be largely attributed to discriminatory housing authority policies, white flight and the fact that most of the economic growth in the Youngstown metropolitan area was located outside of the city. The effects of economic and racial segregation in the Youngstown area were the development of 'a system of geographic, economic, and cultural apartheid'.

Detroit, Chicago and Harlem: segregation, inequality and the meaning of 'whiteness'

Similar patterns to the above are found in Sugrue's (2005) important case study of deindustrialisation processes in post-war Detroit. As the study notes: 'Despite more than half a century of civil rights activism and changing racial attitudes, American cities ... remain deeply divided by race' (2005: xvii). The transformation and decline of Detroit was the result of a combination of three forces that occurred simultaneously. First was the flight of relatively well-paid, secure and unionised jobs. Second was the persistence of workplace discrimination, especially in the private sector, despite legal and civil rights gains. Third was intractable racial segregation in housing, leaving some places behind while others thrived. Sugrue (2005: xviii) argues that segregation led to the uneven distribution of power and resources in metropolitan areas:

the story of metropolitan areas, like Detroit, is a history of the ways that whites, through the combined advantages of race and residence, were able to hoard political and economic resources – jobs, public services, education, and other goods – to their own advantage at the expense of the urban poor.

Sugrue (2005: xviii–xix) goes on to argue that American public policies have encouraged segregation and that policies continue to be blinded as to the causes of the marginalisation of African-Americans in modern American life.

> The transformation of Detroit was not the 'natural' inevitable consequence of market forces at work . . . Still widespread is the assumption that blacks and whites live apart solely because of personal choice . . . Deeply rooted is the belief that unemployment and poverty are the fault of poor people and their deviant attitudes and behaviors, not the consequence of macroeconomic changes that have gutted urban labour markets . . . The fate of Detroit and other cities like it . . . was not primarily the result of the supposedly pathological behaviors of the poor, the lack of a work ethic among African Americans, or the breakdown of the 'traditional' nuclear family in inner cities. Those arguments . . . continue to appeal to those who believe that the causes and solutions of social problems start and end with poor people themselves.

In this and other contexts the 'flip side' of deindustrialisation – capital flight and the introduction of labour-saving technologies – was the process of suburbanisation – the movement of whites from central cities to suburbs – which left in its wake areas devastated and emptied of hope or opportunity.

In contrast to Sugrue, Hartigan's (1999) study of three predominantly white Detroit neighbourhoods – one outlying and two inner-city – argues that for various reasons whites in these neighbourhoods in the metropolitan Detroit area have resisted the pull of 'white flight' to the suburbs. On this basis we are asked to think differently about race and resist the urge to draw abstract conclusions about whiteness and blackness. Such categories, it is argued, are too limited to capture the construction and nuance of ethnic and racial identities and encounters. The study challenges common assumptions that inner-city areas are uniformly disproportionately populated by an African-American underclass, and that racism is necessarily concentrated among working-class whites and particularly within a white underclass. The study found that class backgrounds influence experience and understanding of racial identity and difference. Although it is the case that 80 per cent of Detroit's metropolitan area population is black, whereas its surrounding suburbs are mostly 90 per cent white, and that massive white flight did occur between 1950 and 1990, for whites who remained in the city, especially in the decimated inner-city areas, the significance of race has drastically altered.

Racism was influenced by class distinctions made by whites about other whites such that whiteness itself can be racialised rather than simply being in opposition to blackness. Poor whites, just as blacks, were racialised by more affluent whites, and these class distinctions can be more important than racial distinctions. For example, whites were at least as concerned about growing poverty, the increasing presence of poor whites and rental homes as they were about obvious and inevitable shifts in their neighbourhood's racial composition. Whites also shared a range of frustrations stemming from their precarious economic and social position rather than racial hatred and anxiety. Similarly, although whites in inner-city neighbourhoods felt that Detroit generally was a difficult and dangerous place in which to live, and that the majority of violent crimes that whites encountered were reported as involving black perpetrators, few whites assumed a racial motive for the crime.

Kefalas' (2003) comparable ethnographic study of a white working-class neighbourhood in Chicago's Southwest Side unpicks the construction of white racism in a 'white enclave' contiguous with Chicago's African-American West Side ghetto. This juxtaposition of the connotations 'enclave' and 'ghetto' itself reveals an American nomenclature of class (enclave) and race (ghetto) showing how class and race intersect. Normally, studies focus on race – the opposition of 'blackness' and 'whiteness' – based in a historical narrative that claims that on the arrival of blacks, 'blue-collar' whites violently opposed integration because they appeared to have the most to lose. From their perspective, blacks 'violated racial norms of conduct', threatened to spread poverty and crime, and undermined the sanctity and preserve of white home ownership and white territorial claims on their neighbourhoods. Furthermore, among working-class urban whites unable to flee there is a terror of neighbourhood turnover (Kefalas 2003: 3–4). Just as in Hartigan's (1999) study above, Kefalas shows that this traditional historical account needs to be refined to take account of class-based as well as race-based fears.

In Kefalas' study residents spoke of making 'a last stand' and of defending their neighbourhood against physical decline, poverty and crime. Residents' fears about graffiti and crime were not merely expressions of racism; rather, they reflected their insecurities about what they saw as holding onto 'respectability' and order. In the neighbourhood studied residents recounted how fears about crime and racial turnover had forced working-class whites to abandon sections of the city that were once deemed affordable, safe, stable, working-class, and white. Although proximity to the 'ghetto' underpinned the racial context of working-class fear, race was not the only source of anxiety:

> Beltwayites' racism then can be seen as a byproduct of their efforts to fortify the cultural and moral boundaries between themselves and more stigmatized groups. Class-bound ideologies and boundaries make it difficult for garden [a local, racially loaded description

of the area connoting the 'last stand of a peaceful place' against the ghetto] dwellers to reconcile themselves to [the] existence of *white* teenage mothers, *white* homeless, *white* drug addicts, *white* gangbangers, *white* single mothers, and poor *whites*. Whites are respectable, and respectability keeps people safe from the dangers posed by destructive social forces. (Kefalas 2003: 155; emphasis in original)

Although among white racists of all class backgrounds, 'the category of black is equivalent to the category of poor' (Kefalas 2003: 159), few whites, or blacks, wanted to live in close proximity to high-poverty areas, regardless of race. It was intolerance of poor people, rather than their race, that defined the neighbourhood.

In a different way, Jackson's (2001) ethnographic study of African-Americans in Harlem, New York, rejected simplistic arguments about poverty, class, race and behaviour, arguing that approaches that posit poor people's 'behavioural choices' as primary *causes* of their economic plight, or alternatively, that these behaviours are ghetto-specific *responses* to poverty rather than causes, are both mistaken. Rather, he argued that boundaries are constantly crossed and negotiated, and behaviourally isolated class- and race-based, homogenised groups and places cannot be said to exist in any meaningful way.

Camden, North London: narratives of crime and decline

Turning now to Britain, similar arguments to those presented above have been made about the limitations of homogenising ethnic and class groups into hermetically sealed and fixed social or cultural entities. Watt (2006) studied social and spatial polarisation in inner-London Camden between an impoverished white working class located in council (public) housing estates and an affluent home-owning middle class. The study explored place images, social identity, and the ways in which residents draw on class- and race-based distinctions to describe their neighbourhoods, all of which seemed rooted in narratives of urban decline associated with 'race' and respectability. Again, however, perceived socioeconomic status can easily override race through people making social distinctions of 'taste' and moral judgements of self-worth and the worth of others. In this case Watt points to the ways in which council tenants often become represented as an unruly crime-prone 'underclass', and council tenants draw a distinction between 'rough' and 'respectable' fellow tenants. Just as Jackson (2001) pointed to the salience of supposed behavioural factors in stereotyping judgements in Harlem, so Watt describes how 'roughs' are characterised by violence (whether to people or property), frequent drunkenness and petty criminality, whereas respectability was signified by sobriety, respect for the law, hard work and 'keeping up appearances' by the maintenance of a clean and tidy home.

Watt's study of Camden showed how 'narratives of urban decline' were a prominent theme in the accounts of white working-class tenants who had either been brought up in the area or had lived there for many years. But unlike that found in some other studies, the source of decline was not located in links between the presence of minorities and fear of crime. Instead, Camden residents pointed to local job losses, deteriorating public welfare services, physical decay, paucity of council housing provision, poor youth facilities and so on as sources of this decline. Although gentrification was welcomed by some and not others, of most concern were low-status 'outsiders', 'newcomers', 'problem' tenants and families. Extended social networks – 'knowing people' and 'being known' – were crucial to a sense of security and belonging, and compensated for, and were in tension with, more general narratives of urban decline. Watt (2006: 788) concluded that the main preoccupation of white working-class council tenants in Camden was to maintain respectability: 'The result was a permanent underlying urban anxiety about being *too close*, socially and spatially, to concentrated poverty'. Although crime was a cause for concern, only occasionally was it associated with the presence of ethnic minorities *per se* rather than the presence of 'roughs' and 'problem' tenants.

Competition over local resources: the availability of affordable housing and ethnic enmity

An important source of ethnic enmity in multiethnic settings, especially in places such as London's East End, has been growing competition over scarce local resources brought about by twin processes of deindustrialisation and housing policy since the 1970s. Much of what has happened to council housing in Britain since the early 1980s has been a direct result of government housing policy to encourage home ownership. Central government controls on council house building and the sale of existing local authority properties under right-to-buy legislation (tenants' right to buy their council house at heavily discounted prices), although unsurprisingly highly popular among beneficiaries, resulted in growing shortages of affordable council housing. Lack of new building and the loss of social housing to private ownership meant that, whereas previously council housing had been dominated by white working-class families and married couples in employment, the sector became increasingly dominated by a 'needs-based' allocation of ever scarcer accommodation based on criteria of 'homelessness', disadvantage, overcrowding and family size. As a result, the profile of the council housing population became poorer and more socially and ethnically diverse, while at the same time worsening local employment circumstances linked to economic restructuring and deindustrialisation meant that the number of council renting households containing no one in paid employment trebled from a fifth to two-thirds from 1967 to 1993 (Power and Tunstall 1995; Social Exclusion Unit 1999). Inevitably, as public sector housing came to increasingly accommodate disadvantaged groups, notably minority ethnic groups, female lone parents and young people, housing became a key source of local stigmatising and racialising discourses about race, crime and class, particularly as only slightly better-off locals felt that they or their grown-up children were being denied access to affordable housing.

The implications for race relations of these well-known processes are explored in Dench et al.'s (2006) restudy of the 'new' East End of London. The first study was carried out in the 1950s when the area was much less ethnically diverse than it is today. This, then, is a case study of processes of growing ethnic diversity in the context of growing housing and job scarcity. Since the 1950s, and especially during the 1980s, a new Bangladeshi community had settled which by 2001 constituted a third of the population of the London Borough of Tower Hamlets, and Bangladeshi children made up three-fifths of school enrolments. As elsewhere in Britain, Bangladeshis are likely to be the poorest minority ethnic group. The economic situation of most Bangladeshis in London, like their white working-class counterparts, means they have a low level of access to private housing. During the 1970s relations between whites and Bangladeshis were formed by struggles taking place around housing, particularly tenancy allocation in public housing which allowed established white tenants to secure new tenancies for, and pass tenancies onto, family members. Partly due to housing shortages, this traditional practice was replaced by personal need, especially 'homelessness', as the overriding criterion for allocation, at the expense of long residence in an area, length of time on a waiting list or 'good behaviour'. Thus a younger Bangladeshi population living in overcrowded social housing competed with whites and were seen as being given preferential treatment compared to whites.

This push of social policy in an Americanised direction gave rise to increasingly bitter local white sentiments because it opened up the East End to settlement by outsiders and local control was lost. Although Bangladeshis did not directly compete with whites in the local labour market – their niche was family businesses and catering – changes in the local economy put a premium on formal qualifications rather than traditional informal networks in getting employment. Deindustrialisation and economic restructuring in the 1970s and 1980s and the closing of the Docks left the relatively formally unqualified East End white working class unprepared to compete in the new emerging knowledge-based economy, while some young Bangladeshis were beginning to gain qualifications. This has led to rivalry and resentment in the different relationship of Bangladeshis and whites to schooling. The school success of older Bangladeshi pupils compared to other groups including whites, the growth of ethnic segregation in schools and the flight of white parents to white faith schools all reflected and fed white resentment. Combined with white families' lost influence over the intergenerational transmission of social housing tenancies, the ease with which Bangladeshis have been able to demonstrate housing need due to their overcrowded households, and their perceived claims on the welfare state, this has created the roots of white hostility. Thus state policy in respect of benefit and other entitlements and the paucity of affordable social housing came to have a key role in encouraging racist misconceptions in the East End of London.

Bow and Battersea: why are some places more racist than others?

The mechanisms by which local exclusion and inclusion occur and why some localities are more exclusive than others can be illustrated by Wallman's study. Wallman (1982, 1986) examined local factors affecting ethnic relations in two inner London areas, Bow and Battersea. The two areas had very different 'local styles', such that ethnicity counted for rather little in Battersea, whereas Bow was popularly considered to be a 'racist' area. The study found that in Battersea people's lives overlapped much less than in East London's Bow area. People living in Battersea were less likely to work with or share their leisure time with locals, whereas in Bow most areas of people's lives – from work to marriage – tended to be dependent on family and other locals. In Bow residents relied on local knowledge information about housing, jobs and leisure opportunities; by contrast in Battersea most people had connections of different sorts outside it, and because their ties spread more widely, the friends of their friends reached further, and they were more able to adapt, more able to pull in resources from other areas, they were less dependent on the local core.

As a consequence, in Battersea the only hurdle for the newcomer was finding housing; once successful, he/she was considered a local. Here length of residence rather than colour or ethnicity was more important, whereas in Bow newcomers had to enter all aspects of the local system to be treated like a local, which threw ethnicity into much sharper relief. Because newcomers can only take up options that are there, members of minority ethnic groups who did move into the East End tended to live in ethnic enclaves, felt safer when living close together, and Asian groups in particular felt they had to protect themselves against racist attack. In Battersea neither this sense of ethnic collective danger nor the need to devise ethnic collective responses appeared to be present. The significance of ethnicity and the expression of racist hostility and possibly violence, and fear of crime, vary according to different – open or closed – 'local styles' and the ability and adaptability of local economies and residents to bring in resources from outside. In places like Battersea more inclusive local principles are stronger, and insider status can be achieved by residence and recognition; whereas in places like Bow more exclusive ethnic principles will tend to prevail, and insider status will be ascribed by birth and marrying a local.

Neighbourhood feelings vary by age

Local feelings and responses to ethnic diversity generally vary between young and older residents. In this sense particular attention must be given to the different nature of neighbourhood racism among younger and older people. When there are high levels of neighbourhood racism, young people stand in as proxies for adult concerns and anxieties about 'race'. That is, young people patrol and defend racialised public space on behalf of adults who collude or condone but do not themselves take part in these activities. Younger people are more likely to be the perpetrators of racist violence than adults because of their closer relationship to public space and issues of territoriality. The younger members of 'established' and 'newcomer' groups (Elias and Scotson 1994) within neighbourhoods come to play a particular role in the unfolding story of local hostility such that the established group seeks superiority by virtue of the duration of their residence and therefore differences in their degree of internal cohesion and neighbourhood control. This uneven balance of power is maintained through the exclusion and stigmatisation of the outsiders by the established group through each of the two groups pointing to the worst aspect of the other by referring to 'problem families' or 'criminal elements', but usually the young members of the outsider group. The most ostracised section of the outsider group are children and young people, who are more firmly and cruelly shunned and rejected than their parents, and are more likely to hit back at their exclusion. As the outsider group progressively refuse to internalise the social slur on them and mobilise resources within their reach, they eventually retaliate and the balance of power changes. This change heightens conflict as the established group sense that their former superiority is slipping away.

This sort of analysis is consistent with that of Webster (1996) and Dench et al. (2006) above. As Webster (1996) found in his study of fear of crime and racist violence among white and Asian young people in Keighley, West Yorkshire, England, this changing balance of power between perceived outsider and established groups was expressed through white flight from inner areas and heightened perceptions of areas as 'colour-coded' 'no-go' areas (exclusively 'white' or 'Asian') for one or other of the majority white and minority Asian groups. In a situation of reported high levels of victimisation, especially personal violence among whites, and fear of crime, especially among Asians, what was most marked were the spatial constraints on Asians in terms of going out compared to whites. Large numbers of Asians identified specific places they avoided, while a large number of whites were unable to identify any areas they avoided for fear of being a victim of crime. White estates, some parks and the town centre were all mentioned as places where there was, in effect, a curfew placed on Asian young people. Further, the main reasons cited for avoiding these areas were fear of being attacked and racial harassment. White young people in their turn stated areas they avoided for fear of crime but generally felt much less restricted in their movements than Asians.

Figure 1 shows that whites and Asians mirror one another's fears of areas perceived as 'belonging' to one ethnic group or the other, and therefore to be avoided. Reading the graph from left to right, Braithwaite, Brackenbank, Ingrow and Woodhouse are all white estates, frequently and unsurprisingly mentioned by Asians as places they avoided. At the time of the study Braithwaite and Ingrow were specifically identified by Asians as major sources of perpetrators of white racist violence, although their reputations for violence and crime differed. Parks were seen as dangerous places for both Asians and whites, because they lacked the protection afforded by adult surveillance and because their ethnic use and 'ownership' remain ambiguous and contested. Their contestation arose because they separated or bordered colour-coded areas and were cited by young people as primary locations for racist violence, often involving quite large groups of young people. For example, both Devonshire and Cliffe Castle parks adjoin what were perceived to be 'Asian' areas, and were sites of major skirmishes between groups of white and Asian young people. The ethnic 'ownership' of parks changed so that Devonshire Park, once seen as 'white', was subsequently perceived as 'belonging' to Asians. Young people's imagined fears and their actual victim experiences were found to have coalesced in a strikingly racialised geography of fear (Webster 2003).

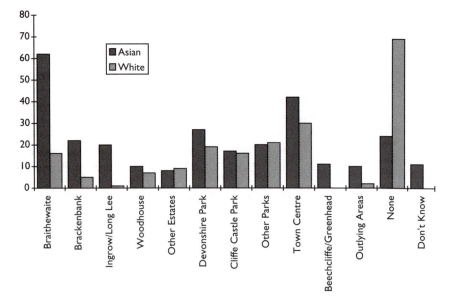

Figure 1 Areas avoided after dark (frequency)

South London: cultural syncretism?

Again, the degree to which some places are fearful and others less so does point to the possibility that the development of negative racial urban situations is not inevitable. For example, Back's (1996) study of inter-ethnic friendship between young people in two ethnically contrasting neighbourhoods in South London shows that inter-ethnic conviviality is possible. Back argues against frameworks of condemnatory moral absolutism in which whites are constructed as 'saints' or 'sinners' – whites are neither singularly racist nor pure advocates of rejecting racism. The ways in which racism enters into the lives of young people and changes can lead to local manifestation *or* rejection of racism. Although one estate was perceived as a white stronghold essentially hostile to black and minority populations, while adults offered racist explanations about the presence of black people in the area, which they associated with decline, drug abuse and crime, young people did not share these adult perceptions. Young people, in contrast to adults, asserted respect and admiration for *local* African-Caribbean youth, but this excluded Vietnamese young people. This was explained by the embracing of particular forms of masculinity and the rejection of others. In contrast, the comparison estate had a strong and established black cultural presence and racist expression was muted within a 'racially inclusive localism'.

Back noted that *white* groups designated 'problem' families and 'newcomers' were as subject to 'outsider' status as blacks and blamed for having caused decline, consistent with the findings of some other studies reviewed here. Nevertheless, Back claims to have uncovered 'cultural syncretism' in both areas, demonstrated in the multiple attitudes of white young people about 'race' and the ways in which being black was seen as prestigious while at the same time other groups were referred to using crude forms of racist imagery.

Understanding race, place and fear of crime

The ordering of ethnic segmentation or syncretism, of enmity or conviviality, in particular locales and place settings can be understood as ways of establishing and maintaining community safety. Although each ethnic group differs from the others in the extent to which it is able to manage safe social relations, there seems to be general 'agreement' about the basis on which associations are considered permissible and safe, or dangerous and to be kept at a distance (Suttles 1968). First, ethnic boundaries tend to form the outermost perimeter for restricting social relations. Second, within multiethnic neighbourhoods each ethnic enclave is an additional boundary which can sharply restrict movement. Although ethnic boundaries are crossed on a regular basis when necessary to shop or go to work, recreation tends to be spent within one's own ethnic enclave. Third, further territorial partitions are present in each ethnic enclave and maintain a degree of segregation between age, sex, and residential groupings. As Suttles (1968: 226) explains:

> The general pattern is one that fans out from the household and is partitioned according to the age and sex of the residents. Females and children are in closest proximity to the household. Males move progressively beyond this perimeter depending on their age.

Devices such as territoriality and distancing operate together to serve to avoid harm, and at the same time, to sort people into groups, which can get along with one another. They help designate the range of associations which an individual may consider *trustworthy*; they help to impose the sorts of *social control* necessary to ensure relatively peaceable social relations; and they impose a mutually *exclusive* character on themselves, which ensures continued participation in neighbourhood groups and thus loyalty and accountability (Suttles 1968: 162).

It is worth quoting Suttles' (1972: 191–2) description of the broad cultural definitions and beliefs that inform the associations of race, place and fear of crime in American society.

> The lawlessness of American cities is notorious, and for good reason. No nation so wealthy and so industrially advanced has such high crime rates and such a regularity in the practice of fraud and deception. In part, the lawlessness of the country derives from its ethnic, regional, and economic pluralism. . . . Americans who differ in ethnicity and wealth are literally so frightened of one another that they carry on a sort of slow-paced, internecine war with one another, triple bolting their doors, buying guns by the carload, and frantically searching for a safe neighborhood or suburb in which to live and bring up their children.
>
> Americans come by this source of lawlessness honestly, for they have inherited much of it from the traditional antagonism and ethnocentrism which the European immigrants brought with them. The United States has added to its lawlessness by a series of heavily loaded stereotypes which presume that poverty and even a low income is such an intolerable condition that disadvantaged people will resort to any means to better their personal situation. The American Dream is largely a dream of pecuniary success without reputable alternatives for those who fail to reach a fairly ample level of economic security. For those of us who believe in the American Dream – or at least those of us who believe that others believe in it – there must exist the lurking suspicion that the poor are wholly dissatisfied and always just at the brink of becoming total opportunists . . . the implications of such a belief must have frightening consequences for low income people in the United States, for they must live in close proximity to one another

and deal with each other in additional realms of life as well. When these stereotypes of low income people are joined to ethnic differences and these to racial differences, the result is an extremely defensive posture on the part of both individuals and ethnic neighborhoods . . . To a large extent this belief is self-fulfilling.

This passage sums up much of the common-sense thought and belief about neighbourhood-based crime in the USA and elsewhere. The status of these beliefs is subject to a detailed and critical review in Chapter 9.

Many of the studies reviewed here tell the stories of local people in terms of how fear of crime is woven into people's everyday lives, and how in some situations fear becomes racialised. They also show how crime and disorder are concerns in which the particular and the local perpetually intersect with wider national and global forces. Taylor *et al.*'s (1996) study of Manchester and Sheffield in northern England examined the different meanings and significance of urban crime and urban fears to differently placed groups. Crime and disorder levels were influenced by recent and dynamic changes in these cities and towns, and it was whether or not these changes had been perceived as positive that influenced different groups' experiences and fears of crime. Anxieties and aspirations occasioned by urban change varied according to age, gender, ethnicity and class. For the majority, however, change was experienced negatively as disruptive of tradition, local identity and attachment to place, and was thought to result in local decline, whereas for the local professional middle class such change was felt to be positive and hopeful. During the period of the study, crime and fear of crime were a particular issue in Manchester but experienced differently against a backdrop of escalating levels of fear and anxiety associated with 'crime'.

The highest rates of increase for both cities coincided with the period of greatest economic and infrastructural decline. One of the key aspects of local perceptions of the crime problem seems to have been the nature of local class structures and urban competition. Furthermore, the relative balance of different populations within a given locality positively or negatively influenced overall prosperity. Proximity to 'the poor' engenders feelings of fear of poverty and its personal implications among concerns that are produced by the fact of living in a city in which there are large numbers of increasingly poor fellow citizens. This development went alongside anxieties that one's own neighbourhood would spiral into decline and become prey to the activities of young men operating on the fringe of the local hidden economy of crime. Implicit in these fears was a sense of becoming corralled within poor areas embedded within the larger city. There was almost an obsession, especially on the part of those who lived outside the inner city and especially within the suburbs, with mapping the precise location of 'the poor areas' of the city and a concern to avoid these areas and the kinds of person and behaviour that it was thought will be encountered there. The sources of these powerful popular theories of 'poor areas' and criminal activity are complex and change, and some different areas and estates become focal points at one time as others emerge. Some areas become fixed in the popular urban imagination and myth as places where moral attributes and 'reputation' are assigned to people and the areas in which they live.

Taylor *et al.*'s discussion of the experiences of black and minority ethnic people in Manchester and Sheffield found that the shopping of all the different minority ethnic groups was centred in local neighbourhoods rather than in the city centre or out-of-town shopping centres. In terms of 'leisure', people very much stayed in their local areas under the protective eyes of 'their' community. Young people, in particular, stayed in their 'own' areas and avoided 'white' areas, moving around in groups as a way of dealing with security in public places, yet as black young people they felt they were constantly perceived as threatening by other users of the city, and also by the police. Young people from minority ethnic groups felt they were restricted to particular territories where they were, in effect, expected to be seen. Overall, though, group respondents in Manchester held many differ-ent views simultaneously – both positive and negative – of different areas, whereas in Sheffield opinions on areas perceived to be 'dangerous' tended to be more polarised and rigid. The study concluded that crime and fear of crime were linked to perceptions of 'local prospects'. More generally, the presence and distribution of anxieties and fears about crime and disorder were quite uneven, and different in expression, in different local areas and in different cities. The study serves as a model for understanding race, place and fear of crime, echoing the findings of most of the studies reviewed here and bringing together many of the themes discussed in this chapter.

Further reading

As discussed in this chapter and Chapter 9, the racial fates of American cities have often been portrayed in terms of the supposedly pathological behaviours of the poor, the lack of work ethic among African-Americans, or the breakdown of the 'traditional' nuclear family in inner cities. Explanations of poverty have often given primacy to culture and behaviour while ignoring or downplaying the political and economic causes of impoverishment. An aspect of these 'culturalist' explanations is to have revamped theories about racial differences in culture, values and intelli-gence. Sugrue's (2005) study of post-war Detroit offers a detailed and close-up refutation of these conservative arguments, showing how economic, urban and political policies, not supposed racial-cultural characteristics, created and wors-ened racial inequalities, as well as how the resulting racial segregation was resisted by residents. In contrast, Patterson (1998) argues that inner-city African-Americans face a severe crisis of family formation with all the ensuing social and psychological problems, including crime, which result from this. Within a very different British context, Dench *et al.*'s (2006) important study of London's East End highlights some of the 'ethnic anxieties', and reasons for these anxieties, found there.

chapter four

Offending and victimisation

Introduction: are cross-national comparisons possible?

Individuals who have not offended by their mid- to late teens are unlikely ever to offend, so this chapter emphasises, although not exclusively, young people's and young adult offending as well as their victimisation. Secondly, although a brief survey of offending and victimisation patterns comparing minorities with the majority populations in European countries is provided towards the end of this chapter, the focus is on data from some English-speaking Western countries, providing an opportunity to highlight the problems with these data. With some exceptions (Junger-Tas *et al.* 1994; Hawkins 1995; Marshall 1997; Tonry 1997), most surveys or studies of race, ethnicity, offending and victimisation are of one country (strict comparisons of self-reported offending using the same culturally sensitive self-report questionnaire devices have been attempted but with mixed results), and are not concerned with the issue of ethnic disparities (see Junger-Tas 1994). This is hardly surprising given the difficulty of comparing race, crime and criminal justice across national jurisdictions. Indeed, strict cross-national comparisons of ethnic disparities in offending, victimisation and criminal justice processes are rendered virtually impossible with existing data because definitions of offences vary between countries, as do criminal processes, sentencing patterns, etc. These difficulties are compounded when it is realised that, with only a few exceptions in individual countries, information on race and ethnic identities is not included in justice system data. In Europe especially, there is widespread ethical aversion to ethnic classifications and monitoring because of the comparatively recent history of genocide. Some countries record 'nationality', which sometimes may be a proxy for ethnicity, but only sometimes. Therefore it is not possible with existing data to make cross-national comparisons of racial disparities in the justice systems of Western countries other than in the major English-speaking countries, which collect official data on race (the United Kingdom, United States, Australia and, to a lesser extent, Canada). Even the usefulness of the data in these countries has been seriously questioned by many – see the contributors to Hawkins (1995), Marshall (1997), Tonry (1997) and below. As a consequence, cross-national surveys of data only compare groups within countries and then attempt to generalise about overall patterns.

Leaving aside ethnicity, offending and victimisation patterns in European countries for later, this chapter starts from a description of offending and victimisation patterns in England and Wales, the USA and Australia where more reliable data are available, ending with a tentative and brief review of race and ethnic disparities in some European countries and some preliminary cross-national generalisations about race, ethnicity, offending and victimisation.

Offending patterns in England and Wales

'Race' or ethnic differences in contact with, and representation in, the criminal justice system are described in Chapter 7. However, much public and academic discussion of 'race' or ethnic differences in offending begins from the premise that suspects and offenders who are arrested, go to court and are in prison are typical of the population of offenders. Therefore, the presence and proportions of black and minority ethnic suspects and offenders in the criminal justice system, compared to whites, are seen as a reliable indicator of their involvement in crime, compared to whites. On this basis the overrepresentation of some black and minority ethnic groups in the criminal justice system, compared to their numbers in the general population, would indicate their greater involvement in crime, compared to whites. The key issue, as always in these discussions, is whether the higher representation of some black and minority ethnic groups (especially black, mixed and Asian suspects and offenders) in the criminal justice system, compared to their numbers in the general population, is indicative of their greater involvement in offending, or their different or discriminatory treatment by the police and criminal justice system. The key problem is whether the ethnic characteristics of suspects and offenders *known* to the criminal justice system – based on police and criminal justice records – can be extrapolated to account for *general* offending patterns among ethnic minorities and the ethnic majority. These issues and problems are addressed after presenting some official data on 'race' and ethnic differences in offending, and involvement in the criminal justice system.

In 2004/5 offences involving offenders aged between 10 and 17 were notified to and dealt with by Youth Offending Teams in England and Wales (Home Office 2006). The data are presented in Table 1. Young black and mixed-background people were very substantially overrepresented compared to white people for robbery offences. Young people from Asian backgrounds also showed some overrepresentation for the same offence.

Table 1 Percentage of offences dealt with by Youth Offending Teams by offence group and self-defined ethnicity, England and Wales, 2004/5

Offence group	Ethnicity of offender				
	White	Mixed	Black or Black British	Asian or Asian British	Chinese and other
Violence against the person	84.9	2.7	6.4	2.8	0.5
Burglary	88.4	2.5	5.3	1.6	0.4
Robbery	54.0	7.7	26.5	7.9	1.3
Theft and handling	86.4	1.9	5.1	3.1	0.7
Vehicle theft	88.3	2.1	4.3	2.7	0.6
Criminal damage	90.5	1.8	3.3	1.4	0.5
Drugs offences	79.4	3.0	10.9	3.5	0.7
Public order	88.8	1.8	4.2	2.2	0.4
Racially aggravated offences	88.0	2.4	4.6	3.1	1.9
Other	82.4	2.3	6.2	3.8	4.8
Total	84.7	2.3	6.0	3.0	3.3
Approx. percentage of the 10–17-year-old population in England and Wales[a]	90.5	0.75	3.0	6.0	1.75

[a] Estimates based on the 2001 Census which divides the age structure of each ethnic group on the basis of different age ranges to the 10–17-year-old group, but this is unlikely to affect the overall trends.

Source: adapted from Home Office (2006), Feilzer and Hood (2004), Owen (2003) and Office for National Statistics (2003).

White young people were very significantly underrepresented for robbery offences. The issue of a striking overrepresentation of young black and mixed-background people requires explanation, and this will be addressed below. These patterns are similar to those evident since 2001. The figures also suggest overrepresentation of young black and mixed-background people for drug offences. The same finding was reported in 2003. Of particular note is the overrepresentation of young black and mixed-background people in virtually every offence group.

Relative to the general population, black people were six times more likely to be stopped and searched than white people, and Asian people were twice as likely to be stopped and searched as white people in 2004/5, similar rates to the previous year. The main and consistent reason over time for conducting a stop and search across all ethnic groups was for drugs. Black people are three times more likely to be arrested than white people, and less likely to be cautioned, although the proportions of individuals from different ethnic groups being arrested for specific types of offence vary significantly across police areas. In June 2005, black and minority ethnic groups accounted for 24 per cent of the male prison population and 28 per cent of the female prison population (including foreign nationals). For British nationals, the proportion of black prisoners relative to the population was 7.1 per 1000 population, compared to 1.4 for white people. People from mixed ethnic backgrounds were more likely to be in prison than white people with a rate of 3.2 per 1000 population. There was variation in the types of offences between each ethnic group (Home Office 2006).

Criminologists have long argued that suspects and offenders who are stopped and searched, arrested, appear in court and go to prison are only a very small and possibly 'unrepresentative' sample of the actual general offender population, and may therefore be atypical of this population (Coleman and Moynihan 1996; Bottomley and Pease 1986). As Bowling and Phillips (2002: 83–4) remind us, the population of suspects and offenders known to the criminal justice system – those who are identified and may end up convicted and sentenced to imprisonment – represent only a very small minority of offences that occur. Therefore we cannot draw inferences about the ethnic and other characteristics of the general population of suspects and offenders from the characteristics of this minority. From reporting an offence to its detection, recording, conviction, sentencing and imprisonment, the criminal justice process suffers 'attrition' through the discretion and decision-making of victims, police officers, court officials, juries and judges. As a result, fewer than 0.33 per cent of all offences that actually occur – according to the British Crime Survey which measures offences that may or may not have been reported – will result in a custodial sentence (Bowling and Phillips 2002). As Bowling and Phillips (2002) argue, this is an insufficient basis on which to reach conclusions about the ethnic or other characteristics of the actual rather than identified offender population. Furthermore, it leaves open the possibility that ethnic differences in offending based on recorded crime statistics may reflect race and ethnic bias in decision-making when victims report and identify suspects, police officers record, arrest, charge and prosecute and courts sentence. Overall, Bowling and Phillips (2002: 86–7) conclude:

> The fact that official statistics such as arrest and imprisonment rates 'over-represent' people of African and Caribbean origin and some people of Asian origin has been taken by some as an indication of greater criminality among ethnic minority populations ... [This] is quite wrong because official statistics are the *product of criminal justice practices*. While data collected by the criminal justice system are 'real', they should be seen as records of organisational decisions, categorisations and actions.

One way of beginning to tackle this issue is to compare patterns of offending known to the police and criminal justice system found in official statistics with self-report offending and victim surveys that reveal offenders and victims' experiences that may or may not have been reported, recorded and/or processed by the police and youth or criminal justice system. Self-report offending surveys provide an alternative measure of offending, which includes those offences and offenders that do not come to the attention of the criminal justice system. As such, they can be used to explore whether self-report offending differs across ethnic groups and to what extent any differences may account for the patterns of disproportionate offending found in official statistics (Bowling and Phillips 2002; Home Office 2005).

The Home Office administered Offending, Crime and Justice Survey (OCJS) (Sharp and Budd 2005) examined self-reported offending, antisocial and other 'problem' behaviours and drug use among different ethnic groups, and explored the extent to which different groups report contact with the criminal justice system and whether variation in different ethnic groups' contact can be explained by their offending behaviour. The OCJS found that, controlling for different age and sex profiles of the groups, white respondents and those of mixed ethnic origin were more likely to say they had offended than other groups across all offences and for both serious and frequent offending. Conversely, black respondents, and especially those of Asian origin, were least likely to say they had offended. Considering only 'serious offences' (any one of vehicle theft, burglary, robbery, theft from the person, assault with injury, or the selling of Class A drugs), 5 per cent of mixed ethnic origin, 4 per cent of white, 3 per cent of black and 2 per cent of Asian respondents reported they had offended in the last year. These patterns will reflect differences across ethnic groups in their profile on 'risk factors' known to be strongly associated with offending (see below). For example, young males are particularly likely to offend and there are a high proportion of young males in the mixed ethnic origin group, which nationally has the youngest age structure of any ethnic group – 65 per cent are aged 0–17, compared to 22 per cent of whites, 25 per cent of Caribbeans and 30 per cent of Asians (Owen 2003). Nevertheless, after age was controlled for, white respondents continued to have a higher offending rate than would be expected from their age profile, while offending rates for people of mixed origin reflected their age profile, and Asian and, to a lesser extent, black respondents still had lower offending rates than would be expected from their age profile. Patterns of drug use across ethnic groups were similar to those for offending, with whites and those of mixed origin being most likely to admit to Class A drug use.

This apparent overrepresentation of whites, and to some extent mixed-origin people, in self-reported offending paints a very different picture than the official one presented earlier. In the official version black, mixed-origin and Asian people are overrepresented in the criminal justice process compared to their numbers in the relevant population. But when asked whether they have offended 'ever' or in the 'last year', white and mixed-origin people are overrepresented and the other groups are underrepresented. This finding is consistent with other British self-report studies. Graham and Bowling's (1995) self-reported offending study based on a sample of 2500 young people aged 14–25, of whom 1700 were white and 800 were from ethnic minority communities, found that white and black respondents had very similar rates of offending, while Asians had significantly lower rates, across a range of offences. Very similar findings are recorded by the 1998/9 Youth Lifestyle Survey (Flood Page *et al.* 2000), which has led Bowling and Phillips (2002: 100) to conclude that 'official crime data exaggerate the extent of offending among ethnic minority communities'. Others have arrived at different conclusions, in particular that ethnic minority respondents to self-report surveys are less likely to admit their offending and drug use to interviewers compared to whites (see Junger 1989, 1990; Bowling 1990; Coleman and Moynihan 1996; Sharp and Budd 2005). One argument is that self-report offending surveys are biased in that they oversample white young people who are in school and are not seriously delinquent, so underestimate more serious offending and ethnic minority offending. Another argument is that if self-reported offending is compared to official police contact and arrest data for the group sampled, then some minority ethnic groups are more likely to 'conceal' their offending (Junger 1989). Webster's (1995) local self-report study of white and Asian young people used a sampling method in which half the sample was Asian, and avoided school-based sampling; it found higher rates of offending – particularly violence offences – among both Asian and whites than evidenced in comparable, often school-based, self-report surveys. Nevertheless, the findings were consistent with Graham and Bowling's (1995) findings that Asian young men were very significantly underrepresented and white young men overrepresented across most offences. There was, however, a group of persistent and serious offenders within both the Asian and white samples, although it was proportionally smaller among Asians than among whites. Sharp and Budd (2005) looked at contact with the criminal justice system in their self-report study in which they asked respondents whether they had been arrested, taken to court and charged with an offence, fined, or given a sentence by a court. They found generally that different levels of contact between ethnic groups reflected different levels of offending. Asians were far less likely to report contact with the criminal justice system than white, black and mixed groups. Black respondents, however, reported levels of contact similar to those of white and mixed groups, despite being significantly less likely to say they had offended.

Overall, despite the disproportionate presence of some minority ethnic groups in the criminal and youth justice system, self-report studies suggest that there is little overall difference between minority ethnic and white groups in offending rates (Graham and Bowling 1995; Feilzer and Hood 2004; Home Office 2004), although Jefferson (1988) argued that we cannot know the *real* black, Asian or white crime rate. This discrepancy between the proportional presence of minority ethnic groups in the criminal justice system and their apparently similar or lower offending rates is explored further in Chapter 7, where the question of alleged bias is addressed.

To conclude this section, we turn to serious violent crime, focusing on homicide. Homicide figures are thought to be more robust than many statistics on offending because homicides are fewer in number, relatively rare, most likely to be reported or discovered, and more extensively investigated and 'cleared up' (solved) than other offences. Murder statistics do not generally suffer the problems of police and other subjective definitions and categorisations that affect other offences. For example, the offences of 'robbery', 'theft from the person' and 'pick-pocketing' are notoriously subject to subjective distinctions that can narrow or blur these offences (Bowling and Phillips 2002: 95). People from ethnic minorities are at greater risk of homicide and also of being suspected of murder than would be expected by their numbers in the population. Although this is most marked for black people it should be realised that the large majority of homicides are intra-racial, not inter-ethnic, both the victim and perpetrator being from the same ethnic group (see Table 2).

According to the Home Office (2006), 11 per cent of all homicides in 2004/5 were of black people, 6 per cent Asian and 3 per cent 'other' minority ethnic groups. A third of black victims were shot, compared to a tenth of Asian victims and 5 per cent of white victims. Table 2 shows that for all groups the majority of homicides are intra-racial, with 74 per cent of all black victims and 88 per cent of all white victims being murdered by suspects from the same ethnic group. As Bowling and Phillips (2002: 98) have pointed out, much has been made of 'black-on-black' homicide and much of this violence is thought to be the responsibility of offenders of Caribbean origin, even though intra-ethnic homicide is more common for all ethnic groups, including whites. Perhaps what is of concern is that black-on-black homicide is much more likely to involve a stranger and also to be a shooting, compared to homicide involving other ethnic groups.

Table 2 Ethnic appearance of recorded homicide victims by ethnicity of suspect: combined data for 2002–5

Victim	Ethnic appearance of suspect					
	White	Black	Asian	Other	Not known	Total suspects
White	1527[a]	103	33	33	31	1727
Black	37	144	5	5	3	194
Asian	32	13	85	3	0	133
Other	25	16	4	50[b]	0	95
Not known	46	6	8	3	17	80
Total	1667	282	135	94	51	2229

[a] Includes 172 individuals killed by Harold Shipman.
[b] Includes 20 cockle pickers drowned in Morecambe Bay.

Source: Home Office (2006).

Case study: street robbery

This chapter began with the presentation of official statistics of known offending patterns among ethnic groups, including whites. Referring back to Table 1, it can be seen that the most striking overrepresentation of an ethnic group in offending was young black people's (mostly young men) involvement in robbery. Despite being only 1.5 per cent of the 10–17-year-old population, 26.5 per cent of robbery offences being dealt with by Youth Offending Teams involved black offenders. Despite the many problems outlined regarding the reliability of official offending data, this disproportionate degree of involvement of black boys and teenagers in robbery is quite striking. How might we explain it? Young people's experience of crime is dominated by street crime, and the majority of offenders and victims of street crime are typically aged between 14 and 19 (Hallsworth 2005). Street crime or street robbery – often evoked by elements in the mass media as 'mugging', so as to racialise it – is the type of acquisitive crime most often associated with young black men (see Burney 1990; Webster 2001; Bowling and Phillips 2002). Across the UK, young black men account for a significantly higher proportion of offenders being supervised by Youth Offending Teams for robbery than would be expected from their representation in the general population. Although in more ethnically homogeneous areas the population of offenders is almost universally white, in ethnically mixed areas black young men are still represented in the population of offenders more than would be expected from their numbers in the local resident black population (FitzGerald *et al.* 2002b; Smith 2003; Hallsworth 2005). FitzGerald *et al.* (2002b) found a positive correlation between levels of unemployment and youth poverty on the one hand, and rates of recorded street crime on the other hand, in London boroughs. Hallsworth (2005) argues that the reason why some areas have disproportionately higher levels of street robbery than others lies in new patterns of economic development in high-crime areas that attract suitable victims to these areas. The problem of offending is bound up with the ruthless socialising of young people into the consumption norms of the free-market capitalist society, and yet their legal consumption avenues are denied. This is a particular problem for multiply disadvantaged communities where the population of offenders is overrepresented. The fact that only some disadvantaged people resolve thwarted consumption choices by engaging in street robbery is explained by their different association with local 'outlaw culture' and 'aggressive masculinity' and the construction of illegal opportunity structures in particular areas.

Evidence about *known* offenders suggests that different ethnic groups are apparently overrepresented in different crimes, including street robbery – whites mostly commit crimes such as burglary and motoring offences. Some of these differences might be explained through the police selectively stopping and searching, arresting and prosecuting available black young men for street robbery. Whether or not minority ethnic young people offend differently or for different or the same reasons as white young people, the cardinal sin in these kinds of discussion is to assume that the ethnic or class profile of the offender population is representative of that ethnicity or class, rather than of the offender group and their particular circumstances, opportunities and constrained choices – in which class and ethnicity play a part.

Victimisation patterns in England and Wales

According to the British Crime Survey (Nicholas *et el*. 2005; Home Office 2006), crime in England and Wales rose from 1981 to reach a peak in 1995 and has declined since. Against this background of declining crime for all groups, the British Crime Survey 2004/5 showed that people from mixed ethnic backgrounds face significantly higher risks of crime than white people. However, there were no other significant differences between people from different ethnic backgrounds on grounds of their ethnicity alone. The issue here is that black and minority ethnic groups *are* at greater risk of crime and experience higher rates of victimisation, particularly common assault and robbery, than whites because they disproportionately live in high-crime urban areas and are younger in their age structure. Black and minority ethnic (BME) groups were more likely than white people to be worried about burglary, car crime and violent crime. The problem with these overall findings is that they do not include people under 16 years old, do not focus on the most victimised groups – young people, particularly young men and women – or the most victimised localities, and they tend to conceal the obvious fact that people generally do not 'choose' to live in high-crime areas unless constrained by ethnic and social class factors found in housing and labour markets (see Chapter 3).

Young people, particularly from minority ethnic groups, are dispro-portionately victimised compared to the general adult population. As a consequence, they experience a heightened fear of becoming a victim of crime while their victimisation is ignored or not taken seriously by the police and other adults. Young Asians, particularly Pakistanis and Bangla-deshis, suffer greater risks of victimisation than any other group, particu-larly from repeated racist violence (Webster 1995, 2003, 2004; FitzGerald and Hale 1996; Percy 1998; Kershaw *et al.* 2000).

As well as acting as proxies for adult fears and anxieties about crime, there is plentiful evidence that young people suffer a heightened sense of having to defend their areas against perceived threats from without while at the same time this reinforces ethnic and other forms of identity within areas. Neighbourhoods and places can be defined as much by who they exclude as well as who they include as 'members'. Young people also experience a heightened fear of certain places or people which reflects their higher rates of everyday violence and crime compared to adults, although this varies according to age, gender and ethnicity (Anderson *et al.* 1994; Aye Maung 1995; Hartless *et al.* 1995; Webster 1995; Loader 1996; Pain 2003). Whether as young people or adults, Asians, particularly Pakistanis, suffer greater risks of victimisation than any other group (FitzGerald and Hale 1996; Percy 1998; Kershaw *et al.* 2000). It has become a crimino-logical orthodoxy that the victimisation of young people is ignored or not taken seriously by the police and other adults, whereas their offending behaviour is exaggerated.

Locally focused victim surveys (Crawford *et al.* 1990; Anderson *et al.* 1994; Webster 1995) conducted in inner-city areas or peripheral estates tend to uncover both geographically concentrated rates of victimisation and age, class, gender and ethnic concentrations. In other words, the risks of victimisation are spread unevenly across areas and social groups in ways that are less discernible in national random victim surveys such as the British Crime Survey. For example, Webster's (1995) local victim survey of Asian and white young people found very significantly higher rates of criminal victimisation than evidenced in national victim surveys. For example, among whites 62 per cent had experienced personal violence. It would be mistaken to underestimate the influence of these levels of cumula-tive violence and abuse on young people's fear of people and places. Fears and anxieties occasioned by such incidents were reflected in young people's 'fear of crime' and the ways in which they identified crime as the main 'problem' in their area.

Offending patterns in the United States

The ethnic and racial contrasts in the United States in respect of offending and victimisation are much more extreme than those found in most western European countries, including Britain. The foreword to Walker et al.'s (2004: xiii) standard text on crime and victimisation patterns, *The Color of Justice*, puts the problem of crime and the issue of race in the USA in the starkest terms:

> Today there are more African American men in prison and jail than in college ... as a result of today's incarceration policies, more African American men will experience the lifelong debilitating effects of incarceration than the lifelong beneficial effects of college.

Nearly one-third of African-American males born today are likely to go to prison, and this rate is very much higher for those living in impoverished, racially segregated urban neighbourhoods.

This massive and growing overrepresentation of African-Americans and Latinos in the US prison and criminal justice systems is discussed more fully in Chapter 7. If, as many argue, disproportionate minority prison and criminal justice populations reflect disproportionate minority offending, then the association of race and ethnicity with crime is justified as this indicates that some minorities have higher crime rates than other groups (Petersilia 1985; Wilbanks 1987; Herrnstein and Murray 1994; Miller 1997; Russell 1998). To understand the situation in the USA – where in some areas race has become virtually synonymous with offending – we first need to briefly describe offending and victimisation rates by ethnicity.

Beginning with offending and offender patterns in the USA, the reality is somewhat different from popular portrayals in which crime is seen as synonymous with armed young African-American men committing robbery, rape, or murder. Again, in the USA, as in Britain and elsewhere, there is disproportionate attention given to street crimes compared to other crimes, resulting in a disproportionately high African-American arrest rate. In 2000, for example, 49 per cent of those arrested for murder, 54 per cent of those arrested for robbery, and 34 per cent of those arrested for rape were African-American (Walker et al. 2004). Even though African-Americans comprise only 12 per cent of the US population they represent 31 per cent of all arrests and 37 per cent of all violent crime arrests (Barkan 2006). Of course, as has already been suggested in relation to Britain, arrest rates are usually a poor indicator of real crime rates (Bowling and Phillips 2002). Even if crimes are reported to the police and the police decide to file an official report, they may be unwilling or unable to make an arrest. In 2000, only 20 per cent of all 'index' crimes (relatively serious crimes) were cleared up by the police, and the clearance rate for serious crimes ranged from 13 per cent for burglary to 63 per cent for murder – the two offences for which African-Americans are disproportionately arrested (Walker et al.

2004). Combining different data from official police records, victimisation reports and self-report surveys, it can be asked whether arrest rates simply reflect different offending rates and patterns among minorities compared to whites (Walker *et al.* 2004). Each of these sources of data, as discussed elsewhere in this chapter, contain well-known problems of police processes, perception and reporting. Taking them in turn, arrest data show that as a percentage of all arrests the typical offender is white except in respect of murder, robbery and gambling, for which the typical offender was African-American, although the latter were arrested at a disproportionately high rate relative to their numbers in the population for virtually all offences, especially for violent crimes. Victimisation survey reports confirm these arrest rate patterns showing that African-Americans are overrepresented as offenders for all offences, especially violent offences. However, comparing arrest data with victims' perception of the ethnicity of the offender, disparities occur for certain offences, particularly in respect of rape, suggesting that whites may be underrepresented and African-Americans overrepresented in arrest data. Overall, though, the different data are consistent in suggesting higher offending rates among African-Americans especially for serious violent offences. Walker *et al.* (2004) argue that differences in offending rates between African-Americans and whites reduce when victim rather than arrest data are used, suggesting some police bias in arrests, and that white and other victims are more likely to report offences to the police when victimised by African-Americans. Nevertheless this was outweighed by the overwhelming evidence of higher involvement of African-Americans in offending. Comparing self-report offending survey data – and there is evidence that some groups, such as African-American male respondents, tend *both* to underreport *and* to be more likely to report some more serious offending behaviour – these data show *least* consistent racial differences in the proportion or frequency with which African-American young people, compared to whites, engage in offending behaviour, particularly in respect of drug use.

Victimisation patterns in the United States

In the USA, as elsewhere, in respect of black and some other minority ethnic men, it is often believed that typically African-American and Hispanic men commit violent crime and mostly against whites. However, as numerous sweeps of the National Crime Victimization Survey (NCVS) have shown, this is not the case. The NCVS, which is similar to the British Crime Survey (but has the advantage of including household members aged 12 or over, whereas the BCS includes those aged 16 or over), asks a large representative sample of household members whether they have been victims of crimes during the 6 months before interview. It is the most reliable source of crime and victimisation patterns available in the USA. It is also worth noting, in stark contrast to the exponential growth in the US prison population over the same period, that overall property crime rates have been declining almost since the survey began in 1973 and violent crime rates have declined since 1994, reaching their lowest level ever recorded in 2004 (Bureau of Justice Statistics 2005).

Although serious violent crime rates have declined in recent years for blacks and whites, in 2004 26 per 1000 blacks compared to 21 per 1000 whites experienced a violent crime against them. Experiences of simple assault and rape/sexual assault were similar for both blacks and whites; however, blacks were three times more likely than whites to experience carjacking. The most striking finding is that, according to FBI reported homicide rates in 2004, 47 per cent of victims were black despite blacks making up only 12 per cent of the US population, compared to 49 per cent of victims who were white. Even more striking, the rate for African-American men is nearly eight times the rate for white men and 24 times the rate for white women. The rate for African-American women exceeded the rate for white women, appearing closer to that of white men. At the height of gun crime between 1987 and 1992, the average annual rate of handgun victimisation was 40 per 1000 for African-Americans aged 16–19 and 29 per 1000 for those aged 20–24 compared to 10 and 9 per 1000 for white men. Hispanics were also overrepresented as victims of violent crime compared to whites. Blacks and Hispanics were very substantially overrepresented as victims of property crime compared to whites, often experiencing double the victimisation rate for whites.

The overall victimisation rate (which combines crimes of violence and personal theft) for African-Americans is 37 per 1000 persons in the relevant population over 12 years old, 28 for whites and 23 for other minority groups. These ethnic differences are much greater for crimes of violence than for crimes of theft, especially for African-Americans (Walker *et al.* 2004). African-Americans and Hispanics are more likely than whites and non-Hispanics to be victims of household and personal crimes. This higher victimisation of African-Americans and Hispanics than of whites is in part explained by the concentration of these populations in core urban areas where victimisation rates are higher for all groups and partly by the younger age structure of different groups.

Offending and victimisation patterns together in the United States

Taken together, much of the above data leaves unresolved the issue of bias in the police and criminal justice system compared to different ethnic rates of offending, and this is discussed in Chapter 7. It does, however, point to an apparently very significant higher rate of offending among African-Americans, especially among males, compared to other groups. Where the popular perception is most at odds with the data is that the majority of known offenders are white, reflecting of course their far greater number in the population compared to African-Americans, who are 12 per cent of the population. In 1997, 67 per cent of arrests were of whites, compared to 30 per cent among African-Americans. On this basis Walker *et al.* (2004: 47) argue that 'the typical victim is a racial minority and that the typical offender, for all but a few crimes, is white'. Similarly, there is a popular perception of crime as involving an act of violence against a white victim by a black offender. The NCVS shows, however, that much crime, as in Britain and elsewhere, is intra-racial. Seventy-three per cent of violent crimes by white offenders were committed against white victims, although African-American robbery offenders are as likely to have white victims as African-American victims. Ninety-four per cent of African-American murder victims were killed by other African-Americans and 86 per cent of white victims were killed by other whites. Eighteen per cent of violent crimes were inter-racial.

A consistent and fundamental weakness of large-scale offending and victimisation data, both in the USA and elsewhere, is the inability or reluctance of official agencies, such as the police, and of designers of surveys essentially aimed at informing official agencies to collect criminologically and sociologically useful data. To compare the patterns and proportions among African-Americans, Hispanics and whites who offend or are victimised, are arrested or enter the criminal justice system, and report to offending and victim surveys, without controlling for demographic factors such as family and age structure, schooling, residential segregation and social class seems perverse. When such factors are taken into account, for example in well-designed self-report surveys, findings such as there being small class differences in offending rates can often seem counter-intuitive when compared to what we know from qualitative studies of the context of offending (Hallsworth 2005; Webster 2006; see Chapters 8 and 9 below).

Walker *et al.* (2004) argue that the US social structure and issues of the extent of racial and ethnic inequality and the relationship between inequality and crime, particularly the growth of the very poor and the African-American underclass, are bound to play a major role in shaping different victimisation and offending rates among ethnic groups. In other words, it should hardly be surprising that some African-Americans are disproportionately engaged in street crime, often involving violence, compared to their numbers in the population, because they disproportionately reside in criminogenic places, disproportionately associate with criminal subcultures found in these places and are disproportionately poor. The problem here is that the majority of ghetto dwellers do not engage in criminality despite experiencing similar structural conditions, and other similarly marginalised minority groups are either not initially disproportionally engaged in offending or their offending reduces intergenerationally as they leave the ghetto for the suburbs, whereas high rates of offending among many poorer African-Americans have been a consistent and persistent feature over many decades.

Offending and victimisation patterns in Australia

There is very little data on ethnicity in Australia, never mind on ethnicity and crime (Collins *et al.* 2000). What little data there is suggests that, despite media panics that some ethnic groups, particularly Lebanese and Vietnamese, were involved in 'criminal gangs', there are very small numbers of young offenders from Lebanese and Vietnamese backgrounds relative to their numbers in the population. Data from the 1990s suggested there was little overall difference between the imprisonment rate of first-generation immigrants and the average rate for the total population. Imprisonment rates for those of Turkish origin were highest, followed by those of Lebanese, Vietnamese and New Zealand origin, all being significantly higher than those of Australian origin. Other ethnic minorities were underrepresented (Collins *et al.* 2000).

Of key significance, and for which data is available, is Australia's indigenous Aboriginal group. In terms of contact with the criminal justice system, indigenous people represented a third of all persons held in police custody in 1995. Another way of grasping this striking overrepresentation of indigenous people in the Australian criminal justice system is that custody rates were 2228 per 100,000 for indigenous people, compared to 83 per 100,000 for non-indigenous people. In other words, Aboriginals and Torres Strait Islanders were 27 times more likely to find themselves in police custody than non-indigenous people, and in Western Australia these groups were 39 times more likely to find themselves in police custody (Cunneen 2001: 18–19). A quarter to a third of indigenous people in police 'protective' custody were there for a non-criminal offence, typically public drunkenness, and a half for public order offences. As well as being more likely to be placed in police custody, largely for reasons of public order or protective custody, indigenous people are disproportionately likely to be arrested and rearrested, with over half of males aged 18–24 years reporting being arrested (Cunneen 2001: 20).

The disproportionate contact with the police and presence in the criminal justice system of indigenous people in Australia are briefly returned to in Chapters 6 and 7. Here, the question is whether the level of Aboriginal overrepresentation in police custody, courts and prisons actually reflects offending levels in this group. Are the types of offences committed by Aboriginal people the types of offences which are more likely to lead to police custody and imprisonment? (Cunneen 2001). Aboriginal people are overrepresented in virtually all offence categories, particularly violence (40 per cent of people imprisoned in Australia for assault are indigenous), and are more likely to have a record of previous offending.

European offending and victimisation patterns

Summarising the data found in the collections by Tonry (1997), Marshall (1997) and Hawkins (1995), Sweden is perhaps the most intriguing example among European countries because of its historically low offending and victimisation rates compared to other European countries, especially Britain. Nevertheless, and consistent with all Western countries, reported crime has risen sharply since the Second World War. Compared with other Western nations, Sweden's non-white immigrant population is very small, although unlike some Western societies citizenship is fairly easy to obtain. Differences between immigrant groups and native Swedes in victimisation rates were small or non-existent, but there have been a growing number of crimes with racist motives. Similarly, self-report studies showed no significantly different levels of offending between Swedes and immigrants (even in public housing with high proportions of immigrants), except for violence, which was higher among immigrants. However, all immigrant groups were overrepresented in official conviction rates, but this disparity was quite small except for homicide, rape and robbery (which were three times the rate for native Swedes). Remarkably, since 1970 there had been no increase in the rate of conviction among native Swedes. The rise had been due to the overrepresentation of immigrants. The highest conviction rates were reported for young immigrants in institutional care, who were particularly overrepresented in serious crimes of violence. These estimates of ethnic disparities in offending and victimisation in Sweden were controlled for legal and social background variables.

Like the other Nordic countries, Sweden has some of the lowest rates of social and economic inequality in Europe. The Swedish model of the welfare state is based on a highly interventionist labour market policy and a universal social security system, each dependent on the other. The social insurance system is generous and virtually universal. This policy has resulted in uniquely low income differentials. Another result, however, is that those who remain outside the labour market, such as immigrants and school dropouts who are unemployed, receive relatively low welfare compensation, because the social insurance system is based on work incentives. The Swedish system depends on a high level of labour market participation and low unemployment to pay for it. However, the jobless rate rose to 8 per cent in the 1990s – and was much higher among immigrants and young people. Despite a growing polarisation of various groups of mostly male young people in large metropolitan areas, overall high levels of social and economic equality may well have contributed to low levels of reported crime by immigrants and ethnic minorities because ethnicity and class do not define each other in the ways found in other European societies.

Albrecht (1997a) has noted how the process of European integration and the abolition of border controls between several European Union countries has put the focus on immigration and cross-border control, shifting public concerns toward issues of ethnicity and international organised crime. Asylum seekers and illegal immigrants especially have become focal concerns, with perceived problems of crime and economic burdens. This in part accounts for the increased significance of recorded violence against ethnic minorities since German unification. In Germany most research on the supposed criminal involvement of minorities is based on police data, which do not properly measure ethnicity. On this basis foreign minorities, especially juveniles and young adults, appeared to be significantly over-represented in arrests (over three times, with respect to their proportion in the population) and criminal involvement appeared to have increased intergenerationally, although there were very significant differences in the degree of criminal involvement between ethnic groups. Again differences are most marked for violent offences, including robbery. Albrecht (1997a) warns, though, that beyond police statistics, when background factors are controlled for, the crime involvement of the male immigrant population aged 18–24 drops to just over twice that of German males. As in Sweden, Albrecht argues that ethnic and foreign minorities did not cause excep-tional crime problems in Germany, and those that there were reflected marginalisation and structural problems in society. For example, the mar-ginal position of Turkish and other minorities with respect to income, socioeconomic position and housing conditions had not improved.

Reliable data on ethnic disparities in offending and victimisation in other European countries are difficult to come by, as already mentioned, and where they do exist they rely on police data, although self-report data are available in the Netherlands (see Junger 1989, 1990; Junger-Tas 1994). According to police and self-report data, visible minority young people were significantly overrepresented in police contacts and arrests, and young people who were not Dutch were responsible for a significant pro-portion of juvenile criminality. Moroccan young men in particular were overrepresented in contacts with the police – 50 per cent of young people involved with the police were of Moroccan origin. Very little was known about ethnic differences in criminal victimisation – the police did not record the ethnicity of the victim and neither did national crime victimisa-tion surveys. Other sources suggested higher victimisation rates among visible minority ethnic groups. Racist victimisation appeared to have greatly increased. Although it is claimed that ethnic segregation between visible minority ethnic groups hardly existed in the Netherlands, such groups tended to live in low-income neighbourhoods and often did much less well at school than whites.

In respect of other European countries, the data are practically non-existent. In France it would appear that when immigration-related offences were removed, minorities offended at twice the rate that would be expected given their numbers in the population, and overall it was apparent that official crime rates in France were highest in those *departements* with the largest official counts of minorities, but this says very little except at a perceptual level. In Spain a disproportionate number of foreigners were arrested, convicted, detained and incarcerated, but it was not known whether they were visible minorities. In Belgium and Italy data do not exist, although in Belgium there were clear tensions between young people from minority ethnic groups and the police, and in Italy there had been a remarkable rise in the numbers of foreigners involved in the criminal justice system.

Again, because of the paucity or unreliability of recent data about ethnic minorities living in European societies, hard conclusions about the social and economic marginalisation of some minority ethnic groups cannot easily be drawn. On the basis of the information available it would appear that there is a very significant unemployment problem among young North African groups – especially Algerian and Moroccan – compared to whites. There has been a long-standing concern that these groups have been economically, socially and spatially excluded and segregated in American-like ghettos, are subject to disproportionate police attention, and that this has led to violence and rioting (most recently in the widely publicised unrest in many French urban areas in 2006). The remarkably precarious situation of foreigners – especially Turks and Moroccans – in the Belgium labour market, due to spectacular increases in unemployment, is another example of European-wide deindustrialisation and economic restructuring initiated in the 1970s and 1980s which has hit some minority ethnic groups hardest. Marshall (1997) concluded that common explanations across national jurisdictions for ethnic disparities in offending and victimisation are discrimination and deprivation, or structural inequality, that socially and economically disadvantage minority groups. He adds that in virtually all European countries the media focuses on foreigners as criminals, or on organised crime as an 'alien' threat.

Conclusions from cross-national data on offending and victimisation

Tonry's (1997: 1) collection of analyses of racial and ethnic disparities in crime and criminal justice in Germany, England and Wales, Sweden, the Netherlands, the USA, Switzerland, Australia, Canada and France concluded that:

> Members of *some* disadvantaged minority groups in every Western country are disproportionately likely to be arrested, convicted, and imprisoned for violent, property, and drug crimes. This is true whether the minority groups are members of different 'racial' groups from the majority population ... or of different ethnic backgrounds ... or – irrespective of race or ethnicity – are recent migrants from other countries ... [However, n]ot all economically and socially disadvantaged groups are disproportionately involved in crime.

For example, according to Tonry's cross-national survey, disadvantaged

Bangladeshis, Pakistanis and Indians in Britain, and Turks in the Netherlands, were underrepresented in offending, whereas disadvantaged African-
Americans in the United States and African-Caribbeans in Britain were
disproportionately involved in crime and the criminal justice system. From
the data presented for each country (and remember that much of the data
is flawed or even non-existent for some countries), Tonry (1997: 11–19)
suggested that there were some robust and consistent findings that could be
generalised across national boundaries. First, in every country, crime and
incarceration rates for members of some minority groups greatly exceeded
those for the majority population. This was the case for both visible and
non-visible ethnic or national minorities, not simply blacks or Aborigines.
Second, minority groups characterised by high crime and imprisonment
rates were also characterised by various indicators of social and economic
disadvantage. However, not all disadvantaged groups exhibited high crime
rates. Third, in countries in which research had been conducted on the
causes of racial and ethnic disparities in imprisonment, group differences
in offending appeared to be the principal cause, not invidious racial or
ethnic bias. This research examined official decisions made on a case-by-
case basis taking into account relevant variables – both qualitative and
quantitative – at every stage of the justice process from police stops to
parole release, aggregate statistical analyses of national crime data and
imprisonment data and victimisation studies. This kind of data appears to
have been available only for the USA, England and Wales, Australia and
Canada and, as we shall see, does not necessarily control for non-legal
factors such as social class. For Tonry (1997: 19) what is most striking
about these findings is that they come from so many countries 'in which
some groups are substantially less successful economically and socially
than the majority population'.

The relationship between minority disadvantage, offending and victimisation using cross-national data is, according to Tonry (1997), far from
straightforward, as the many examples of disadvantaged minorities having
low offending rates attest. Nevertheless, many of Tonry's – and Marshall's
– contributors point to the salience of minority disadvantage as a factor
in offending patterns. Albrecht (1997b: 37) presents a particularly clear
statement of the problem:

> Apparent overrepresentation of offenders and victims from various
> ethnic minorities to some extent may be explained by deprivation and
> control theories. But criminology needs to move beyond such theories.
> As society becomes segmented along ethnic lines, the lowest segments
> are increasingly composed of members of immigrant groups that are
> most likely to be affected by unemployment, bad housing, poverty,
> and insufficient education and vocational training and are likely to
> remain in this situation for a considerable time. . . . Structural theories
> should focus on black markets and subcultures in which ethnic and
> foreign minorities are heavily involved.

For Albrecht (1997b: 67–8), heightened offending could be explained by a range of often competing theories, but these are unlikely to be specific to immigrant, foreign or ethnic groups. Theories of deprivation predict higher levels of crime among immigrants, just as indicators of disadvantage explain crime involvement among those who are similarly situated in the majority population. For immigrant populations, therefore, it is not specific cultural expectations that produce conflicts resulting in criminal offending, because the very same variables account for crime among immigrants that explain crime in the general population. Similarly, control theory suggests that the disproportionate crime involvement of some immigrant populations occurs because of reduced opportunities to develop bonds to conventional society, yet this same lack of attachment is found among crime-prone members in the majority population. Finally, Albrecht (1997b) argues that when proper controls are introduced into research designs and data analysis, offending is less or no more widespread among resident ethnic and foreign minorities than it is among comparable national (majority) groups. This raises the question of whether or not specific discrimination-based theories are needed in deciding whether some minority groups have elevated crime rates or whether elevated crime rates are an artifice of discrimination by the police and in the criminal justice system.

The immigration and crime thesis: intergenerational crime patterns?

A key aspect of findings from cross-national analysis is the claimed consistency of the immigration and crime thesis. This thesis states that

> first-generation immigrants are typically more law-abiding than the resident population, that their children and grandchildren suffer assimilation problems that produce higher-than-normal offending and imprisonment rates higher than those of either their parents or the resident population, and that subsequent generations have crime experiences indistinguishable from those of the general population. (Tonry 1997: 19)

Marshall (1997) also argued that first-generation immigrants typically have a low level of involvement in crime, which then rises among second- and third-generation immigrants and minorities due to their higher expectations that are then disappointed as they meet discrimination. However, European research suggests that this multigenerational immigration and crime model based on American experience is simplistic and only partly true. Tonry (1997: 22–5) found that voluntary economic migrants from many Asian cultures in the USA (Chinese, Japanese, Koreans) and England (Indians, African Asians, South and East Asians) have lower crime rates than the resident population in the first *and* in subsequent generations. Second, he found that cultural difference between structurally similarly situated immigrants, independently of the age or class composition of the group, can result in sharply different crime patterns, just as cultural differences may predict greater criminality. Third, some countries' policies for aiding immigrants' assimilation may reduce crime rates, including among second- and third-generation descendants. So, for example, Sweden's social welfare and settlement policies may have reduced differences in crime rates among the second generation. Fourth, the reasons why groups migrate may be a powerful factor that shapes criminality as reduced self-esteem and alienation are expressed in reduced self-control and in social isolation. These reasons may also encourage successful adaptation. Finally, some categories of migrants have economic or social characteristics, such as being middle-class and relatively well educated, that discourage offending. This issue of intergenerational crime patterns is explored empirically below and more theoretically in Chapter 8, in respect of African-Caribbeans in Britain and African-Americans in the United States.

Smith (2005) argues that divergences in rates of crime between second-generation disadvantaged British minority groups cannot be explained by levels of poverty and disadvantage. Although Bangladeshis and Pakistanis are the most disadvantaged, crime rates rose sharply in the second generation among African-Caribbeans but not among the South Asian groups. Smith argues that this is because of the legacy of slavery and unfulfilled cultural expectations of British life among Caribbeans (see Chapter 8). This legacy of slavery led to rapid changes in the African-Caribbean family after migration that loosened constraints on crime, and unfulfilled cultural expectations of British life led to experiences of rejection and then rebellion against white authority, leading to elevated crime rates. This argument is extended to include American, European, Australian and Canadian minorities to show that only some, not all, disadvantaged minority groups are disproportionately criminalised. Although all of the minority groups with higher rates of crime or incarceration are socially and economically disadvantaged, some disadvantaged ethnic minority groups do not have higher rates of offending. One implication of Smith's (2005) and Tonry's (1997) arguments is that, despite procedures and practices of criminal justice that work to the disadvantage of ethnic and immigrant minorities, most of the explanation for higher rates of offending and imprisonment among some minorities is not found in direct racial or ethnic bias against them. Another implication is that differences in levels of deprivation and educational levels do not easily map onto differences in rates of offending. For example, crime rates have increased and persisted from one generation to the next among African-Caribbeans that cannot be explained by detrimental changes in social, educational or economic disadvantage. Levels of deprivation are considerably higher among Pakistanis and Bangladeshis than among African-Caribbeans. Among the original migrants Caribbeans were better qualified than Bangladeshis and Pakistanis, and this continued into the second and third generations, so that neither level of education nor level of educational progress can explain the higher crime rate among African-Caribbeans.

There are a range of problems with these claims about intergenerational crime patterns between different ethnic groups. First, and most importantly, as Chapters 6 and 7 demonstrate, Smith seems to ignore the history of conflict in the relations between African-Caribbeans *and* Asians and the police in Britain. Second, the social and economic conditions of most working-class and second- and third-generation minority ethnic young people in Britain from the early 1970s to recently worsened quite substantially (and there is a parallel though different history in the USA in respect of African-Americans; see Chapters 8 and 9). Although the responses of young people growing up at this time were complex and varied, one adaptation was criminality and disorder, the latter first among African-Caribbeans *and then* Asians, as well as wide-scale criminalisation by the police of African-Caribbeans. Thirdly, in measuring intergenerational crime patterns, Smith relies on the assumption that arrest, prosecution and imprisonment data indicate crime rates rather than bias among the police and in the criminal justice system, and yet there is plentiful evidence of a strong historical bias by the British police against African-Caribbeans in particular from their arrival in the 1950s and in subsequent generations (see Chapter 6).

Understanding offending and victimisation

Analysing the causes of offending, studies often identify 'risk factors' such as 'poor' parenting, truanting, school failure and drug use that may encourage the likelihood of offending, and 'control factors' such as a strong 'bonding' to family, school, cultural institutions and employment that may discourage offending among individuals (Laub and Sampson 2003). Victimisation surveys and studies often identify individuals' 'lifestyle' activities and environmental factors as contributing to being prone to or being at risk of victimisation. However, to fully understand offending and victimisation processes we need to understand the ways in which individual risk and control factors interact with demographic, social-structural and area factors to encourage or discourage offending and vulnerability to crime (Bowling and Phillips 2002; Webster 2003, 2006; Goodey 2005). This seems particularly the case in deciding the contribution of ethnicity compared to other factors such as social class differences to greater risks of victimisation, offending and coming to the attention of the police and criminal justice system. As Goodey (2005: 72) argues in respect of, for example, victimisation theories:

> As theories they encourage consideration of social-structural opportunities and constraints which impact on differential experiences of

routine daily activities. However . . . their remit needs to be extended to consider the relative impact of power and powerlessness on social-structural opportunities and constraints which affect social groups differently. So, for example, if you encounter racist violence in a public place as a young African-Caribbean male, this needs to be interpreted with respect to your demographic characteristics, your encounter with an offender in time and place, and the social-structural impact of racism. In other words, not only is your victimisation proneness exacerbated by your youth, by you being male, and by you being out in a public place, but fundamentally it reflects your 'place' in white British society.

Ethnic minority populations are generally younger and often fit a strikingly different social and economic profile from the bulk of the white population, live in the most disadvantaged areas with the highest risks of crime victimisation, and are often employed in the riskiest and lowest-paid jobs.

The impact of social-structural change in destabilisation of neighbourhoods, the creation of local fear of crime and racial conflict was addressed in Chapter 3 and is returned to in the context of social disorder in Chapter 6. Numerous neighbourhood-based studies have consistently shown that, regardless of whether children and young people have accrued individual risk factors associated with chronic offending, serious offending is significantly more likely in the most disadvantaged neighbourhoods, particularly those experiencing high levels of concentrated poverty, weak residential stability and high transience of populations. Conversely, predictions of offending based on risk fail to materialise in the case of individuals living in more affluent neighbourhoods (Lizotte *et al.* 1994; Sampson *et al.* 1997; Wikstrom and Loeber 1998; Lupton 2003). Within neighbourhoods themselves the sort of 'social capital' to which residents have access – the advantages and disadvantages that can come from longer-term commitment to the social networks in which people operate – and the nature of their peer groups can both have a decisive influence in encouraging or discouraging criminality (Field 2003). The effects of some sorts of 'social capital' or peer group association can be highly limiting of alternative opportunities, or in the case of criminal and/or dependent drug-using networks, potentially destructive (Perri 6 1997; Hallsworth 2005). Nevertheless, local social networks can be important in accompanying, supporting and encouraging criminal and/or drug-using identities, offering protection and criminal opportunity. Continued involvement with particular sorts of peer group, and an associated particular form of *masculine identity*, is a process that, for some, sees the emergence of a group forum that initiates sustained criminal careers (Collison 1996). These neighbourhood issues in understanding ethnicity, offending and victimisation, particularly the alleged emergence of an 'underclass' in poor neighbourhoods, and place-specific cultural generation of deficient individual or parenting factors most closely associated with the onset of offending, are discussed in Chapters 3, 8 and 9.

Finally, individual risk factors in offending and victimisation as they relate to ethnicity – supposed low intelligence, being raised in a lone-parent family, poor parental supervision, family conflict, being brought up in care, regular truanting and school failure, peer influence, living in a poor area, dependent drug use, joblessness, and, later, not forming a stable family of one's own – are shown in different social-structural contexts of race, ethnicity and crime in Chapters 3, 5, 7, 8 and 9. Care is taken in these different contexts to contrast and critique criminological explanations of offending and victimisation that focus on individual level explanations (see Sampson and Laub 1993; Graham and Bowling 1995; Farrington 2002; Piquero *et al.* 2003) and sociological studies that have focused on blocked opportunities, arguing that delinquency and criminality are one type of group 'solution' to lack of opportunity. For example, racial discrimination, racial stratification and social and economic inequality have both direct and indirect effects on crime, victimisation and criminal justice (Box 1987; Reiman 1990; Lea 2002; Walker *et al.* 2004; Cook 2006). The next chapter, however, begins with the sort of victimisation most central to understanding race and crime.

Further reading

Readers should turn to Tonry (1997) for a description of cross-national offending and victimisation patterns and some possible explanations for what appears to be a convergence of the race and crime debate across a number of countries. Poynting *et al.* (2004) offer an insight into the criminalisation of some ethnic minority groups in Australia. Walker *et al.* (2004) comprehensively describe victimisation and offending patterns in the USA from a social-structural perspective, and Bowling and Phillips (2002) offer a comprehensive look at the evidence in Britain from a very well-argued 'minority perspective'. An excellent recent study of racialised street crime is Hallsworth (2005).

chapter five

Racist violence

Introduction: the British context of reform

Arguably the patterning and understanding of racist violence or racist 'hate crime' are highly specific to different national and local contexts, as are police and legal responses (or lack of responses) found in different jurisdictions. Different emphasis is placed on the dimensions that go to make up racist violence, whether assessments of the intent and motivation of perpetrators, the experiences and perceptions of victims as well as bystanders, witnesses or audiences of racist violence. In Britain, for example, it is only recently that attention has shifted from recognition and documenting of victim's experiences (see, for example, Chahal and Julienne 1999) to understanding the motivation of perpetrators, whereas in the United States the focus has been on perpetrators for some considerable time. Racist violence in many advanced societies is poorly understood. An understanding of racist violence is hampered not only by the difficulty of comparing quite different national and local contexts but also by the range of actions that might be said to constitute racist violence, from lynchings, the actions of neo-Nazis and communal race riots to individual racist 'hate crimes' (Blee 2005). For the sake of clarity and coherence, this chapter mainly focuses on a British narrative and analysis of racist violence and police and legal responses. However, a discussion of the history of lynching and extralegal punishment in the USA is included in the next section, not least because of the importance of this uniquely American form of racist violence in influencing race relations and subsequently the American system of capital punishment. The overall approach of this chapter uses an integrated framework that emphasises the importance of understanding the interaction between perpetrators, victims, witnesses, audiences and police and legal responses, as well as the history and context of violence (Webster 1996, 2003, 2004; Bowling 1999; Ray *et al.* 2003, 2004; Ray and Smith 2004; Blee 2005).

Any discussion of racist victimisation in Britain is overshadowed by Sir William Macpherson's inquiry (begun in 1997) into the failed police investigation of the racist murder of Stephen Lawrence, a young black man, in South London in 1993. The inquiry report (Macpherson 1999) received widespread publicity and support – its recommendations being endorsed by the British government and the police – and succeeded in bringing the issue of racist violence from the periphery to the centre of law and order policy in Britain.

The inquiry arose from a long-standing campaign by the victim's parents, Doreen and Neville Lawrence, to seek justice, yet no one has been convicted of the murder. Announcing a string of initiatives and changes in policy and the law since the inquiry, the UK government both reflected and led changes in the ways that racist violence came to be popularly perceived. It had been helped in this task by the support of the *Daily Mail* newspaper, which led a campaign supporting the Lawrences' fight for justice. This was a key development since this traditionally right-wing newspaper's readership includes that constituency of 'respectable', 'middle class' and 'middle England' voters crucial to the outcome of British general elections. This influential, mostly white group – traditionally aloof, indifferent and sometimes hostile to the plight of Britain's black and minority ethnic urban population – seemed persuaded of the injustice and seriousness of racist violence directed towards Britain's black and minority ethnic population. These wider implications are seen in the ways that the Macpherson report subsequently

> set the tone and the content of the British government's commitments to ethnic minority communities on issues of crime and community safety. These commitments were unprecedented in that not only were they explicit and high profile but they were also attached to a wide-ranging programme of action. (FitzGerald 2001: 145)

This chapter begins by recounting the history of racist violence in Britain and the USA. Racist victimisation and crime are understood in their historical and geographical context, showing that their patterns and meaning change between localities over time. This is followed by a recent case study on the processes and events surrounding the racist murder of Stephen Lawrence and the findings of the inquiry into the failure of the (London) Metropolitan Police to successfully apprehend his killers. Some implications of the inquiry are noted, and there is a critical discussion of these implications and assessment of the subsequent effects in respect of policing racist victimisation and changes in the law. Racist victimisation involves a social and power relationship between the police, victim and perpetrator, and this relationship changes (e.g. better policing, rises in racism, the ability of victims to defend themselves) and outcomes are unpredictable. It is, however, important to inquire about perpetrators as well as victims. Finally, the extent of racist victimisation in England and Wales is outlined to show trends and changes in self-reported victimisation, victimisation reported to and recorded by the police, and in the prosecution of perpetrators by the Crown Prosecution Service and the courts. After considering what theoretical framework might explain racist victimisation, the chapter ends with a prognosis of changes in racist victimisation and of police effectiveness.

Historical background to racist violence in Britain

The pattern of development of racist victimisation in Britain is from an earlier period of larger-scale white 'race' riots involving attacks on black people and the places they lived to a more recent, smaller-scale, 'routine', lower-level harassment. Often hidden in the recent period are occasional outbursts of usually unreported street skirmishes between groups of black and minority ethnic and white young people. Although large-scale immigration from the Indian sub-continent and the Caribbean began in the post-1945 period, earlier settlement of black and minority ethnic residents had occurred in Britain's ports. Thus the white 'race' riots of 1919, which occurred in nine British ports, are seen as having most significance in the history of English racist violence. In the same year, July 1919, whites and blacks battled for a week on Chicago's South Side. Although by this time bloody urban riots were not unheard of, the Chicago riot was unusual in that blacks actively defended themselves from white violence – they fought back. As we shall see, visibly opposing white supremacy was no trifling offence, especially in the Southern states, where it usually resulted in death at the hands of a white mob (Tolnay and Beck 1995). It is important to emphasise that the victims of white violence were not passive as black people reacted to, and resisted, racist attacks through organised forms of self-defence, and on occasion with equal violence (Hiro 1991; Jenkinson 1993). For example, widespread violence against black people and property in the Notting Hill area of London in August 1958 resulted in black people forming vigilante groups which patrolled the area in cars.

Histories of racist violence point to the importance of local factors and specific events that precipitate and join with underlying racist hostility and anti-immigration feelings, based in a wider background of nationalist and post-colonial anxieties about social change and economic insecurity (Pearson 1976; Layton-Henry 1984; Holmes 1988; Colley 1992; Panayi 1993; Solomos 2003). For example, Pearson (1976) pointed to racial hostility as a response to the decline of the cotton industry and the culture that went with it in North-West England. Here local perceptions find expression in forms of 'racial anxiety' rooted in a local lore of economic decline and depression of wages associated with the arrival of Pakistani migrants.

Violence against Asians reached a climax and became national news during the 1970s, particularly as a result of skinhead attacks, culminating in two murders of Asians in the latter part of the decade. The response to these kinds of attacks became increasingly politicised through the organisation of the Asian Youth Movement and its complaints that the police were unwilling to protect Asian areas (CARF/Southall Rights 1981; Hiro 1991). Racist victimisation became entrenched in certain areas because of their histories of immigration and other peculiarities such as insularity and traditions of extreme right-wing political behaviour in London's East End (Husband 1982) and a defensive economic logic in North-West England's cotton manufacturing areas (Pearson 1976). An important aspect of this entrenchment was the contesting of territory between majority and minority groups of young people (Hesse *et al.* 1992; Webster 1995). In this sense racial hostility and resentment take different although linked forms among young people and adults. Among adults hostility tends to be focused on perceived competition for access to welfare entitlements and public services, including education and, crucially, housing (Collins 2004; Dench *et al.* 2006). Among young people hostility focuses on the struggle over public space because of their closer proximity to street culture (Webster 1995, 1996, 2003). Young people's and adults' hostility are linked, however, because in localities where white hostility towards black and Asian people is common and widely accepted, perpetrators of racist violence – usually young people and young adults – draw support from the broader adult 'perpetrator community', who, although they may not carry out racist acts themselves, tacitly condone them by their expression of racist attitudes within the group (Sibbitt 1997).

Despite the historical longevity and entrenchment of racist violence in British localities, and plentiful evidence of the scale and seriousness of attacks against British Asians in particular in the 1960s and 1970s (see Pearson 1976; Layton-Henry 1984; Hiro 1991), official recognition of the problem only began in 1981 with the publication of a Home Office report on racial violence (Home Office 1981). This official endorsement began to spawn surveys and monitoring exercises which counted the prevalence of racial attacks and pointed to the inadequacy of police statistics, reporting practices and police responses to racial 'incidents' (Bowling 1999), to the extent of highlighting racial harassment by the police against black people (Greater London Council 1984). The Home Office report on racial attacks in 1981 was followed by the Home Affairs Select Committee report on racial attacks in the following year (Home Office Affairs Committee 1982). The subsequent Home Office report, *Racial Attacks* (Layton-Henry 1984), provided an initial policy impetus to change in statutory agencies' attitudes to racial harassment. It revealed that Asian people were 50 times more likely to be attacked on racial grounds than white people, and Black people were 36 times more likely to be attacked. Controversies surrounding the definition, reporting and recording of racist victimisation, and responses amongst policy-makers, have continued (see below). For example, the House of Commons Home Affairs Committee in its report in 1986 defined racial harassment as 'Criminal or offensive behaviour motivated wholly or partly by racial hostility' (Home Affairs Committee 1986), and the Greater London Council (1985) concluded that harassment includes:

> Racial name-calling, rubbish, rotten eggs, rotten tomatoes, excreta, etc. dumped in front of victims' doors, urinating through the letterbox, door-knocking, cutting telephone wires, kicking, punching and spitting at victims, serious physical assault, damage to property, e.g. windows being broken, doors smashed, racist graffiti daubed on door or wall.

Smith's (1994: 1106) definition perhaps best captured the nature of racist victimisation as:

> victims of a pattern of repeated incidents motivated by racial hostility, where many of these events on their own do not constitute crimes, although some crimes may occur in the sequence, so that the cumulative effect is alarming and imposes severe constraints on a person's freedom and ability to live a full life.

A common thread throughout the history of racist victimisation in England and Wales are complaints by black and minority ethnic communities that they are overpoliced and underprotected (Bowling 1999; Webster 2004). There is clear evidence that in respect of the earlier white 'race' riots mentioned previously, the police not only did not protect victims or their property and blamed the presence of minority ethnic communities for the disorders, but also colluded with or offered tacit support to the white rioters. Here, as later, there was a marked distrust between the police and minority ethnic communities. Whitfield (2004) has shown how deterioration in relations between the police and London's Caribbean community went unnoticed or was treated with indifference during the crucial early years of immigration. This downward spiral was, at least in part, a consequence of the indifference shown by the police to racist violence, which would inevitably erode black confidence in the police still further.

Bowling (1999) has argued that despite senior police managers in the recent period prioritising racial attacks on members of minority ethnic groups, the police continue to be ineffective in the prevention of incidents, protection of victims, and prosecution of perpetrators. The explanation, according to Bowling, lies in police discretion towards racist incidents and the lack of importance they are accorded in officers' hierarchy of the 'police relevance' of crime events. Rank-and-file police work is dominated by a working common-sense understanding of the law, and the more discretionary and ambiguous the legal matter, the greater the opportunity for occupational, common-sense values to enter operational matters. Because racist incidents are not taken seriously, even assaults occasioning injury, this makes a strenuous law-enforcement response less likely.

Bowling goes on to suggest that racist incidents are seen as legally ambiguous – indeed, officers consistently question or deny the importance or relevance of racism or racial motivation to crimes. They are seen more as 'neighbourhood disputes', 'anti-social acts' or 'disturbances' than as serious crimes. Victims and perpetrators tend to be people of 'low social status', so the police perceive there to be a low likelihood of detection or arrest, or the victim might withdraw the allegation at a later point. Police officers identify and have sympathy with the viewpoint of the 'white community', seeing its resentment and its expression in violence as 'natural' and understandable. Perpetrators are perceived as indistinguishable from ordinary yobs and victims as inherently or naturally vulnerable.

Summarising the history of racist victimisation in England and Wales, the longevity of and resistance to racist victimisation can really be said to have reached a climax in the 1970s and 1980s. Of particular note, this period saw an increase in organised forms of 'self-defence' by black and minority ethnic young people, claiming, for example, to be defending the Asian community from threats by far right organisations to march through Asian areas. The 1990s saw a marked increase in the reporting by whites and/or recording by the police of racist incidents involving Asian on white attacks (Webster 1995, 1996; FitzGerald 2001). Throughout these periods faith in the police to tackle racist victimisation remained low.

A peculiarly American form of 'popular justice': lynching and extralegal punishment in the United States

Contemporaneous reporting of lynchings and white race riots in the Southern, Western and Midwestern United States (cited in Ginzburg 1988: 10, 200) reveal much about this uniquely American form of racist violence:

> Sam Holt, the negro who is thought to have murdered Alfred Cranford and assailed Cranford's wife, was burned at the stake one mile and a quarter from Newnan, Ga., Sunday afternoon, July 23, at

2:30 o'clock. Fully 2,000 people surrounded the small sapling to which he was fastened and watched the flames eat away his flesh, saw his body mutilated by knives and witnessed the contortions of his body in his extreme agony . . . Mrs. Cranford, the rape victim, was not permitted to identify the negro. She is ill and it was thought the shock would be too great for her. The crowd was satisfied with the identification of Holt by Mrs. Cranford's mother who did not, however, actually see Holt commit the crime . . . On the trunk of a tree nearby was pinned the following placard: 'We Must Protect Our Southern Women.' (*Kissimmee Valley Gazette*, 28 April 1899)

Maryland Witnesses Wildest Lynching Orgy in History
In the wildest lynching orgy the state has ever witnessed, a frenzied mob of 3,000 men, women and children, sneering at guns and teargas, overpowered 50 state troupers, tore from a prison cell a Negro prisoner accused of attacking an aged white woman, and lynched him in front of the home of a judge who had tried to placate the mob.

Then the mob cut down the body, dragged it through the main thoroughfares for more than half a mile and tossed it on a burning pyre. (*New York Times*, 19 October 1933)

By the 1920s and 1930s lynching began to decline, and the last confirmed lynching was in California in 1947 (Pfeifer 2004). This popular form of ritualised and lethal white violence against mostly African-Americans for alleged 'crimes' ranging from homicide and rape to theft and minor transgressions of racial 'etiquette' was the key method of controlling blacks and maintaining white dominance through terror. Lynching is the illegal or 'extralegal' (as opposed to legal state- and court-sanctioned) killing of individuals by groups or 'mobs' (Tolnay and Beck 1995; Patterson 1998; Pfeifer 2004; Vandiver 2006). The sheer scale of the crowds involved in some lynchings can be judged by Fedo's (2000) detailed case study of the lynchings in Duluth in 1920. Explanations of the phenomenon of lynching fall into four overlapping areas: socioeconomic; cultural; socio-legal; and race theology. Each of these approaches will be considered in turn.

The legacy of racist violence in the United States offered by lynchings rests on a long-standing white accusation that African-Americans were 'prone' to violence and crime, and were sexual predators on white women. Lynching was popularly accepted and rationalised as just an alternative method of punishing law violators. Leaving aside the facts that many victims were falsely accused and that alleged guilt, by definition, was never tested by due process, many lynchings occurred in response to only the slightest, if any, provocation against white mores and racial etiquette – alleged insubordination, a 'look', a disagreement, dispute or argument – in which no alleged 'crime' whatsoever had taken place. Another commonly heard justification was that the existing legal system was too slow and inefficient, whereas lynching delivered swift and certain 'rough justice' (Pfeifer 2004; Vandiver 2006). Apart from these kinds of wholly spurious rationalisations and justifications, we need to look at the complex relation-ship between Southern whites and blacks during the period (Tolnay and Beck 1995). For whites, blacks posed an economic, political and social threat to the racialised Southern caste system. The 'postbellum' South and 'post-Reconstruction' period (these terms refer to the period after the American Civil War and the era of lynching) saw the rise of racist mob violence against blacks in the 1880s, peaking and then receding during the First World War, resurgent during the early 1920s, and finally dwindling during the 1930s (Tolnay and Beck 1995).

This periodisation is important in pinning down the historical dynamics of race relations that explain lynching. In the wake of the Civil War, the Thirteenth Amendment ended legal slavery and the absolute control whites had over Southern blacks. As a result, labour shortages ensued as blacks sought better working conditions or moved, and Southern whites responded by seeking to regain control over the black labour force. Southern states enacted the 'Black Codes' – laws and statutes regulating the supply of black labour and restricting the rights of freedmen – to re-establish the pre-war status quo. In reaction to these developments, Congress passed sweeping civil rights legislation in 1866 that threatened to topple the class structure and racialised caste system of Southern society. Thus began the violent repression of blacks through white race riots and lynching, not only to ensure their subordination to white economic domin-ation but also to terrorise politically active blacks, black civil servants, blacks who were economically successful, and blacks who refused to defer to white supremacists (and any white sympathisers and whites who taught blacks). White supremacy was to be 'defended' at all costs through both popular unorganised violence and organised terrorism enacted by the Klu Klux Klan – who in the early 1870s appeared to control much of the state of South Carolina – and other white supremacist organisations. Through-out the South federal attempts to enforce the Fourteenth and Fifteenth amendments that guaranteed civil rights to blacks failed. Tolnay and Beck (1995) argue that from this point the federal government abandoned all ideals of civil rights in the South, leaving matters in the hands of Southern state assemblies and local courts, in the context of growing economic dislocation due to the decline of the plantation economy.

The lynching era of 1880–1930, in which it is estimated that at least 2462 African-American men, women and children (some estimates put the figure at 5000; see Patterson 1998) met their deaths through mob killings and lynchings, can be portrayed as the eradication of specific persons accused of crimes against the white community. But the latent functions of lynching were as a mechanism of state-sanctioned terrorism designed to maintain control over and neutralise or eliminate African-American com-petitors for social, economic or political rewards. Their ritual and symbolic nature also affirmed the unity of white supremacy, seen in the fact that a majority supported outlaw mob violence (Tolnay and Beck 1995). The historical and geographical variation of lynching can be explained, according to Tolnay and Beck, through an understanding of lynching as an integral part of the Southern economy and class structure that emerged during the 1870s and 1880s to replace slavery – in particular, the role of the cotton economy. Gains in the real price of cotton in the Cotton South between 1883 and 1930 were associated with years of reduced lynching activity against blacks, controlling for demographic factors, generalised violence and black crime. This relationship weakens after 1906 when economic factors became less important. Thus lynching was an indirect method for controlling and maintaining the supply of black labour at times of high demand for this labour. Of course, this reliance on exploited black labour was also mixed up with white aggression and racial economic competition at times of economic stress, as well as the racist ideology bequeathed by the legacy of slavery that weakened constraints against racist violence. A second relationship between lynching and black out-migration occurred later with the great migration of African-Americans to the urban North in the 1920s and 1930s. Lynching encouraged migration and at the same time was a violent response to it, although the overall effect of black out-migration from the Southern states saw the demise of lynching. The failure to halt the exodus – and the economic threat it posed – through intimidation and force led to a reduction in the level of violence directed at the black community. As the 1930–60 period shows, lynchings did not disappear completely from the Southern United States with the exodus of black labour to Northern urban areas during the 'Great Migration' (Tolnay and Beck 1995). As popular support for lynchings waned during the 1930s, and as the South began a profound transformation of its agricultural economy, so the class structure changed, and lynchings became increasingly uncoupled from the Southern rural economy. As Southern industrialisation and urbanisation developed, the new urban middle and upper classes opposed racist 'rough justice' traditions embedded in the rural white working class (Pfeifer 2004).

This socioeconomic explanation for lynching perhaps takes too little account of considerable variation in patterns, frequency and the meanings of lynching across Southern society. For example, Vandiver (2006) explored the relationship between legal and extralegal executions over the lynching period in different localities and found that the function and meaning of lynchings and executions varied over time, by place, and by circumstance. In north-west Tennessee very few legal executions were carried out but a large number of lynchings were – whether the alleged offence was a serious crime or a trivial caste violation – whereas in other areas legal executions were substituted for mob violence in cases of alleged sexual assault. Nevertheless, chance and circumstance were as much factors in deciding lethal punishments as the kinds of systematic explanation offered by Tolnay and Beck (1995).

Cultural explanations of lynching take two main forms – those emphasising cultural change in class relations (Pfeifer 2004) and others emphasising the ritual and religious meaning of lynching (Patterson 1998).

Pfeifer (2004: 2–3) argues that lynching was an aspect of a 'cultural war' over the nature of criminal justice waged between rural and working-class supporters of 'rough justice' and middle-class advocates of due process. Impatient of abstract, bureaucratic and allegedly lenient legal solutions, mobs enforced direct, harsh, personal, informal 'justice' to maintain race and class goals through ritualised, communally based punishment of what was perceived as serious criminal behaviour – through the prism of race, gender, class, and circumstance. Lynching was not, as Tolnay and Beck (1995) had argued, only a means of defending the racialised and segregated class structure of 'cotton culture', rather lynching reflected a perspective on law based on 'popular sovereignty' as well as serving the goal of white supremacy and 'racial order'. From a different perspective, Patterson (1998: 171) reminds us that 'lynching', although rare, has continued into the modern era, citing the tying and dragging by truck of an African-American musician by three white men in 1998 at Jasper, Texas. His main argument, though, is that a significant minority of lynchings were 'sacrificial murders', 'laden with religious and political significance' (Patterson 1998: 173) indicated by the sadism, torture, mutilation and burning of victims – a kind of 'ritual cannibalism', redolent of primitive religious sacrifice.

The era of lynching still has resonance today in the American criminal justice system. The decline of lynching and the rise of the death penalty in effect sustained the goals of rough justice across the United States (Pfeifer 2004). There is a strong connection between the historical practice of lynching and the present pattern of capital punishment in the United States (Bedau, Zimring, both cited in Vandiver 2006). As demonstrated in Chapter 7, African-Americans are astonishingly overrepresented on death row and in modern lethal executions. Like historic executions and lynchings, modern death sentencing is strongly influenced by location and race. Zimring (2003) argues that the regional distribution of modern executions reflects the historic regional pattern of lynchings. Comparing the regional distribution of lynchings occurring between 1889 and 1918 and legal executions between 1977 and 2000 by region of the country, Zimring (2003) found that the South had 88 per cent of the lynchings and 81 per cent of the executions, and that this correlation held for all other regions in the United States, and is much stronger for historic lynchings than for historic legal executions. Zimring (2003) explains the overwhelming Southern preponderance of modern executions in terms of a Southern tradition of localism and vigilantism and a contempt for state monopoly of punishment, compared to other regions. This tradition has continued to the present, and is seen in a tolerance of lethal punishment, disregard for due process, and community-approved white violence against blacks. In the past, those who opposed lynching often urged executions as a substitute. Today, modern defenders of capital punishment, like historic defenders of lynching, argue for states' rights (Bedau 1997).

Case study: the racist murder of Stephen Lawrence

Stephen Lawrence, accompanied by another young black man – his friend Duwayne Brooks – was racially abused and engulfed by a group of five or six young white men while waiting at a bus stop. Despite being stabbed twice by his assailants, he ran over 100 yards with his friend to escape his attackers, whereupon he collapsed and later died as he was taken into hospital. His attackers ran off. The Macpherson inquiry subsequently uncovered a litany of police actions and attitudes towards the victim, his friend, the victim's parents and in the conduct of the murder investigation that betrayed – perhaps unwitting – racist assumptions among the investigating officers. From the very beginning – their arrival at the murder scene – police officers were insensitive, unsympathetic, suspicious and stereotyping in their assumptions, attitudes and actions.

The police seemed more interested in questioning Duwayne Brooks than tending to the victim before the ambulance arrived, stereotyping him as unpleasantly hostile and agitated rather than traumatised. The police took a line of questioning that assumed Stephen Lawrence had been in a fight rather than that he had been the victim of an unprovoked racist murder. There was a lack of urgency in pursuing suspects early in the investigation. The underlying message of Macpherson was that because the victim was black this disqualified him from being considered an 'ideal victim' (Goodey 2005) by the police – someone wholly innocent and deserving of an urgent, dedicated, determined and professional police investigation to catch his killers.

Macpherson (1999: 317) concluded that the investigation of Stephen Lawrence's racist murder was 'marred by a combination of professional incompetence, institutional racism and a failure of leadership by senior officers'. The victim was not given first aid by police officers; officers did not take any immediate proper steps to pursue the suspects; the parents of the victim were treated with insensitivity and lack of sympathy; the investigating officers misjudged and delayed the arrest of suspects, and did not take responsibility for their failure to act; and the course of the investigation was marked by 'a series of errors, failures, and lack of direction and control' (Macpherson 1999: 320). For Macpherson (1999: 321), the overall explanation for these failures was the existence of institutional racism in the police, which he defined as follows:

> 'Institutional Racism' consists of the collective failure of an organisation to provide an appropriate and professional service to people because of their colour, culture or ethnic origin. It can be seen or detected in processes, attitudes and behaviour which amount to discrimination through unwitting prejudice, ignorance, thoughtlessness, and racist stereotyping which disadvantage minority ethnic people.

Macpherson has been criticised on a number of counts, not least because of the methodological difficulty of grounding the concept of institutional racism in an investigation of a single incident of a failed murder inquiry (Lea 2000).

Macpherson and its aftermath: policing racist victimisation and the law

FitzGerald (2001) assessed what had been achieved post-Macpherson with regard to the handling of racist incidents. One of the central thrusts of Macpherson was that the failure of the police to deal adequately with racist incidents had resulted in a lack of trust in the police among minority ethnic groups. FitzGerald argues that government commitments to ethnic minorities arising from Macpherson are in tension with other government priorities, particularly in respect of disproportionate stops and searches of black people. Historically, the recording of racist incidents required police officers to identify racial motivation. In response to criticism the police adopted a wider definition of what constituted a 'racial' incident, and officers were not to have the last say as to whether an incident was racially motivated or not. Finally, Macpherson offered a wholly victim-centred definition, whether there was actual independent evidence of racial motivation or not. According to FitzGerald, the main effect of Macpherson was to have greatly increased the willingness of the police to record incidents as racist, thus closing the gap between what the self-report British Crime Survey had revealed about the number of racist incidents and what the police recorded – the gap between underreported and underrecorded incidents and actual incidents. Police forces however, were still not addressing 'low-level harassment' – as demonstrated by the London figures during and after the Macpherson inquiry. Perhaps of most significance is that, following the publication of the Macpherson report and the embracing of a definition of racist incidents irrespective of the ethnicity of the victim or perpetrator, the proportion of recorded incidents involving white victims has increased and the proportion of victims from visible ethnic minorities has declined, and although whites were still the main perpetrators, a higher proportion of suspects were recorded as black than previously.

FitzGerald concluded that the Macpherson effect was to have greatly increased reporting of racist incidents during 1998–9 – a sustained period of sympathetic media coverage and senior police commitment – but that this increase seemed mostly based in the London Metropolitan Police area rather than elsewhere. At the same time, in some police circles and amongst some whites, there was a backlash against the perceived privileged treatment of ethnic minorities, which may have encouraged the reporting by and recording of white victims. FitzGerald reserves her most telling criticism of Macpherson for the label of institutional racism. This concept not only exacerbates rather than resolves underlying racial tensions, it is tautological in that it merely describes what requires to be explained in the first place – police racism. It is unhelpful because abstract, denies personal responsibility and 'may generate a sense of impotence at best and resentment at worst' (FitzGerald 2001: 162). John Lea (1986, 2000), Rowe (2004) and others have made similar arguments, adding that the concept of 'institutional racism' fails to locate the causes of racism within the structure of operational policing and the relationship between police and minority communities. If, as Macpherson insists, racism is generated by the way institutions function, intentionally or otherwise, rather than by the individual attitudes of their members, then we still need to know *which* institutional processes, dynamics and unintended consequences of the working of institutions encourage racism. Although Macpherson blames a restrictive police occupational culture – lack of contact between white officers and black people outside a policing context – Lea suggests that policies that flow from this explanation have a long history of failure. For Lea the problem lies elsewhere, in power and community relations between the police and economically and politically powerless groups, including those within the white population – groups towards whose demands the police have little incentive to respond, who are most likely to be disproportionately stopped and searched and who are as likely to be discriminated against because of their social class and area of residence as because of their ethnicity – a crucial factor ignored by Macpherson.

Nevertheless Macpherson's contribution in drawing attention to the unintended consequences of the workings of institutions and linking the handling of racist victimisation and disproportionate stop and search, both engendering distrust of the police, was an important if undeveloped advance on previous official views. The chapter now turns to Macpherson's effect on changes in the law in respect of racist victimisation.

The Crime and Disorder Act 1998 introduced into law the concept of specific racially aggravated offences in relation to violence, harassment, public order and criminal damage. The Anti-terrorism, Crime and Security Act 2001 extended this concept to include religiously aggravated offences. Whereas previously police forces recorded racist incidents on the basis of a definition that relied on the police officer's interpretation of the presence of racial motivation or an allegation of racial motivation by any person (Association of Chief Police Officers 1985), in 1999 the police adopted Macpherson's (1999) definition that 'any incident which is perceived to be racist by the victim or any other person is racially motivated'.

In respect of racially or religiously aggravated offences, however, it must be shown that the offender demonstrated hostility towards the victim around the time of the offence, or that the offence is motivated (wholly or partly) by such hostility, based on the victim's presumed membership of a racial or religious group (Home Office 2005). This shift to a legal definition, which includes hostility to the victim's presumed membership of a racial or religious group, marks a very significant change in how the police and criminal justice system have come to perceive racist incidents and racial motivation.

Recorded aggravated offences increased 3 per cent between 2001/2 and 2002/3, and 13 per cent between 2002/3 and 2003/4 – more than was the case with recorded racist incidents. For both recorded racist incidents and aggravated offences, police forces vary widely in the number and type of offences recorded, cleared up, prosecuted, convicted, cautioned, not tried or acquitted. In 2002/3 the Crown Prosecution Service saw a 12 per cent increase in defendants for prosecution of a racist incident from the previous year of whom 74 per cent were successfully prosecuted. Overall, about one-third of both racially and non-racially aggravated offences were cleared up by the police. There was a 17 per cent increase in persons cautioned or prosecuted by the courts for aggravated offences in 2003 compared to 2002 (Home Office 2005).

This growing formalisation of racist victimisation in law and the recognition that such offences have a basis in hostility to the victim's membership of a group reflect wider changes in Britain's cultural values and how these changes have influenced English law. This shift from laws and a criminal justice system that assumed a culturally and ethnically homogenous society to a system that increasingly recognises cultural and ethnic heterogeneity may lead to the law and criminal justice system becoming inconsistent, confused and contradictory, or perhaps fairer. As David Smith (1997) notes, the fundamental ideal of liberal democratic justice is that everyone is equal under the law after specific case characteristics have been taken into account. On the other hand, in practice, justice may discriminate on grounds of ethnicity or race (Hood 1992; Feilzer and Hood 2004) and in generating disproportionate attention to the arrest, prosecution and punishment of one social or ethnic group rather than another (Hudson 1996). This raises parallel issues not just for the treatment of offenders, but also for the recognition of victims of racial and 'religious' crimes. In February 2006, Parliament debated a controversial Bill to make 'incitement to religious hatred' a criminal offence, with uncertain outcomes as to how it will be enforced, whether the offence mistakenly confounds and confuses religious and racial hatred (see Spalek 2002) and with unforeseeable implications for free speech.

The legal and criminal justice implications of changes since Macpherson are a fundamental and novel tension between a tradition which concentrates on securing fairness for the individual and more recent developments that recognise and seek fairness for groups. As Smith (1997: 1045) has previously argued, from one point of view,

> equal treatment does not mean the same treatment. Hence there is room for different treatment of groups according to their specific needs: for example, for the police and other agencies to take special action to meet the needs of ethnic minorities as victims of racial attacks.

This takes us back full circle to our earlier discussion of balancing an encouraging and increasing recognition among whites that black and minority ethnic populations are disproportionately racially victimised whilst discouraging any white backlash – especially among poor whites – that may perceive BME groups as receiving preferential treatment. As the next two sections will show, a survey of the historical background to racist victimisation and the recent trends and extent of racist victimisation in England and Wales reveals a complex but clear story of disproportionate racist victimisation of black and minority ethnic people.

Extent of racist victimisation: patterns and trends

The police have recorded racist incidents since 1986. There is some evidence that the number recorded rose steadily to a peak in 1986/7 then declined until the early 1990s (Home Office 1981, 1989; Home Affairs Committee 1989; Webster 1995; Bowling 1999) but this whole period is marked by the problem of severe underreporting, especially among black and minority ethnic groups compared to whites, and underrecording by the police (Home Affairs Committee 1989; Hesse *et al.* 1992; FitzGerald and Hale 1996; Bowling 1999). FitzGerald and Hale (1996) compared racist incidents reported to the 1988 and 1992 British Crime Surveys and established that ethnic minorities are more likely to be victims of crimes and serious threats than whites, because of their younger age structure, their socioeconomic characteristics and the type of area they live in, as well as because of their ethnicity. Significantly, in areas where racial attacks are *perceived* as a problem, both minority and white respondents tend to have higher levels of fear of crime. Most importantly, the BCS provided no evidence of the large rise in racist incidents between 1988 and 1992 suggested by police reported crime figures, but shows a large gap between racist incidents reported to the police and those actually recorded over that period (FitzGerald and Hale 1996).

The dramatic rises in reported racist incidents from 1998/9 shown in Figure 2 can almost certainly be accounted for by a greater willingness to report and changed police recording practices – especially in London – directly as a result of the Macpherson inquiry and changes in the law. This second cycle of rises in recorded racist incidents from 1996/7 to a peak of 54,370 in 2001/2 then saw a fall until 2002/3. Importantly, the increase until 2001/2, set besides the BCS finding of a decline over this period, suggests a progressively fuller recording on the part of the police and possibly increased confidence in reporting to the police (Home Office 2004). There were, however, wide variations in whether recorded incidents rose or declined between police force areas over time. Although the number of racist incidents recorded by the police rose by 7 per cent between 2002/3 and 2003/4 (following a 10 per cent fall the previous year), those recorded

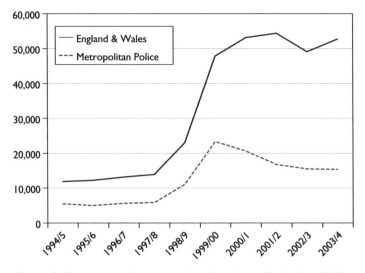

Figure 2 Ten-year trend in reported racial incidents (England and Wales and London)

Sources: Home Office (2004, 2005); Nicholas *et al.* (2005).

by the Metropolitan Police showed a slight decline, and the BCS showed little change over the period. Overall, the BCS has shown that the number of racially motivated incidents has fallen since the mid-1990s (see Clancy *et al.* 2001) but may have recently begun to rise again.

According to the BCS 2002/3 and 2003/4, Asians appear to be far more at risk of crime than other ethnic groups and whites, all of whom experience comparable risks. However, BME groups, and Asians in particular, face significantly higher risks of personal crime than whites. The noteworthy exception to this overall pattern is that blacks face dramatically greater risks of homicide and are much more likely to be shot than any other group. These findings require caution because, after allowing for age, Asian people face only slightly higher risks of crime than others. Young people are generally more at risk of crime than others, and the Asian population is younger than average. What are striking are the experiences of people of mixed origin[1] who faced higher risks for burglary, robbery and vehicle crime than any other group. The BCS 2003/4 found that over the previous 12 months 26 per cent of whites and blacks, 31 per cent of Asians and 39 per cent of people of mixed origin were victimised. Most of the greater risks of crime faced by BME groups can be attributed to demographic factors such as area of residence, age, social class and income. The same cannot be said for the mixed group whose higher risks do not disappear even after allowing for age, and the type of area (affluent/deprived) in which the person lived. The BCS 2004/5 found a 10 per cent increase for both recorded less serious racially-aggravated wounding and racially-aggravated harassment, and reductions from 8 to 5 per cent in racially-aggravated common assault and damage to a dwelling, between 2003/4 and 2005/6.[2] In both years the detection rate for racially aggravated violence and harassment increased by 40 per cent compared to less serious offences such as racially aggravated damage to dwellings and vehicles. Two per cent of all common assaults in 2004/5 were racially or religiously aggravated (Nicholas *et al.* 2005). These findings – the most recent – found a narrowing of the gap between ethnic groups in crime risks compared with earlier sweeps of the BCS, but also the emergence of a mixed-origin group especially vulnerable to crime.

As was argued in Chapter 2, groups living in relatively high-crime, deprived areas – disproportionately BME groups and poor whites – tend also to be more at risk of racist crime (Webster 2003). The BCS asks all crime victims whether they thought that the incident was racially motivated. Risks of racially motivated victimisation were higher for people from all the BME groups than for white people and highest for those from a mixed background.

As numerous studies have shown, the majority of racist incidents recorded are either damage to property or verbal harassment, regardless of jurisdiction in the United Kingdom (Maynard and Read 1997; Clark and Moody 2002; Jarman 2002; Home Office 2005), although an early local self-report survey found much higher levels of violent compared to damage to property incidents (Webster 1995). This and other findings again should counsel caution in how we interpret overall statistics, given local and temporal variation. The 2002/3 BCS – consistent with previous sweeps – found that risks of racially motivated victimisation were higher for people from all the BME groups than for white people. However, just as we saw the emergence of the mixed-origin group as having the highest victimisation rates in respect of crime, so they also have the highest rates of racially motivated victimisation. Results from the 2002/3 BCS showed that less than 1 per cent of white people had experienced a crime that they thought was racially motivated, compared to 2 per cent of black people, 2 per cent of Chinese and those from 'other' minority ethnic groups, 3 per cent of Asian people and 4 per cent of mixed-origin people. People of mixed origin were least likely to report crimes (31 per cent) and Asians were most likely to report (42 per cent). Among BME groups, Asian people had higher levels of worry about violent crime compared to people from other groups (Home Office 2005).

To summarise from the data presented thus far, the larger BME groups face crime risks that overall are similar to those faced by white people, although Asian people have slightly higher victimisation rates, but this is likely to be because of the relative youth of the Asian population and where they live.

There remain considerable problems with survey data. Risks of racist victimisation between groups take into account the age profile of the group, social class and area of residence to see whether these comparisons hold. According to the Home Office (2004) and the BCS, there appears to have been some convergence of crime risks over the last few years, except for those who are of mixed ethnic origin – whose risks are significantly higher. White people reported the lowest rates of racially motivated offences, but again, although this picture is unlikely to change dramatically, a somewhat different picture may emerge if groups are disaggregated according to age (e.g. the BCS does not ask under-16s about their victimisation), area of residence (e.g. whether affluent or deprived, ethnically mixed or not) and social class and income.

If the apparently greater but declining risks faced by Asians in respect of racist victimisation can be explained by the younger profile of this population, and where they live, compared to some other BME groups and whites in particular, there remain some unanswered questions. First, this does not take account of local conditions and smaller area risks influenced by events and the entrenchment of racist attitudes and victimisation in some areas and not others. Second, comparing victimisation rates and risks with the demographic characteristics of the group – that it is younger and young people are more likely to be victimised – also needs to take into account the extent to which the victim population are available not just their age profile. For example, young Bangladeshi men in particular tend to reside in overcrowded housing, pushing them to spend their leisure time on the street. Third, to what extent does an area accommodate motivated racist offenders because of the peculiarities of the area and whether local influences encourage or discourage resentment and hostility? Fourth, guardianship may or may not be available depending on whether potential victims are able to defend themselves or use avoidance strategies, or whether the police are able to police racist victimisation effectively. For example, there may be an interaction effect in so far as perpetrators perceive that victims are vulnerable and available in a context they perceive will have few consequences and little redress against them. Fifth, we still know far too little about racist victimisation among children and young teenagers. Sixth, the emergence of a hitherto ignored group – people of mixed origin – who suffer by far the highest risks of both criminal and racist victimisation compared to other BME groups and whites, is still to be explained. Finally, there are important grounds for differentiating white ethnic victimisation in respect of poor British white, Irish and Jewish groups (Stenson 1996; Watt and Stenson 1998), although this does not take away from the fact that visible minority ethnic groups have and are likely to continue to experience heightened, intensive, repeated and prolonged risks of racist incidents compared to other groups – a quite different qualitative experience than that of most whites (Sampson and Phillips 1992).

If we ignore these contextual factors of reporting – to the police, the BCS or a local survey – then we ignore the particular social context in which information, experience and knowledge are influenced, given and received. National and aggregate statistics about racist victimisation tell us an important part of the general picture about *whether* incidents are increasing or not for certain groups, but they do not tell us *why* what they describe is happening, nor do they tell us where, to whom, or to what we should look for an explanation (Webster 1996).

Have understanding and policy towards racist victimisation improved?

What longer-term evidence is there of improvement in the policing, handling, reporting, recording, prevention and understanding of racist victimisation since the Macpherson inquiry? In particular, have changes in police and other agency codes and practice and the law been more consistent and effective in increasing victim satisfaction with the handling of racist incidents? These questions can begin to be answered from the review presented here. A recent Home Office assessment of progress (Docking and Tuffin 2005) has concluded – through surveys of all police forces and local authorities in England and Wales, and in-depth studies of attitudes and practices of individuals in three areas – that police and other agencies' policies and practice have improved. As would be expected, there was regional variation in this improvement, but overall both reporting and recording have increased, although some officers continued to see most incidents as minor and not worth bothering about or failed to understand why something may be interpreted as racist. There remained major problems in schools and local education authorities in monitoring and recording racist incidents. Overall, police and agencies' treatment of victims and witnesses had very significantly improved since the Lawrence inquiry, in terms of increased sensitivity and understanding of the issues and greater willingness to deal with racist incidents, particularly among specialist rather than operational officers. Officers criticised the Crown Prosecution Service for not taking racist offences more seriously. Despite some promising Probation Service work, relatively little work was being carried out to tackle perpetrators' views or prevent potential perpetrators from committing racist offences or holding racist views. The main conclusion, however, from Docking and Tuffin's (2005) assessment is that although trust and confidence in the handling of racist incidents by the police and other agencies has improved, the recording of incidents perceived by victims to be less serious, but which might have a cumulative impact, continues to be neglected.

As is fitting, given earlier arguments, the chapter concludes with Ray and Smith's focused study of racist offenders (2004: 693) in which they argue that

> the figures on racist incidents have been produced by a greater readiness on the part of whites than of Asians to report incidents they believe to be racially motivated, and willingness to believe this has itself been encouraged by the police and the media accounts of the problem since the mid-1990s.

Meanwhile, 'White residents of areas close to neighbourhoods with a large Asian population feel threatened and at risk, and become more likely to report to the police incidents that might have gone unreported in a less fearful environment' (2004: 694). This is perhaps one of the most significant unintended consequences of changes since Macpherson and the accompanying recent improvements in reporting and greater trust of the police in handling racist victimisation.

Despite its limitations, the Macpherson inquiry is a watershed in understanding of and policy towards racist victimisation in England and Wales. On this basis alone it is to be welcomed. In the post-colonial and post-Lawrence policing climate found in Britain, however, improvements and gains in the policing of racist victimisation can be overtaken by events such as the 'War on Terror', when once again concerns with racist violence are overtaken by concerns with stop and search, public disorder and alleged black or Asian criminality. In Britain, as elsewhere, the key to understanding racist victimisation is to recognise how different forms of racism and the groups targeted by racism change over time and according to context, and policies aimed at ameliorating racist victimisation need to respond accordingly.

Understanding racist violence

The motives and characteristics of perpetrators and those who condone or collude in racist violence have received less attention than the experiences of victims. This was understandable at a time when racist violence was not taken seriously and its prevalence had to be established through victim surveys and victims' accounts. Today, however, simply condemning perpetrators and ignoring why they perpetrate racist crimes adds little to our understanding of the causes of racist victimisation. In some cases such blanket condemnation can lead to the self-righteous moral absolutism that argues that all members of a particular group – working-class whites – are racist or collude in racism, including violence (see Collins 2004; Dench et al. 2006). Some relatively recent studies have begun to bring the perpetrators of racist violence and the contextual nature of racist violence back into the picture so as to better understand factors – both direct and indirect – that encourage or discourage racist hostility and on occasion its extreme expression in violence.

In their study of racist violence in Walthamstow, London, Hesse et al. (1992) noted how violence persists and becomes entrenched in some multi-ethnic neighbourhoods and not others. They use the concept of the 'local ethnoscape' to characterise urban neighbourhoods as composed of segmented population groups who reflect on who and where they are in relation to who is around ('core' places) and who surrounds them ('marginal' places). These social encounters may reinforce or challenge ethnic identity

in the social landscape and are based on the power of one group to dominate another (Hesse *et al.* 1992: 168). The term 'ethnoscape' captures the
different ways in which multiethnic neighbourhoods are 'seen' by their
members and links comprehension of personal safety with awareness of
their positions of ethnic and other forms of power.

A local study of the changing patterns and relationships of racist violence between 16–25-year-old Asians and white victims and perpetrators
over 5 years (Webster 1994, 1995, 1996, 1997) found that the power
perpetrators had over their victims changed over time, with the result that
an initial high level of white on Asian victimisation was very significantly
reduced. Harassment, intimidation and violence were reduced as Asian
young people grew older, formed defence and vigilante groups and were
able to defend themselves from racist attack. They established, designated
and defended 'safe' areas – various parks and areas deemed to 'belong' to
Asians – while avoiding 'white' areas. What had begun as a defensive form
of street masculinity that altered local power relations had by the end of
the study reduced perpetrators' opportunities and motivation; created
Asian-only youth centres that reduced the availability of victims on the
street; won the cooperation, support and protection of some local police
and schools; and successfully competed for scarce urban resources – at
the expense of less powerful and less well-organised young white men. The
study also found a wide variation of response to racist victimisation within
Asian and white groups and the wider community. Although racist attitudes
and beliefs were widespread within the white community, particularly
among young people, there were different degrees to which individuals
rationalised, condemned or condoned racist violence. Similarly, some
Asian young people were considerably more at risk of becoming racially
victimised than others, and responses to violence ranged from the 'respectable' (denial that it was taking place and/or blaming the victims as 'looking
for trouble') to *ad hoc* self-defence and sustained vigilante activity that
targeted and meted out 'rough justice' to alleged perpetrators. A key finding, however, was that widespread racist hostility among the wider white
community seemed to offer legitimacy to the few who perpetrated violence.
A threefold typology on a continuum of 'normal', 'aggressive' and 'violent'
racists was employed to capture this wider local context. Another key
finding was that perpetrators did not 'specialise' in violent racism but were
also involved in more general violence and other forms of criminality. Also,
there was considerable ambiguity in the minds of white (and Asian) young
people about what constituted 'racist violence' and racist victimisation.
Many interviewees described different race encounters and conflict as 'just
fighting between individuals and groups of young people' in some situations, and as 'racist' in others. Finally, in the course of the study both
official victim report and self-report data revealed that proportionally
more whites than Asians were being racially victimised, which indicated
changes in the willingness of whites and reluctance of Asians to report
incidents in the context of a changed power relationship between the two

groups, increased victimisation of whites by Asians (whether in 'self-defence' or not) and a more open-ended police definition of what constituted a 'racist incident'.

Some of these themes and the analytical framework were subsequently developed by other writers and studies. Sibbit (1997) referred to what she called the 'perpetrator community' – the majority living in an area – who, although themselves not involved in harassment or violence, did not necessarily condemn such actions, or if they did, did so in the context of espousing a 'common-sense' racism that held back from linking their shared low-level racist hostility to its expression in harassment and violence. It is to this wider local context that we now turn to find answers as to why racist hostility arises that can form a backdrop to harassment and more extreme expressions of hostility in racist violence. In employing the concept of 'perpetrator community' here it is important to understand that it refers to a local ethos of a perhaps influential tolerance of low-level racist hostility, not to the views of the majority of residents. It is also important in this type of discussion not to draw too many inferences about local conditions – examples of which are given below and elsewhere in this book – directly leading to or causing individual instances of racist violence, because other contingent factors in individuals' lives also have to be taken into account.

Developing some of the themes introduced earlier, Larry Ray and colleagues studied young adult and adult racist offenders under the supervision of the Probation Service and in prison in Greater Manchester in the North of England (Ray and Smith 2004; Ray et al. 2003, 2004). They argue that, on the one hand, a single focus on the individual motives and intentions of racist offenders ignores the grounding of such offences in wider cultural and social contexts of violence, social exclusion and marginalisation. On the other hand, the 'dominant images of the racially violent offender are one-dimensional and exaggerate the degree to which such people are politically conscious "haters" ' (Ray and Smith 2004: 682). As white working-class communities displace 'resentment at economic decline and social decay onto apparent representatives of a "cosmopolitan" culture' (Ray and Smith 2004: 695), encouraged in this by local media representations and far right political parties, these wider crises of deindustrialisation and neighbourhood destabilisation become displaced onto the biographies and structures of feelings of individuals, including racist offenders. These processes involve the transformation of offenders' unacknowledged shame rooted in multiple disadvantages and perceptions that Asians are illegitimately given preferential treatment and are more successful than they. Shame turns to fury and rage directed against Asians within a cultural context in which violence and racism are taken for granted (Ray et al. 2003, 2004).

The drawing of boundaries in the formation of identity and enunciation of racial and cultural difference, often expressed in abusive language, exclusionist practices and sometimes violence, seems connected to anxiety, uncertainty and ambivalence arising from inter-ethnic contact in contexts of neighbourhood and social change. Boundary drawing and boundary defence seem defining features of the conditions underlying the emergence of racist victimisation and violence, yet perversely ethnically or racially defined groups are locked together through the service each one renders to the other group's search for identity. If racist victimisation and violence are conceived as a series of 'border skirmishes', this is not to downplay their seriousness, and not all such victimisation and violence can be explained in this way. This would be to ignore the criminal yet dangerous, transgressive and redemptive possibilities of racist and other forms of violence found among some individuals and groups (see Katz 1988; Presdee 2000).

Further reading

The standard work on policing racist violence in Britain is Bowling (1999); it is both grounded empirically and supplies a convincing theory of the police organisation as a basis to explain police inaction towards racist violence. Ray and Smith (2004) and Ray *et al.* (2003, 2004) put the motivations of perpetrators of racist violence in social context, and FitzGerald (2001) and Lea (2000) began the important debate about the consequences of the Macpherson Inquiry for official policy towards tackling racist violence. Webster (1996, 2003) draws out the links between racist violence and wider issues of crime and public disorder.

Notes

1 For the first time the 2002/3 BCS used the new 2001 Census classification of ethnicity that includes a 'mixed' category.
2 There is a discontinuity in the police recorded trend for violence (including racially aggravated violence) in 1998 and 2002 when new offence categories were added.

chapter six

Race, policing and disorder

Introduction: the centrality of policing in black and minority ethnic groups' experiences

Some perspectives on police–minority relations have narrowly focused on crime-fighting aspects of policing or police treatment of victims, to address the issue of whether the police treat suspects and victims from minority ethnic groups differently than they do the white majority. This can ignore the wider function of the police as arbiters in the maintenance of public order and their role in policing race and ethnic relations. The role of the police in mediating and representing 'race' and ethnic relations as an apparently 'public order' issue cannot be separated from their role of 'fighting crime'. The mere presence of black and minority ethnic groups in Britain and elsewhere has been deemed a 'problem' of social order, in the context of often shared assumptions within police occupational culture about the moral worth of people according to their age, race, sex and class (Brogden *et al.* 1988). What seems undeniable, however, is Kalra's (2003) assertion that policing has had a consistently significant impact on the lives of many minority ethnic populations. Such populations are not only policed but in large measure also constructed by police activities that set and mark out, create and maintain distinct bounded ethnicities.

There is plentiful evidence of particularly fraught patterns of contact and conflict between some minority ethnic groups and white working-class groups and the police. One of the main aims of this chapter is to ask how this hostility and conflict arose and to describe the escalation of conflict to the point of serious public disorder. Although compared to mundane encounters such escalation is comparatively rare, given that the main function of the police is to maintain public order through the disciplining of groups deemed a threat to police authority and thus social order, larger-scale conflict is likely (Choongh 1997; Johnston 2000). Although the focus is on Britain, evidence from other Western English-speaking countries, particularly the United States and Australia, is introduced to show different instances and histories of policing race and ethnicity.

Lore and disorder: history of minority–police conflict in Britain

It was noted in Chapter 5 how a downward spiral occurred in relations between the London Metropolitan Police and London's Caribbean community from the 1950s. An early study (Glass 1960) of London's West Indian community pointed to an overt 'colour bar' in housing and places of public entertainment, which the police did nothing to discourage. The defining moment for how the police and the public would first come to perceive race relations in Britain, however, was the white race riots in Nottingham and Notting Hill and elsewhere in London in August and September 1958, which involved numerous attacks on West Indians and their houses. This would not be the last time that race relations and public disorder would come to be seen as synonymous. Responses to the disorders were mixed. There were those who condemned the white rioters while identifying 'the colour problem' as predicated on the presence of a 'coloured minority'. Other commentators voiced their concerns over prostitution associated with the areas in which West Indians lived, against a background of growing unemployment, a chronic housing problem, concerns with crime and violence, 'Teddy boys' and licensed drinking clubs. Again not for the first time, the murder of Kelso Cochrane, a 32-year-old West Indian carpenter on the night of 17 May 1959 in Notting Hill Gate, London, ignited a different kind of debate, about the vulnerability of black men to violent racism and the role of racist groups (Glass 1960). Meanwhile, Whitfield (2004) shows how the Metropolitan Police marginalised reports of any negative aspects of community relations and were unable to accept that community and race relations were anything more than the preserve of social workers. Londoners in general and police officers in particular began to view immigrants in an increasingly negative manner and as a threat to law and order. In particular, the police became obsessed with the gambling and prostitution alleged to exist within the West Indian community, reinforcing negative police stereotypes.

It is important to realise that the antagonism between police and black communities pre-dated any suggestion of black overrepresentation among offenders. Neither was this antagonism limited to young people (Keith 1993). It is the case, however, that although the new generation of African-Caribbeans inherited their parents' experience of racial exclusion and isolation, they faced very different conditions and problems of schooling and employment (Phillips and Phillips 1998). Hall *et al.* (1978) famously described and analysed how young black men and their alleged disproportionate involvement in street robbery came to symbolise a crisis in state authority amidst the growing economic crisis in which black and white working-class young people faced collapsing youth labour markets. Again not for the first time, panics about law and order and the linking of crime to race and ethnicity came to stand in for deeper underlying political and economic problems. Beginning in 1975, the police made a series of highly public statements claiming disproportionate black criminality. Collusion between the police and the media ran this story for the next decade. Thus in 1983 the *Sun* newspaper ran a headline 'BLACK CRIME SHOCK' and carried the statement: 'Blacks carried out twice as many muggings as whites in London last year' (cited in Lea and Young 1993: 105). Some studies argued that, in effect, the police consciously conspired to construct young black people as a serious threat to law and order so as to enhance their own powers and resources as the 'thin blue line' holding back a tide of alleged black criminality (Cashmore and McLaughlin 1991; Gilroy 1987). Others noted an interaction effect between disproportionate black crime that reflected disadvantage and police harassment. Whatever the truth of these claims, the police routinely used their discretionary powers to stop and search, harass and criminalise large numbers of young black men they believed 'suspicious' (Lea and Young 1993).

The means by which some black young men attempted to 'redress' the balance between the police's power and their powerlessness are now well known (Benyon and Solomos 1987; Rowe 1998; Solomos 2003). The 'riots' in 1980 and 1981 in Bristol, Brixton and Southall in London, Toxteth in Liverpool, Moss Side in Manchester and Handsworth in Birmingham involved a cross-section of the black community as well as large numbers of young black men. Triggered by the local arrest and police detention of young black men, often without charge, and alleged police harassment that heightened black collective identity and hostility to the police, the under-lying issue was the funnelling of black youth into unemployment or unproductive and uncreative work at the bottom of the labour market (Hall *et al.* 1978; Cashmore and Troyna 1982). In 1982, for example, 60 per cent of black 16–20-year-olds available for work were without a job (Muncie 2004). It is difficult not to agree with Keith's (1993: 232) conclusion that: 'In the 1980s the variables of race, crime and public order did not just interact, they came in part to define each other.'

Just as the white race riots in 1958 had marked the beginning of a new era of race relations in Britain, so too did the 1980s disorders. Keith (1993) argued that the 'uprisings' of the 1980s were instrumental in the systematic racist criminalisation of British black communities so that 'blackness' became represented as innately criminal. By this account 'cause' should not be confused with 'blame'. The cause of the rioting was not simply police racism but police–black conflict deeply rooted in the local histories and experiences of particular communities. In some places the police routinely raided social clubs used by blacks excluded from mainstream pubs. Other places became notorious for the deaths in police custody of black people, and still others for police drug raids of certain cafés, and so on. All of these events precipitated conflict and confrontation with the local police, but almost none of them had anything to do with significant or serious criminal activity. Keith (1993) concluded that although policing was clearly central to the underlying causes of civil disorder in the 1980s, it was not individual police racism or crime fighting as such which was to blame, but the changing role of the police in maintaining public order and sustaining the systematic racial subordination of one class of British citizens, in the context of the economic restructuring of British society. It is the structural position of police forces within society as a whole and the historical change in the nature of conflict, rather than the reification of the problem of police racism, that explained the disorders.

It would be inaccurate to assume that British minority–police conflict has only involved the African-Caribbean community. British Asian workers involved in strikes against workplace racial discrimination and segregation from the late 1950s to the late 1970s were sometimes policed in adversarial ways. This period was also marked by campaigns against the policing of immigration law. From the late 1970s and early 1980s Asian young people organised politically to defend their areas from marches and incursions by far right organisations (Webster 2004; Ramamurthy 2006). In July 1981, for example, 12 young Asian men were arrested on charges of conspiracy to manufacture petrol bombs in Bradford, West Yorkshire. They were able to produce a successful defence that they were defending their communities from threats by far right organisations to march through an Asian area. The acquittal of the 'Bradford 12', as they became known, in April 1982, marked a decisive moment for the Asian youth movement in places like Bradford and Southall in London and, most unusually, seemed to offer legal legitimacy to efforts of minorities to defend their areas from attack in the face of threatened racist violence. 'Self-defence' was to become a recurring theme which was later to have considerable consequences for police–Asian relations and in the recent period.

From the mid-1980s to the early 1990s racist violence against Asians increased, along with a marked increase in the reporting and recording of Asian on white racial incidents (Webster 1995, 1996, 2003; FitzGerald 2001). This period seemed to follow a similar pattern to that which had occurred in relations between the police and the African-Caribbean community in the 1970s and 1980s. Again, collusion between the police and media constructed 'Asian' ethnicity in the language of criminality, alleging the widespread involvement of Asian young men in street rebellion, gang violence, crime and drugs (Webster 1997; Goodey 2001). Eventually, the serious disorders in the North of England involving young Asian and some white young men in Bradford in 1995 and in Bradford, Burnley and Oldham in 2001 marked the abrupt end of the 'multicultural settlement' that had governed race relations in the 1980s and 1990s (Kalra 2003; Webster 2003). The current period has seen a particular escalation of the threat some young British Asians are said to pose through terrorist acts, with profound implications for the policing of Asian communities (Pape 2006; Richardson 2006). Each of the periods reviewed here constituted a particular relationship of Asian communities to the police as governors, arbiters and enforcers of public order and marked a shift in that relationship. The recent and current periods are discussed later.

Policing black and minority ethnic communities in Britain

'Suspect populations'

It is well established that the police routinely identify 'suspect populations' they believe are likely to be involved in criminality to which they return and harass on the basis of how the police perceive and judge their social status, age, ethnicity and gender, as well as their known criminality and availability on the street (McAra and McVie 2005). In their study of contact between the police and white children and young people in Edinburgh, Scotland, McAra and McVie (2005) concluded

> that the police do disproportionately target certain groups of children who might accurately be described as the 'usual suspects'. This suspect population comprises (for the most part) young boys from lower class backgrounds and broken families, who live in areas of high social deprivation, who have an active street life (and who consequently form a core component of the population available for policing). Importantly, analysis indicates that it is the volume and seriousness of their offending, which is *key* to understanding why children *first* come to the attention of the police. However, once identified as a

trouble-maker, this status appears to suck young people into a spiral of amplified contact, regardless of whether they continue to be involved in serious levels of offending.

In contrast, Bowling and Phillips's (2002: 166) comprehensive review of evidence about policing British minority ethnic communities concluded that there is

> a widespread tendency for black and Asian communities to receive greatly inferior treatment by the police ... and that ethnic minority communities are considered to be 'suspect populations' in a way which transcends their class position and is defined specifically by police officers in terms of 'racial' characteristics as individuals and as a collective.

These seemingly contradictory conclusions are not necessarily in disagreement because they refer to different ethnic contexts and places. However, they require some refinements and the adding of some caveats. While the police construct 'suspect populations' on the basis of class as well as race, the fact that Asian people's experiences of contact with the police is more mixed, ambiguous and complicated than is sometimes the case with black people's experiences can offer new insight into the relationship of race, ethnicity and class in policing situations and processes.

Attitudes towards the police

Smith (1997) has argued that Asian experiences of police and criminal justice processes are different than those of African-Caribbeans. Although police racism towards Asians is evident, it takes a different form from racism directed towards African-Caribbean people, and this is reflected in different contact and conflict between the police and Asian people. Gordon (1983) concluded that although there was a strong perception within particularly African-Caribbean neighbourhoods that they were 'overpoliced' (i.e. harassed and subject to racist abuse and brutality by the police) this was much less the case among Asians, including young people. More recently, the growing paradox in the policing of British Asian communities is that on the one hand community members seek more effective policing to reduce crime and disorder, while on the other Asian communities have become increasingly perceived as sources of criminality, disorder and terrorism (Webster 2004). Studies appear to show that attitudes towards the police, whether from direct or indirect contact with them, are different between white, black and Asian people. Waddington and Braddock (1991) found that 'cultural attitudes towards the police' varied in that both white and Asian groups of young people included those who viewed the police as either trusted guardians of law and order or bullies, whereas the study's black sample almost exclusively regarded the police as 'bullies' in uniform.

These two fundamentally different conceptions of what the police are – their role and function in society as either trustworthy and efficient or epitomised in terms of arbitrary authority and racial discrimination – arise from the ways in which the police are seen to use their discretion, as impartially or not. Such studies, however, usually ignore the social class background of young people. Numerous studies of attitudes towards the police (see, for example, Crawford *et al.* 1990; Aye Maung 1995; Sims and Myhill 2001) have consistently found that either Asians disapprove less of the police than African-Caribbeans or whites, or tend to hold views which place them between African-Caribbeans and whites in their disapproval ratings, although some studies lump Asians and African-Caribbeans together, take insufficient account of age, and few disaggregate 'Asian' or class background. Similarly, Asians were less likely to believe that police misconduct occurred frequently than whites and African-Caribbeans.

Contact with the police: stop and search

Studies of police-initiated contact can permit inferences to be made about police attitudes towards and different treatment of minority ethnic groups (see Phillips and Brown 1998; Bowling and Phillips 2002; FitzGerald *et al.* 2002a). For example, Norris *et al.*'s (1992) observation study of a routine police patrol in inner-city London found that black people, particularly young black men, were disproportionately likely to be stopped. Although they were unable to isolate whether race or some other factor leads to a particular police action, nevertheless the intensity of surveillance that young black men collectively experienced gave rise to high levels of hostility towards the police. Overall, Asians are stopped and searched by the police to a lesser extent than blacks, but more than whites. The most common reason for searching black and Asian people is for drugs, and despite wide variation between police force areas, black people were more likely to be stopped for this reason than any other group (Home Office 2000b, 2006). In 2004/5 black people were six times as likely, and Asian people twice as likely, to be stopped and searched as white people (Home Office 2006). The search rate for black and Asian people under the Terrorism Act 2000 was four and five times that for white people (Dodd and Travis 2005). Indeed, throughout the 1990s police discretionary and legal powers to stop children and young people in the street were significantly extended, and predictably these powers were much more likely to be used against Asians and African-Caribbeans (Muncie 2004). Studies appear to show that some police officers are more suspicious in their attitudes towards Asian and black young people, and are more likely to stop individuals belonging to these groups on 'speculative' grounds for some types of offences, especially robbery and drug offences, than white young people. In general, there is evidence of 'overpolicing' black and minority ethnic communities (see also Chapter 4) through heightened suspicion of drugs possession, stops being more likely to result in a search and formal action, trawling for arrests on speculative grounds, and using stop and search to socially control young people (FitzGerald 1999; Phillips and Bowling 2002).

Arrests

Nine per cent of arrests in 2004/5 were of black people and 5 per cent Asians, and this disproportionate arrest rate – black people were three times more likely to be arrested than white people – had increased from the previous year (Home Office 2006). Arrest rates for Asians were generally greater than for white people but below those for black people, although this varies according to their representation in the local population and the location of the police station (Phillips and Brown 1998). Of those arrested, whites and Asians experience similar cautioning rates, higher than for blacks, although some studies have found that Asians were significantly less likely to be cautioned than white suspects (Phillips and Brown 1998). Black and Asian people are overrepresented in arrests for fraud, forgery and drugs (Home Office 2000b, 2006). It is possible, though, that earlier studies are out of date and that since the mid-1990s police suspicion towards Asians may have intensified in the context of recent disorders and growing anti-Muslim feeling (see Miles and Brown 2003).

Police beliefs

Some have claimed that, compared to African-Caribbeans, Asians suffer little discrimination at the hands of the police despite being similarly disadvantaged, and that this reflects both their actual lower offending rates and the belief among police that they offend less (Smith 1997, 2005). Although evidence has been available for some time that (some) police officers *do* hold stereotypes of Asians (Graef 1989; Webster 1997; Bowling 1999), it has not been clear whether these incorporate the *belief* that Asians offend more or less than other groups or offend more than they were thought to have done in the past. As Bowling and Phillips (2002) make clear, their victimisation tends not to be believed by the police. Low offending rates among Asians have traditionally been explained as the result of strong informal controls said to inhere in 'Asian culture and family life' creating a criminological and police consensus about the law-abiding nature of Asians (Mawby and Batta 1980; see Webster 1997). Wardak (2000) examined the decisive influence of community institutions in the Pakistani community in Edinburgh in discouraging or controlling deviance and delinquency, cultural institutions that paradoxically had grown in importance in the face of white hostility and high levels of deprivation.

Recent studies continue to suggest that Asian young people's experience has been different from that of black young people, being similar to or more favourable than that of whites at each stage of the police process, from stop and search through to remand decisions (Webster 2004, Home Office 2006). Whether different treatment of Asians is as significant as it is for African-Caribbeans might be clearer if studies disaggregated Asians, particularly Pakistanis and Bangladeshis living in poor neighbourhoods (see Clancy *et al.* 2001).

Bowling and Phillips (2002: 129) amply summarise the sources of black–police hostility as more intensive surveillance, higher rates of stops and arrests by the police, and harassment, citing

> pervasive, ongoing targeting of black areas involving 'stopping vehicles 'often on a flimsy pretext', persistent stop and search on the streets, commonplace rude and hostile questioning accompanied by racial abuse, arbitrary arrest, violence on arrest, the arrest of witnesses and bystanders, punitive and indiscriminate attacks, victimisation on reporting crime, acting on false information, forced entry and violence, provocative and unnecessary armed raids, and repeated harassment and trawling for suspects.

Taking into account all stages of police processes (including cautioning and being held at the police station), Bowling and Phillips (2002) concluded that when black young people came into contact with the police, whether as victims or witnesses, when they reported crime, sought information, or as suspects, their position in terms of the treatment they received and their perceptions and experiences of the police tended to be worse than comparable Asian and white young people.

Police racism

Some studies have challenged this view of pervasive police racism on grounds that there is a disjuncture between the attitudes and behaviour of police officers – between their private attitudes and their professional behaviour – noting that the prevalence of racism and stereotyping has little impact in terms of the way in which officers go about their duties (Waddington 1999). Alternatively, it might be – as claimed by Macpherson (1999) – that the police organisation is 'institutionally racist' and police officers are unwittingly racist (see the critical discussion in Lea 2000; Rowe 2004). Another study has challenged the view that racial disproportionality in police stop and search is attributable to officers selectively targeting minority groups. Waddington *et al.*'s (2004) direct observation study argues that the 'available population' – those who use public spaces on a regular basis – does not have the same demographic or ethnic characteristics as the resident population against whom disproportionate stops are usually compared. They concluded that, compared to the 'available population', those stopped and searched are not disproportionately drawn from minority groups. In general, the disproportionality in stop and search experiences by young men of *all* racial and ethnic groups may simply attest to their greater availability for being stopped and searched, rather than any particular selectivity on the part of the police. Factors such as the visibility of police targets, elderly vehicles, the available population at different times of day and night, variation between police force areas, etc., were more important factors in police decisions to stop and search than ethnicity *per se*. The evidence presented here and in Chapter 4 suggested that black people *are* disproportionately stopped, searched and arrested for *certain* offences – street robbery and drug possession – even when their greater (demographic) 'availability' in the local *population* is taken into account, but this is a different matter than their availability and visibility on the *street*, to which Waddington *et al.*'s (2004) study alludes.

Policing black and minority ethnic communities in the United States

In the USA controversy surrounding situations of contact and conflict between the police and minorities has mostly centred on the experiences of African-Americans. From being personally 'hassled' – being stopped or closely watched by a police officer, having not done anything wrong – and disproportionate arrest rates, to being shot by a police officer, African-Americans have a strong sense that they are treated unfairly by the police, compared to whites and other groups (Miller 1997; Russell 1998; Walker *et al.* 2004). The most widespread source of this perception is what is claimed to be 'racial profiling' – the use of race as an indicator in the decision to stop and search a suspect (Russell 1998: 34) – but this is only part of a larger pattern of racial disparities in the criminal justice system (see Chapter 7). Racial and ethnic minorities are arrested, stopped and questioned, shot and killed by the police out of proportion to their representation in the population. African-Americans represent only 12 per cent of the population but 28 per cent of all arrests, 33 per cent of all index crime arrests, and 38 per cent of all violent crime arrests (Walker *et al.* 2004). Police processes and activities, from the most routine to the use of deadly force, show a consistent pattern in the relationship between the police and racial and ethnic minorities that suggests the existence of police racism. However, this pattern is complicated by variation between different minority groups, between different police departments in their treatment of minorities, between the police and minorities of different socioeconomic status, and between different parts of the police organisation in their impact on minority groups.

As in Britain, there is a long history of conflict between the police and racial and ethnic minorities involving large-scale public disorder and rioting, often provoked by police abuse and mostly involving Hispanics and African-Americans, notably in 1917–19, 1943, 1964–8, 1970 and 1971, and in the riots of 1992 in Los Angeles and 2001 in Cincinnati. This should alert us to the fact that race and ethnicity are consistently the most important factors in shaping attitudes about the police, but, similar to the position of South Asians in Britain, virtually every survey of public attitudes about the police in the USA shows that Hispanic attitudes of confidence in the police fall in between white and African-American attitudes. The real differences in favourable or unfavourable perceptions of the police, however, are found among poor African-Americans and young people, regardless of race, both groups being the most hostile. The heart of the conflict between police and minorities involves young people, particularly young men, and especially those in poor neighbourhoods (Miller 1997; Russell 1998; Walker *et al.* 2004). African-Americans have much less favourable attitudes toward the police than any other group, and they report higher levels of use of excessive force against them, although this varies according to local police policy on the use of physical or deadly force, and some argue that class rather than race is the determining factor in the use of excessive force.

Arrest data suggest that people from racial minorities, especially African-Americans, are arrested far more frequently than whites. This is likely to be because of *both* some minorities' greater involvement in serious crime *and* the persistence of some discrimination against African-Americans (Walker *et al.* 2004). To the extent that it can be said to exist, racial profiling seems of less significance than 'class profiling' – the disproportionate and harsh policing of poor young people in poor or wealthy areas, as well as African-Americans in white areas. Overall, minorities are more likely than white Americans to be shot and killed, arrested, and victimised by excessive force, but this reflects the broader patterns of social and economic inequality in US society discussed in Chapters 3, 7, 8 and 9. These inequalities are based on both race and class, and the injustices suffered by racial and ethnic minorities at the hands of the police are a result of both discrimination and the disproportionate representation of minorities among the poor.

Policing black and minority ethnic communities in Australia

The situation between the police and minorities in Australia was touched on in Chapter 4, particularly the overwhelming use of police custody for low-level public disorder offences in relation to the Aboriginal population. Describing and analysing police processes in Australian contexts, Collins *et al.* (2000), with reference to the policing of young Lebanese men in urban areas, and Poynting *et al.* (2004), with reference to the policing of Arabs and 'terrorism', found police discrimination. For example, Collins *et al.* (2000) found fraught patterns of contact and conflict similar to the USA and Britain between the police and minority young men in Sydney. Again, though, the key focus here is the relationship between the police and Aboriginal people, a relationship explained, according to Cunneen (2001: 75), by the history and nature of paramilitary colonial policing in Australia: 'the legal order which police came to enforce was very much the law of a colonial state which excluded Aboriginal people and sought their control'.

Indigenous people in Australia were from quite early on in the colonisation process subjected to widespread terror, violence and massacres in the context of a suspension of the rule of law. Police summary executions of Aboriginal people, in response to their resistance to the expropriation of their land without compensation, were followed by authoritarian legislation to prevent their movement and keep them in designated reservations. The police assisted in maintaining indigenous people in a position which denied them fundamental human rights and afforded them little protection under the law (Cunneen 2001). They were subject to paramilitary policing, racialised and routinely discriminated against, using levels of violence and, later, levels of police surveillance that did not apply to any other group. From the 1960s onwards, even as legislation to protect Aboriginal people was being introduced, there was increased contact between Aboriginal people and the police around 'street offences' and the control of behaviour in public places. The policing of alleged street offences by Aboriginal people during the 1980s and 1990s was continuous, extensive and disproportionate. This overpolicing eventually gave way to 'zero tolerance' policing and a renewed concentration on the policing of street offences, again public order offences that particularly targeted Aboriginal people.

Cunneen (2001) identified the fundamental relationship between the police and indigenous people as one organised around social space and social order, and the regulation, contestation and policing of space. These ideas and themes are taken up in the next section in a very different national and racial context.

Explaining conflict and hostility between black and minority ethnic young people and the police

Working-class young people – white, Asian and black – are treated as 'police property'; as Muncie (2004: 232) notes, 'histories of police–youth relations are replete with examples of the proactive policing of young people's use of public space'. Reiner (1985: 132) concluded that 'the disproportionate black arrest rate is the product of black deprivation, police stereotyping and the process by which each of these factors amplifies the other'. A report by the Commission for Racial Equality (2005) suggests it unlikely that we have entered a more benign 'post-Macpherson' policing era, as lessons about racial targeting by the police had still not been learnt and had not percolated down the police ranks. What *is* certain is that police processes are important triggers that can recruit and propel young people into the criminal and youth justice system, as the next chapter demonstrates.

So far, an emerging pattern is discernible that draws our attention to a particular source of police–minority conflict found in the policing of all young men (and women) in public space, regardless of race or ethnicity. Can we therefore separate race, class and age effects in the policing of public space and public order? Both in terms of their experiences of over-policing and underpolicing – that is, that minority and other young people feel that they are subject to a double injustice of disproportionate police attention as a suspect population while not being protected as vulnerable victims – are these the sources of their hostility and conflict with the police? It would seem so. Webster (1995) found that Asian young people had a stronger perception than whites of the police as unlikely to be sympathetic to them as victims. Yet they were also more worried about becoming victims of crime and were more likely to report their victimisation.

Anderson *et al.*'s (1994) groundbreaking Edinburgh study of white young people found that young people are generally reluctant to report their victimisation to adults or the police. Instead they employ peer support as a means of security, self-reliance and self-defence that relies on the 'solidarity' of those it protects (loyalty and not 'grassing'). To 'break with this is to threaten the whole basis of the strategy – and with it the personal and collective safety of all' (Anderson *et al.* 1994: 152). The consequence is that in developing their own strategies for coping with crime and policing in an attempt to reduce the impact that crime has on them, without reference to the adult world, young people risk exacerbating and inflating its importance. At the same time, a 'vicious circle' is set in train whereby because young people are not taken seriously by adults or the police, or are even held in some way responsible for their victimisation, they do not report, their victimisation remains hidden, adult and police incredulity increases, the police are deprived of the information they require to investigate crime successfully, and, faced with this situation, the police are left to resort to the very adversarial methods that contributed to this lack of information in the first place (Andersson *et al.* 1994: 158). Loader (1996) has noted this vicious circle effect, adding that the frequency with which the police move on young people is matched only by the rarity with which young people call the police as victims of crime. When there is evidence that the police consider young people in public places as their 'property', judge them in terms of respectability and ethnicity, question and apprehend them on suspicion of technical delinquency and generally routinely supervise their use of public space, then the circle is closed (Loader 1996; McAra and McVie 2005).

Case study: the British 'Asian' disorders of 1995 and 2001

The history of apparently racially based public disorder and minority–police conflict in Britain at its most spectacular has involved large-scale urban rioting – notably involving African-Caribbeans in the 1980s. As the 1990s progressed, a different group of disaffected young men began to appear on the streets of Britain to show their direct opposition to the police.

The disorders of June 1995 involving large numbers of Asian young men in the Manningham area of Bradford, in the North of England, were triggered when two police officers intervened against a 'noisy group' of young Asian men playing football in the street, entered a house and allegedly knocked down an Asian woman in a struggle, during which three young men were arrested (Bradford Congress 1996). The report of a local community organisation concluded that the disorders occurred in the context of a 'severe loss of confidence in the police' and provocative and unreasonable police action. Unlike the subsequent Bradford disorders of 2001, the 1995 disorders were at the time widely seen to be primarily anti-police riots. Anecdotal evidence suggested paradoxically that Asian young men in the area alleged tolerance and neglect by the police of prostitution, street drunkenness, rowdiness and abusive and intimidating behaviour by whites coming into the area from outside, all of which were deemed an affront to the mostly British Muslim Pakistani and Bangladeshi populations living there. Despite or because of the occurrence of public disorder, their resentment towards the police seemed to rest on a perception of them being unable or unwilling to maintain order and civility on the street or address their concerns about crime.

Their particular concern to supposedly protect Asian women from affronts to public morality and propriety was perhaps perversely linked with the action that had sparked off the disorders, which in their eyes demonstrated disrespect among police officers towards Asian women. Somehow this was also linked with the inability or refusal of police officers to rid the area of street prostitution, as Asian young men acted as vigilantes driving prostitutes out of the area. These actions had also spurred resident white and black women to leave the area, as they felt harassed and perceived as prostitutes. The imagery was of high levels of distrust and hostility towards the police and their ability to tackle incivility in the area.

In contrast, the immediate events leading to the serious public disorders that took place in the Northern English ex-textile towns of Oldham, Burnley and Bradford in spring and summer 2001 appeared to be a confused series of well-publicised violent 'racist' clashes and attacks against people and property involving Asian and white young people. The context was a climate of fear and rumour within Asian communities that the British National Party and/or the National Front – both far-right racist political parties – were going to march into Asian areas despite banning orders authorised by the British Home Secretary. The National Front had visited Oldham from all parts of the country to demonstrate their 'support of the white population against racist attacks', and the relative electoral success of the British National Party in Oldham and Burnley seemed to affirm significant support for ideological racism. The overall effect was reversion among Asian young people to 'self-defence' in the context of these perceived threats. There is a considerable literature analysing the disorders (see, for example, Kundnani 2001; McGhee 2003; Webster 2003; Burnett 2004; Hussain and Bagguley 2005; Robinson 2005; Worley 2005), mostly criticising the narrowness and agenda setting of the official reports, the abandonment of multicultural policy and questioning the efficacy of the notion of 'community cohesion'. Here the focus is on the policing dimension and implications for the policing of Asian communities, before attempting to explain some causes of the rioting in Bradford, Burnley and Oldham.

Official local and national reviews and reports on the disorders and the conditions preceding them (Clarke 2001; Ouseley 2001; Ritchie 2001; Cantle 2002; Denham 2002) were generally uncritical of the police in terms of either any historical role they might have played or in their operational handling of the events themselves. Significantly, however, most of the reports emphasised that their consultation with local Asian communities had revealed that most people, including young people, wanted the police to be more evident on the streets and have a stronger and more visible role. Consistent with anecdotal evidence surrounding the 1995 Bradford disorders, locals alleged that the police had tolerated virtual 'no-go areas' by not tackling drug crime and even colluding with non-intervention in relation to inner-city drug sale and use on the streets, and had underestimated the extent to which 'low-level' persistent offences and harassment creates fear of crime and lack of public safety. Meanwhile, it was felt that Asian young men in gangs remained untouchable and the police report and inquiry into the Burnley disorders argued that drug-related criminality within an Asian and a white group sparked the disorders, rather than racism (Clarke 2001).

This recurring and paradoxical theme in the policing of inner-city Asian communities – that, in effect, they are underpoliced rather than over-policed and that the police seem unwilling or unable to enforce the law against prostitution, drug dealing, anti-social behaviour and low-level per-sistent offending – sits uneasily alongside perceptions of the inadequacy of police responses to racist violence, and the punitive criminalisation of large numbers of Asian young men involved in the disorders. Cantle (2002) asserted that minority communities must face the fact that over time the police have adopted a toleration of certain types of criminality.

Webster (2003) examined socioeconomic, ethnic, demographic, hous-ing, crime and racist violence data from Oldham, Burnley and Bradford that pointed to some underlying structural issues to policing Asian com-munities in these areas. He concluded that the disorders in Oldham, for example, should be seen against a backdrop at the time of high and increas-ing rates of crime, especially violent crime, and large increases in reported racist *violence*, against national trends. In particular, although the majority of repeat victims were Asian and twice as many perpetrators were white as were Asian, there was willingness by whites to report incidents against them that they perceived as racist and to identify the *suspect* as Asian, reflecting a belief among whites of an increase in violent attacks upon them by groups of Asians and a belief among Asians that certain areas and housing estates were 'no-go areas' for them. Areas that suffered the highest rates of unemployment and social and economic disadvantage – areas of

Asian and white working-class residence – were also seen as the most violent and disorderly. These or adjoining areas were where the disorders took place. British Pakistanis and Bangladeshis living in Oldham, Bradford and Burnley, like elsewhere in Britain, are among the poorest minority ethnic groups (see Chapter 7).

Explaining the Asian disorders: 'parallel lives'?

Denham's (2002: 1) Home Office report on the disorders opened with the claim that Asian and white communities were living 'parallel lives'. Herman Ouseley's (2001) report on Bradford set the agenda for how the disorders subsequently came to be understood, pointing to the existence of self-styled and unrepresentative 'community leaders' who encourage segregation and fear to maintain their power base. Ouseley (2001: 1) argued that there were growing divisions along race, ethnic and social class lines, noting 'the very worrying drift towards self-segregation' in a city that apparently 'now finds itself in the grip of fear'. Alleged growing ethnic segregation was partly fuelled by 'self-segregation' based in fear of racist harassment and violent crime, and partly by the promotion and protection of identities and cultures. Further, certain community policing styles had themselves contributed to segregation in the past by mistakenly seeking the views of unrepresentative adult 'community leaders' while ignoring the views of a wider constituency, including young people. These claims of self-segregation as a main contributing factor explaining the disorders are next examined.

The main basis of explanation and subsequent discussion about the 2001 disorders in Northern English cities were claims of residential concentration, self-segregation and polarised (particularly Asian) communities. Some writers have examined these claims by measuring whether increased segregation has taken place over time, using the 1991 and 2001 Census. Simpson (2004) found that, contrary to the widely held belief that residential areas in inner-city Bradford had become more segregated by ethnicity, the Asian population living in these areas of original settlement was growing naturally and through continued immigration (mostly through marriage partners coming to Britain), not through self-segregation. Not only was there no movement of South Asian residents towards areas of South Asian concentration, but on the contrary Asians were dispersing from these to other more ethnically mixed areas. Earlier studies had noted a dispersal over time of African-Caribbeans born in London but a concentration of Bangladeshis, yet concluded that there are no ghettos in British cities. Simpson (2004) argues that this is also the case for British Asians when residential movement over time rather than the size of the population at any one time is taken into account. Others (Ratcliffe 1997; D. Phillips 1998; Webster 2003) have found that many Asians, particularly young adults, would like to move to 'better' and mixed areas outside the current inner-city settlements but are not easily able to do so because of a paucity of affordable and suitable housing, lack of social networks for support, racial discrimination in the housing and labour markets, and fear of harassment. It is clear, though, that the predominant housing aspirations among *both* whites and Asians of where to live identify areas characterised as being among 'decent people', having good-quality housing and local amenities, and low levels of crime and violence, regardless of their ethnic composition. Overall, these studies concluded that self-segregation on the basis of ethnicity is a myth, and in Britain (in contrast to the USA; see Walker *et al.* 2004) residential segregation on the basis of social class is much more significant than segregation on the basis of ethnicity (Dorling and Thomas 2004; Simpson 2005).

A counter-argument is put by others that aspirations about where to live and evidence of some dispersal of Asians from original settlement areas are beside the point, because of the *de facto* proportional growth of Asian populations in these areas due to their younger demography. This is held to be more important in deciding whether segregation has increased than the movement of people into and out of areas. For example, Johnston *et al.* (2005) argue that the Bradford Asian population is becoming more isolated residentially. Increasing 'concentration' – the proportion of an area population who are Asian – in Bradford points to increasing segregation – isolation from the remainder of the population, over time. In other words, despite Asians moving to more ethnically mixed or white areas, this has not equalled the amount of Asian in-movement and population growth in traditional areas. Finally, Burgess *et al.* (2005) point to high levels of school and neighbourhood ethnic segregation across England, especially among British Pakistani and Bangladeshi children, and claim that areas of particularly high segregation for Asian pupils coincide almost exactly with the locations of public disorder in 2001 (in Bradford, Oldham, Burnley, and nearby Blackburn where no disorders took place). Whether Asians can be seen as living 'parallel lives' depends on how segregation is understood. Asian populations are growing faster in traditional areas of Asian settlement because of the youthfulness of the population. But this is a different matter than whether segregation is desired or chosen – 'self-segregation'. The evidence is that Asians, like other groups, including the white majority, wish to live in affluent areas whatever the ethnic make-up of those areas, but are prevented from doing so because they cannot afford it and/or are discriminated against in the housing and labour markets. These factors are ignored in the reports on the disorders.

Understanding race, policing and disorder

The policing of African-Americans, especially young men and women, has to be seen in the context of a more racially segregated urban society than is found in Britain and over a much longer period, involving an overt attempt to contain and control African-American communities and maintain white supremacy. This is even more the case seen in the policing of Aboriginal people in Australia, where the paramilitary policing of indigenous people was part and parcel of colonial policy.

The history of the deterioration of relations and subsequent conflict between African-Caribbeans and the police in Britain has rightly been emphasised as a key aspect of the processes that led to escalation of these and outright confrontation and public disorder in the 1980s. Although each disorder arose from local conditions and specific histories of grievance and conflict, the scale of the disorders across urban Britain pointed to a general crisis in the relationship between African-Caribbean communities and the police in the 1980s. This crisis was unlikely to have arisen from significant criminality within the African-Caribbean community – although police obsession with marijuana possession was, and probably still is, very apparent – but from pervasive conflict and adversarial policing against African-Caribbean young men at the time. By contrast, relationships between the police and Asian communities in Britain have until recently received comparatively little attention and have therefore been emphasised here.

Conventional views of race, policing and disorder, as well as ignoring local histories of police and ethnic relations that can lead to conflict, see the police's role as responding to or containing disorder in very difficult circumstances. What is usually left out of this account is the role the police may themselves have played in precipitating disorders in the first place through the (often oppressive) ways they have policed certain neighbour-hoods and groups, particularly the young and the poor who already experience wider discrimination in education, housing and labour markets. The police's historical dislike of, and independence from, political control and their lack of introspection have helped form many of their attitudes, while at the same time their experience of hostility has informed officers' broader perspectives of the black and Asian community as being 'anti-police'. It is tempting to argue, as some might, that the police cannot 'win' in public disorder situations. They are pilloried by rioters and their supporters for being racist, and by officialdom and the public for having been too 'soft' on the supposed criminality that is said to lead to such disorders.

Whether minority groups are treated differently or more harshly than whites by the police is often couched in terms of *either* the police's 'justi-fiable' suspicion that certain groups – primarily young working-class white and black men living in poor areas or being in the 'wrong' areas, or simply being on the street or driving certain vehicles – are more likely to be involved in offending, *or* the police making unfounded generalisations about individuals and groups based on stereotyping and racism. The prob-lem with this 'either/or' scenario is that it precludes the possibility of 'both', that is, that the police believe that some groups are disproportionately likely to be involved in offending and/or public disorder *and* that this informs their different judgement and treatment of individuals according to their availability on the street, time and place, where they live, and their age, gender, ethnicity and social class. The police return again and again to the 'usual suspects' – those the police themselves help construct as a 'suspect population'. From a policing perspective, such criminal stereotypes are an inevitable part of police work. Lea (1986: 160) characterises this perspective as follows: 'If, for every offence committed, the police directed their attentions and suspicions equally to all sections of the community, then no crime would ever be solved.' Criminal stereotyping on the part of the police seems inevitable whether visible race is present or not. Here we enter a self-confirming vicious circle in which if the police believe that young black men are disproportionately involved in particular types of crime (say drug offences or street robbery), then a disproportionate number of the group may be stopped and arrested, which may then amplify the original involvement of the group in crime, while confirming police stereotypes of criminality. This magnification process, reflected in police arrest statistics, then serves to intensify the concentration of police resources deployed against the group, further artificially magnifying its arrest rates, and so on (Lea 1986).

Much of the debate surrounding racist stereotyping in the police has conceptualised the problem as an issue of the peculiarities of police 'canteen culture' or 'cop culture' – the informal occupational attitudes, values and ideologies said to inhere in the police. 'Cop culture' has been described by Reiner (2000) as embodying seemingly contradictory senses of mission/ commitment and cynicism; isolation and solidarity from the wider community and an omnipotent belief that only the police 'really' understand the problems of wider society; that the police represent the 'thin blue line' between social order and chaos while being parochial, insular, suspicious and stereotyping in attitudes. Although, as Reiner argues, many of these beliefs are functional for police work to be effective and succeed, they can easily result in racist stereotyping. This cultural explanation tends to ignore the question of power or the ways in which the police are structurally positioned towards poor and black and minority ethnic communities – as unaccountable and powerful – as well as the wider society. Chan (1997), in particular, has pointed to weaknesses in cultural explanations, drawing attention instead to broader institutional, social and structural dimensions of policing. Comparing the occupational subculture model and wider explanations resting on social structural issues of inequality and power-lessness, certainly subculture plays a part in creating resistance among the lower ranks to what they regard as politically driven 'top-down' 'anti-racist' management initiatives, such as the post-Lawrence reforms (Rowe 2004).

Junior officers jealously guard the power and discretion conferred on them in enforcing the law and in their dealings with the public, including minority ethnic communities. Among officers, 'not to be racist' in using these powers may seem to them as an interfering and politically motivated special interest – one among many competing demands placed on them

– rather than a fundamental principle of fair and democratic policing. Chan's (1997) study has shown, in the Australian context, that police reform is fraught with difficulties of implementation on the ground, and can easily be overtaken by events. For example, there is growing evidence that Asian young men are being disproportionately stopped and searched under the Terrorism Act. Yet as Richardson (2006) convincingly demonstrates, terrorist risks have been *both* greatly exaggerated *and* enhanced by the ill-judged reactions of the USA and her allies to the attacks of 11 September 2001. And, as Pape (2006) demonstrates, suicide terrorists are wholly atypical of members of Asian Muslim communities in Britain and elsewhere. Paradoxically though, they carry out suicide attacks from altruistic motives and with a perverse sense of duty towards their communities.

Finally, the structurally powerful position of the police *vis-à-vis* some of the communities they police is discussed by Choongh (1997), who argues that negative police attitudes to poorer minority ethnic and other areas can lead to aggressive and antagonistic policing strategies that discipline particular segments of the population, legitimised in terms of the maintenance of public order. Johnston (2000: 51) argued that late modern policing combines this disciplinary function with 'policing communities of risk'. British Asian Muslim communities have come to embody perceived 'risk' in ways hardly imagined a decade ago, while at the same time, as Hussain and Bagguley (2005) found in their study of British Asian Muslim young people, they demand 'recognition', acceptance and equal rights as British citizens – an acceptance they believe is often denied to them.

Further reading

The historical context and process of the deterioration of relations between the police and British Caribbeans in London is catalogued by Whitfield (2004). The standard British work on race, policing and disorder is Keith (1993), but readers should also seek out Lea and Young (1993) for a 'left realist' perspective, and Cashmore and McLaughlin (1991) for a 'radical' perspective. Choongh (1997) and Chan (1997) provide excellent grounded theoretical accounts of police functions and police culture, respectively, that go a long way in explaining the underlying reasons for police–minority contact, conflict and hostility. Waddington et al.'s (2004) important and innovative study of disproportionality in police stop and search challenges some long-held criminological assumptions. Finally, Rowe's (2004) useful overview of recent debates in policing and racism serves as a clearly written and argued primer on these debates. Russell (1998) and Walker et al. (2004) again offer good critical reviews of the American literature, and Cunneen (2001) does so for Australia.

chapter seven

Race, criminal justice and penality: difference or discrimination?

Criminal justice processes cannot be examined in isolation or divorced from their wider context in other institutional processes and processes of social and economic change. These wider processes can have a direct impact on who ends up in the criminal justice system and in prison and an indirect effect on how they are treated and judged having arrived there. Studies of race, criminal justice and penality have often ignored the 'indirect' effects of racial discrimination and injustice outside the criminal justice system – in schools, among the police, in care homes, in neighbourhoods and housing and labour markets – on criminal justice processes, instead just focusing on evidence of discrimination within the criminal justice process itself. This chapter attempts to redress this imbalance between a sole concern with processes internal to the criminal justice system and a complementary concern with factors in the wider social and institutional environment in which the criminal justice system operates. There is also a particular, although not exclusive, focus on the youth justice system and young people, partly because individuals who have not offended by aged 15 or 16 are unlikely to do so, and partly through limitations of space.

The chapter first describes the overrepresentation of black and minority ethnic groups in criminal justice systems across a range of national jurisdictions, focusing particularly on Britain and the United States where the data are most reliable. Second, it explores how this overrepresentation might be explained – whether it is because of different or elevated offending rates among some black and minority ethnic groups compared to whites, or because of discrimination in criminal justice processes, or whether there might be *both* higher offending rates among some groups (see Chapter 4) *and* discrimination both within and outside criminal justice processes. Third, the chapter discusses perceptions of fairness and equality about the criminal justice system in Britain and America. Finally, it places the criminal justice system as one institutional site on a continuum of crime and social control institutions in the context of wider changes in social, welfare and criminal justice policies, social and economic change, and the creation of prison and custodial populations.

Race and criminal justice in England and Wales

Overrepresentation

Generally, black and minority ethnic groups are overrepresented in the criminal justice system when compared to their representation as members of the population as a whole. This is especially true for black and Asian suspects and offenders. Black and Asian people experience a greater likelihood of being stopped and searched. Asian and especially black defendants are more prominent in the Crown Court caseload, although this is partly due to a tendency to elect for jury trial more than other ethnic groups, including whites. Furthermore, black people are also overrepresented in the prison population, reflecting, at least in part, the longer average sentences imposed upon them (Home Office 2006). These data are presented in Table 3.

What is particularly striking about Table 3 is the very significant overrepresentation of black people, and to a lesser extent Asian people, at every stage of the criminal justice process compared to their proportions in the relevant general population. What is at issue here is whether black and Asian people are treated differently because of their supposed racial background or ethnicity. Feilzer and Hood (2004: 30) warn that

the research carried out on this issue over several years has failed to

Table 3 Percentage of people at different stages of the criminal justice process by ethnic group, England and Wales, 2004/5

	Ethnicity			
	White	Black	Asian	Unknown/not recorded
Stops and searches	74.7	14.1	7.1	2.6
Arrests[a]	84.3	8.8	4.9	0.6
Cautions[a]	83.8	6.4	4.4	4.2
Youth offences[b]	84.7	6.0	3.0	3.3
Crown Court	75.7	13.0	7.4	–
Prison population[c]	76.8	13.5	5.4	0.7
Prison receptions[c]	80.8	10.2	5.4	0.5
General population (aged 10 and over, 2001)	91.3	2.8	4.7	0.0

[a] Notifiable offences.
[b] Proportion for mixed background 2.3%.
[c] Sentenced prisoners only. Proportion for mixed-background prison population 2.7%; prison receptions 2.4%.

Source: Home Office (2006).

reveal any findings that conclusively prove whether these different outcomes for minority ethnic people have been due to discrimination, either direct or indirect – or the result of other factors.

After all, ethnicity is just one of a complex of socially constructed experiences, which may or may not take on significance in particular circumstances or situations. Some visible minority ethnic groups of young people are decidedly underrepresented in self-reported crime and in the youth justice system compared to their numbers in the population. Dozens of studies over 25 years have shown that black people, both men and women, have been overrepresented at every stage in the criminal justice process and whites have been underrepresented relative to their numbers in the population. However, Asian people were not overrepresented. These ethnic differences have not significantly changed, and are as marked among young people as they are among the adult population (Bowling and Phillips 2002; Home Office 2004). Because the Census breaks down the ethnic population by age ranges that are not the same as the youth justice system, which deals with 10–17-year-olds, the following figures should be treated as indicators and not exact comparisons. In 2001, black people aged 10–17 made up 3 per cent of the population in England and Wales, but accounted for 9 per cent of 14–17-year-olds arrested, 6 per cent cautioned and 15 per cent of young people aged 15–17 serving a custodial sentence. On the other hand, Asian young people aged 10–17 were substantially underrepresented in arrests, cautions and youth custody (Feilzer and Hood 2004). Nationally, black and mixed-parentage young people are very substantially overrepresented among those remanded in custody or receiving detention and training orders compared to other groups (Feilzer and Hood 2004). More locally focused studies of youth justice have found that black young men and women were very considerably overrepresented, and white and Asian young men and young women were underrepresented relative to their numbers in the relevant local population, although the extent that this was the case varied by area (Feilzer and Hood 2004).

Disproportionality in the criminal justice system: difference or discrimination?

Previous studies have found evidence of racial discrimination at different stages in the criminal justice process, while other studies have found little or no evidence of such discrimination. The methodological strengths and weaknesses of these studies have been discussed at considerable length (Mhlanga 1997; Bowling and Phillips 2002). The main criticisms have been that studies contain minority ethnic samples that are too small for meaningful statistical comparison between groups. They have not been able to capture cumulative decision-making at each stage over the course of criminal justice processes from prosecution to sentencing. They have not measured or analysed all the factors – offence characteristics, legal and social factors – that go into making sentencing and other decisions, so as to establish the significance or not of racial or ethnic background in decision-making. Perhaps most importantly, they have not been able to discover the subjective grounds and attitudes of criminal justice officials when making their decisions. Studies aim to establish that there is a residual element of different treatment of ethnic minorities which is not explained by the offence characteristics of the case and legally and socially relevant factors such as seriousness, social or employment status, unstable family background or homelessness. In other words, studies seek to demonstrate that black people receive harsher treatment which is not to do with their greater criminality, by taking into account such 'legally relevant' variables as type or seriousness of the offence or previous convictions (Hood 1992). Early critics of this approach suggested that it was practically impossible to take into account more than a few variables (Reiner 1993). For example, Walker (1988) studied the court disposal of young males, by race, in London in 1983, and was hampered by missing data about previous convictions or cautions, and seriousness of offence – data that simply were not available. This was, however, one of the first studies to control for economic and social characteristics of defendants, and concluded that since the police tended to deal with people of lower social class, and black people also tend to be of lower social class, it is to be expected that black people are overrepresented in the criminal justice system compared to the general population of London (Walker 1988: 442). Walker (1988) found that a higher proportion of blacks were acquitted and a higher proportion were given a custodial sentence, and that the police more readily prosecuted black people on insufficient evidence. In Walker's (1989) later study of older defendants, the main finding was that a considerably higher proportion of blacks were tried in the Crown Court and thus more likely to receive a custodial sentence than whites or Asians, although again, a full explanation why this might be the case could not be established. More recently, a growing sophistication of statistical analysis can be seen in the use of multivariate analysis by which many more variables can be analysed simultaneously, offering a more powerful test of the effect of different factors. The following are examples of studies that have been able to use multivariate analysis to good effect.

Unfortunately, studies of minority ethnic young people in the youth justice system are few and so dated that social and demographic change may have invalidated their findings. What is the evidence about the continuing disproportionately large population of African-Caribbean youths in the youth custody system? Mhlanga's (1997) was the first systematic study of youth justice prosecution and court decisions among 10–17-year-old Asian, black and white children, living in the London Borough of Brent between 1982 and 1987. The study found that there were racial differences in the treatment of young offenders that could not be explained by a myriad of other factors, both social and legal, such as significant racial differences in the nature of and involvement in criminality. For example, the police seemed more ready to presume guilt and prosecute black young people on insufficient evidence and were more lenient towards white and Asian young people, against whom they were more likely to take no further action or to caution. Black young people were more likely to receive a custodial sentence than their Asian and white counterparts. Hood's (1992) study of the Crown Court sitting in various places in the West Midlands, England, included people under the age of 21, but age did not affect a disproportionate use of custody against black defendants. After taking into account all legitimate factors, Hood concluded that black defendants had a 5 per cent greater probability of being sentenced to custody than their white counterparts. Regardless of whether they pleaded guilty or not guilty, black and Asian defendants received longer sentences than whites. Hood concluded that 7 per cent of the overrepresentation of black males in prison was the result of the use of custody in ways which could not be explained by legitimate factors. Crucially, the proportions of ethnic minorities sentenced to custody at the different sittings of the Crown Court studied were even larger. The proportion of blacks sentenced to custody was 17 per cent higher than for whites at the Dudley Crown Court, but racial differences at Birmingham Crown Court disappeared when legal and social factors were taken into account. This implies that judges at Dudley were influenced by race when sentencing, with easily foreseen consequences of rises in the black prison rate.

Feilzer and Hood's (2004) recent study of minority ethnic young people in the youth justice system examined 17,054 cases of white, Asian, black and mixed-parentage 12–17-year-olds, male and female, in eight Youth Offending Team areas. This, the first study to systematically explore decisions relating to minority ethnic groups at all the various stages of the youth justice process, used multivariate analysis to examine decisions by the police, the Crown Prosecution Service and the courts. The study collected information on a wide range of relevant legal and social variables such as education, school exclusion, employment status, family structure and other 'risk factors', which might singularly or together influence decision-making. It was found that among those prosecuted, convicted and sentenced, a higher proportion of black and mixed-parentage males had been remanded in secure conditions and a higher proportion had been committed for sentence at the Crown Court. Although this would predict a higher likelihood of a custodial sentence, no evidence was found that either black or mixed-parentage males were more likely to receive a custodial sentence than white males, once the characteristics of their cases had been taken into account. However, youth court magistrates were more ready to commit marginal cases involving black young people to the Crown Court than they were white young people. An unexpected finding was that Asian young people were more likely to be sentenced to custody than expected from their case characteristics (but the proportions sentenced to custody were the same as whites). Asians and mixed-parentage – but not black – young males were more likely to be sentenced to a more restrictive community sentence than whites. Young females, including those of black ethnicity, were treated more leniently than their male counterparts, and black females appear not to have been treated differently from their white counterparts. The study found overall, though, that there were at different stages of youth justice processes, different outcomes that were consistent with discriminatory treatment of Asian and black males, and especially mixed-parentage males and females, in respect of prosecution, remand, conviction, the use of more restrictive community penalties and longer sentence. The key finding was that large differences or discriminatory treatment of minority ethnic young people were found between Youth Offending Team areas. This was tantamount to youth justice by race and geography. The study raises important issues in respect of discriminatory treatment against mixed-parentage young people. It also points to the problem that aggregate studies of police and criminal justice process decisions across several courts and jurisdictions may minimize the extent and concentration of race discrimination, because sizeable discrimination may be revealed in individual police and court jurisdictions (Russell 1998: 28).

When we turn to criminal justice outcomes, there was an 80 per cent increase in the South Asian male prison population compared to an increase of a third for white males and a doubling of African-Caribbean males between 1985 and 1999. Among Asians this increase began from a low base when Asian males were underrepresented in prison relative to their numbers in the general population. Currently the Asian prison population is proportional to their numbers in the general population (from 2 to 3 per cent over the period). What is particularly significant, though, is the doubling of Muslim – particularly British Pakistani – prisoners between 1990 and 1999 (Home Office 2000a; Bowling and Phillips 2002). At time of writing the prison population is approaching 80,000, the highest it has ever been, while offending levels since 1995 have steeply declined, and the two – a rising prison population and declining crime rate – are unlikely to be significantly related.

Perceptions of fairness and equality

Black people in particular have displayed a lack of trust and confidence in the police and criminal justice system for some considerable time. However, the 2002/3 British Crime Survey found that, except in relation to the police, Asian and especially black people gave significantly higher ratings of confidence in different aspects of the effectiveness of the criminal justice system than whites, including the youth courts, although those of mixed origin showed the lowest police rating of all groups (Home Office 2004; Nicholas and Walker 2004). Shute *et al.*'s (2005) qualitative study of ethnic minority perceptions of fairness and equality of treatment in the criminal courts (even after they received custodial sentences) lends support to the thesis that black people's experiences of treatment in the courts have improved. However, this somewhat encouraging picture is contradicted by evidence from the Home Office Citizenship Survey which shows that black respondents, especially younger people, rated their trust in the police and the courts less favourably than all other ethnic groups, and were more likely than white people to expect discriminatory treatment. Overall, the police and prisons continue to be agencies distrusted and believed to be unfair among black, especially young black, people (Home Office 2004).

Race and criminal justice in the United States

Racial disparities in America's justice system are paralleled by comparable minority group disparities in other countries. However, as was found in the discussion of offending and victimisation patterns in the USA in Chapter 4, so with criminal justice outcomes in that country – the contrasts are much more extreme than those found in most western European countries.

Overrepresentation

Perhaps what is most striking in respect of criminal justice processes in the United States are their outcomes, shown in the ethnic composition of the US prison population. Over half of all prisoners in the USA are

African-American, despite blacks representing only 12 per cent of the US population. The incarceration rate for African-American men is seven times the rate for white men (3250 per 100,000 compared with 461 per 100,000). Hispanics comprised 10 per cent of the US population but were 17.5 per cent of all prisoners in 1996 and are the fastest-growing group within the prison population (Walker *et al.* 2004). There are similar patterns of overrepresentation among female prisoners: African-American women are over half the female prison population, while Hispanic women are a quarter of the female federal prison population but are not overrepresented in state prisons. A total of 68,000 black women were locked up. In 1999 close to 800,000 black men were in custody in federal penitentiaries, state prisons and county jails, corresponding to one male out of every twenty-one and *one out of every nine* aged 20–34 (Wacquant 2000). On any given day, over one-third of African-American men in their twenties are under supervision of the criminal justice system – imprisoned, on probation or on parole – and this often exceeds two-thirds in Northern deindustrialised cities (Tonry 1995; Wacquant 2000).

In a recent critical review Wacquant (2005: 5–6) has argued that America's 'carceral boom' started in 1973 and amassed nearly 1 million more inmates during the period 1985–95. As of 30 June 2000, the population held in county jails, state prisons, federal penitentiaries and juvenile custody had broken the 2 million barrier. Southern states such as Texas and Georgia were incarcerating over 700 per 100,000 residents. And this imprisonment rate does not tell the whole story. By 2000, the population placed under correctional supervision (including offenders placed on probation or released on parole after having served the greater part of their sentence) approached 6.5 million – 3 per cent of the country's adult population and one American male in 20 (Wacquant 2005: 7). The 'penal economy' of the United States now consumes a third of direct public expenditures devoted to crime control; for the first time, local governments spend more on criminal justice than they do on education, and the system continues to grow.

How can we explain this growth in the criminal justice system, and what are the implications for black and minority ethnic groups in the USA? Official justifications rested on the idea that the carceral boom is a response to the relentless growth of crime, especially violent crime. Wacquant (2005) argues that this common-sense argument has no foundation in evidence. First, with only a few localised exceptions, crime rates have stagnated and then declined over the last three decades. Next, the vast majority of new convicts are non-violent offenders. And, finally, fear of crime is unjustified and unfounded as most Americans have little reason to fear violence, which remains strongly concentrated in deprived inner-city areas (see Chapters 4 and 9). Violence and homicides are not 'random' as is often believed – thus, between 1975 and 1995, the murder rate of whites remained consistently one-sixth that of blacks – and the spectacular upsurge of murders between 1985 and 1993 concerned essentially unemployed young black men in the poor neighbourhoods of big cities, as murderers and as murder victims, and connected to the withdrawal of welfare support, joblessness and the booming crack trade becoming an important employment sector for some young black people. Finally, Wacquant (2005) argues that the ultimate causes of America's 'carceral hyperinflation' are, firstly, changes internal to the criminal justice system seen in the demise of rehabilitation – the idea that imprisonment aims to reform the criminal with a view towards his or her eventual reintegration into society – and its replacement by the idea that the primary aim of the prison is to punish, segregating the 'wicked' from the rest of society; and secondly, changes in the ways criminality was used by politicians and the media – in particular, the claims by these 'authoritative' sources, from the late 1960s, that the 'problem' of growing urban disorder required a restoration of government authority. The 'war on crime' became part of a political repertoire and 'bulwark' against the expansion of the welfare state to reduce both poverty and racial inequality (Wacquant 2005: 17; see also Garland 2001 for a similar argument). Crime and fighting crime had become a continuously running moral panic, nearly all of it directed towards young black men in poor neighbourhoods. The ways that crime was thought about – in dichotomous moral terms for electoral purposes – 'cemented the association between dangerousness and blackness' (Wacquant 2005: 18).

As the prison population soared, with the use of longer sentences, mandatory minimum sanctions for a wide range of offences, the imposition of life sentences for the third violent crime or felony (the 'three strikes and you're out' policy), the 'war on crime' was joined by the 'war on drugs' (Tonry 1995). The proportion of prison inmates convicted for drugs-related offences soared from 9 per cent in 1980 to a third in 1995. During the same period, the share of African-Americans among admissions to federal and state penitentiaries nearly doubled. Tonry (1995) argued that it could easily have been foreseen that the 'war on drugs' would disproportionately affect young black men (see Chapter 9). Wacquant (2005: 19) suggests that a point has been reached whereby *the penal system has partly supplanted and partly supplemented the ghetto* as a mechanism of racial control'. The massive overrepresentation of African-Americans in penitentiaries in the USA is only partly explained by them proportionately committing more crimes than whites, as Chapter 9 shows, owing to differences in class composition, socioeconomic stability and extreme levels of residential segregation. Other reasons are the preferential enforcement of those laws most likely to lead to the arrest and prosecution of poor African-Americans. The elevated incarceration rate of African-Americans is directly related to the onset of the 'war on Drugs' inaugurated by Richard Nixon, continued by Ronald Reagan and amplified by his successors (Tonry 1995). As Wacquant (2005: 20–1) defines it:

> the federal anti-drug campaign has concentrated squarely on the declining dark ghetto. As a result, the arrest rate of blacks for narcotics

violation has shot up tenfold in ten years . . . As a result, the number of blacks caught in the snares of the penal apparatus has exploded, and with it the litany of deleterious consequences for their employment and family life: if one adds those on probation and parole to jail detainees and prison inmates, nearly half of young African Americans in the big cities are currently under criminal justice supervision. The result is that a deep *structural and functional symbiosis has emerged between the ghetto and the prison*. The two institutions interpenetrate and complement each other in that both ensure the confinement of a population stigmatized by its ethnic origin and deemed superfluous both economically and politically.

Racial disproportionality in the US criminal justice system, according to this argument, rests on political and cultural choices that penalise poverty.

Disproportionality in the criminal justice system: difference or discrimination?

Imprisonment is a possible final outcome of the criminal justice system. What of discrimination or difference at earlier stages of the process? An early study by Petersilia (1985) attempted to provide an overview of racial disparities in the US criminal justice system, at a time when African-Americans made up only 12 per cent of the population but over half of the prison population. The study conceded elevated crime rates, especially in respect of street crimes, among African-Americans, but then went on to argue that socioeconomic conditions among blacks may be more consistently related to crime than they are among whites. Criminal justice officials may perceive unemployment as an indicator of recidivism (rather than a mitigating circumstance in crime), decide accordingly and dispense harsher and longer sentences to blacks or any unemployed offender (Petersilia 1985: 25–6). In examining court processes, Petersilia concluded that:

> minorities are treated differently at a few points in the criminal justice system, [but the study] . . . has not found evidence that this results from widespread and consistent racial prejudice in the system. Racial disparities seem to have developed because procedures were adopted without systematic attempts to find out whether they might affect various races [sic] differently.

Walker *et al.* (2004: 145), in their summary of the evidence, note the long-standing and explicit historical racism of American courts, especially in the Southern states, but argue that much has changed since then. Nevertheless, despite these changes in court procedures, the situation today is one of persistent inequities: 'Racial minorities, and particularly those suspected of crimes against whites, remain the victims of unequal justice.' Within the cautionary context of inconsistent and contradictory evidence for different stages of the trial process, Walker *et al.* (2004: 172) are able to conclude:

there is evidence that defendant race/ethnicity continues to affect decisions regarding bail, charging, and plea bargaining. Some evidence suggests that race has a direct and obvious effect on these pretrial decisions; other evidence suggests that the effect of race is indirect and subtle.

To the extent that racial discrimination exists – and it seems likely – it will tend to operate mostly at the pre-trial and sentencing stages. Indeed, discrimination during the pre-trial stage of the criminal justice process can have profound consequences at trial and sentencing. If ethnic minorities are more likely than whites to be represented by incompetent attorneys or detained in jail prior to trial (because unemployed and poor), they may, as a result of these differences, face greater odds of conviction and harsher sentences. It is likely that discrimination in sentencing remains a reality at the final stage of the criminal justice process, after previous offending, seriousness of offence and the indirect effects of race (poverty, homelessness, family instability, etc.) are taken into account (Crutfield *et al.* 1994; Walker *et al.* 2004).

A note on the death penalty in the United States: the case of Alabama

In the discussion of lynching in Chapter 5 we saw how those states currently having the highest rates of capital punishment were historically those at the centre of extralegal punishment and lynching. Since the death penalty was upheld as constitutional and re-established in 1976, 90 per cent of jurisdictions that employ the death penalty exhibit patterns of racial bias in capital charging or sentencing of defendants accused of killing white victims (Stevenson 2004). The death row population in Alabama has doubled since 1990, and since 1998 that state has sentenced more people to death per capita than any other. Alabama has successively made the application of the death penalty more widespread, and has called for the death penalty for non-homicide offences, including drug dealing.

Of those persons executed in Alabama between 1975 and 2000, 70 per cent were African-American. Although nearly 65 per cent of homicide victims in Alabama are African-American, 80 per cent of Alabama's death row prisoners have been sentenced for crimes involving victims who are white. Racial bias in jury selection is an important cause leading to all-white or mostly white juries in capital cases, although the African-American population in each county is between a third and a half. The only respite from (or alternatively, exacerbation of) the likelihood of being sentenced to death is that judges can override juries in the decision (Bedau 2004). In Alabama there is no state-funded public defender system and most defendants are poor. There is a racist double jeopardy in death penalty processes in the United States: extreme harshness towards black perpetrators when their homicide victim is white, combined with a devaluing of the status of black homicide victims compared to white victims (Kleck 1981).

Race and criminal justice in other countries

Perhaps the country that stands in starkest contrast to the United States (and Britain) in terms of penal policy is Sweden, where average prison sentences are short and prisons often open, although there is evidence of a more punitive direction in penal policy since the 1980s focused on foreign offenders, in the context of debates about immigration policy (Marshall 1997). In Germany there has been since the mid-1980s a sharp increase in the use of imprisonment for foreign offenders, who account for approximately 25 per cent of the prison population. Drug offences played a crucial role in this rise, especially among Moroccans, Columbians and Spaniards (Albrecht 1997a). Similarly, in Italy, there has been a remarkable rise in the numbers of foreigners involved in the criminal justice system, but the paucity of official and criminological data makes it difficult to draw any hard conclusions. Nearly a third of the prison population in France comprised minorities, and this proportion is growing. In Spain a disproportionate number of foreigners are arrested, convicted, detained and incarcerated. But Spain, like many European countries, does not collect ethnic data so we do not know whether they are visible minorities. Despite a historical reputation for tolerance and low imprisonment rates in the Netherlands, a recent dramatic change in penal climate as a response to alleged soaring crime rates has tripled the prison population.

The historical and social context of criminal and youth justice in Britain

Focusing in this section on black and minority ethnic young people in Britain, criminal and youth justice processes can be understood better in the context of the cumulative, intergenerational crises faced by black and Asian young people as they attempt to adopt new identities and adapt to economic and social change from the 1970s to the present. Changes in schooling and youth training, in eligibility and entitlement to welfare benefits, in youth labour markets and drug markets, and changes to their neighbourhoods marginalised and polarised their experiences. Minority ethnic young people's offending and their victimisation, their complaints about and conflict with the police, and their treatment by the youth justice system cannot be understood outside the impact of these changes. Minority ethnic young people's transitions to adulthood often take place in inner-city neighbourhoods and peripheral estates characterised by deindustrialisation, destabilisation, deprivation and high levels of crime and violence.

This contextual understanding has a number of components (see also Chapter 1). First, black and Asian young people's experiences of the police (see Chapter 6) and youth justice system are explained by changes in their social conditions through the interaction of social class, place and race. Second, a consistent – but unexplained – finding of statistical studies of the influence of race on crime rates, policing and youth justice is that different or discriminatory treatment by the police or the courts appears to occur in some areas and jurisdictions but not in others. This geography of race, crime, policing and youth justice has often remained unexplained because studies have lacked local contextual data, whether of a particular neighbourhood, court, or a local history of police racism. Third, sources of racism and racial discrimination are found in changing social relations between majority white and minority ethnic working-class groups, in relations between social control professionals and their minority ethnic clients, as well as between employers and employees. In consequence, the ways in which white ethnicity is formed become important to understanding discrimination. Fourth, not only is it the case that race and ethnicity on their own do not tell the whole story, but also their meaning changes. Although social class, gender, race and ethnicity continue to have salience in reproducing disadvantage and identity, it is recognised that young people in particular subjectively experience these social relationships differently from the past. As class and ethnic identities become both differentiated *and* polarised, they give way to more individualised and heterogeneous experiences of disadvantage. On the other hand, as the discussion of the disorders in Bradford, Burnley and Oldham in 2001 in Chapter 6 showed, for some Asian young people, the opposite may be true, as their singular collective sense of identity is strengthened by an embattled and growing sense of threat and hostility (Webster 2003). By the same token, ways of talking about and acting on class, ethnic identity and disadvantage have become more 'coded' – racial connotation has become less explicit in public discourse and social practices. Offending is talked about by reference to group and individual deficits and 'risks' rather than by reference to race and class, although the former may simply substitute for the latter (see Feeley and Simon 1994).

Change and continuity in the lives of black and Asian young people

This section sketches some of the changes that occurred in the lives of minority ethnic young people resulting from the sustained economic depressions of the post-1973 years. If the 1970s were years of crisis, the 1980s brought the 'solutions' to this crisis – a series of cumulatively repressive measures against working-class young people in general and black young people in particular.

Whitfield (2004) has noted how the deterioration in relations between the police and London's Caribbean community went unnoticed during the crucial early years of immigration. Although the new generation inherited their parents' experience of racial exclusion and isolation, they faced very different conditions and problems (Phillips and Phillips 1998). As the 1970s began black youth unemployment began to rise, but it was their experience of school that marked the new generation. ESN ('educationally subnormal') special schools and approved schools contained disproportionate numbers of black children because of the influence of teachers' prejudice and low expectations of black children's abilities and performance (Coard 1971; Cashmore and Troyna 1982). The 1970s and 1980s were marked by repression. Black youth constituted over a third of detention centre and borstal populations in the south of England. The numbers of 14–16-year-old males – whites and black – sent to custody more than doubled between 1971 and 1981. Periods of intense politicisation of youth crime – 1970, 1979–83 and 1992–98 – were punitive and intensely racialised (Webster 1997; Goodey 2001; Pitts 2001; Solomos 2003).

The 1990s followed a similar pattern but took a different turn. Again, collusion between the police and media constructed 'Asian' ethnicity in the language of criminality, alleging the widespread involvement of Asian young men in street rebellion, gang violence, crime and drugs (Webster 1997; Goodey 2001). Parlous deprivation, high levels of imposed residential segregation, school failure, increasing conflict with the police and high levels of local racism all conspired to racialise and criminalise young British Pakistanis and Bangladeshis (Webster 1996, 2003, 2004; Goodey 2001). As Chapter 6 showed, this complex of factors eventually resulted in widespread disorders in Bradford in 1985 and in Bradford, Burnley and Oldham in 2001. These events marked the abrupt end of the 'multicultural settlement' that had governed race relations in the 1980s and 1990s (Kalra 2003; Webster 2003).

'Offender' populations and their context

Despite a large body of literature documenting changed transitions from teenage years to young adulthood, it is often forgotten, and can remain hidden, that during the economic restructuring of the 1980s and 1990s the social conditions of working-class young people substantially worsened. Incomes, benefit entitlements, job availability and security previously enjoyed were taken away, first from those aged 16–17 and later from those aged 18–25. As a consequence, transitions have become increasingly extended, precarious and sometimes chaotic for working-class white, Asian and black young people (Furlong and Cartmel 1997; Fergusson 2002; Mizen 2004; Muncie 2004; Webster *et al.* 2004; MacDonald and Marsh 2005). Some of these processes of social exclusion are discussed more fully in the next chapter. For now we can note that offender populations are disproportionately drawn from young people not engaged in education, employment or training (NEET), and from those who have lived in the care system (Pearce and Hillman 1998; Social Exclusion Unit 1998, 1999;

Bentley and Gurumurthy 1999; Britton *et al.* 2002). Estimates suggest that up to 20 per cent of 16- and 17-year-olds are NEET and at least 9 per cent of the NEET population appears to be from minority ethnic groups. Young people who are NEET are concentrated in deprived areas, and African-Caribbean, Bangladeshi and Pakistani young people are especially at risk of becoming NEET (Coles *et al.* 1998; Social Exclusion Unit 1999; Stone *et al.* 2000; Britton *et al.* 2002). The main predictors of becoming NEET (and offending) are early truancy and school exclusions, which disproportionately affect young African-Caribbean men and children in care (Social Exclusion Unit 1998). Often, studies have simply causally related truancy and school exclusions to offending without explaining why truancy occurs. Britton *et al.*'s (2002) qualitative study of white, black, Bangladeshi and Pakistani 16–17-year-olds' intermittent routes into NEET found that disaffection and boredom at school were linked to troubles and traumas outside school, so that early school disaffection, truancy, troubled early and later lives and negative experiences of being in care were linked. For minority ethnic young people the disadvantages of care interact with their experience of racism in care.

Although the increased precariousness of youth transitions and disengagement from education, employment and training disproportionately affects some minority ethnic young people, for other groups this has not been the case. Growing polarisation between and within different minority ethnic groups complicates processes of social exclusion and disadvantage in respect of these groups. There is evidence of both upward and downward inter- and intragenerational educational and occupational mobility (Kalra 2000; Mason 2003; Pilkington 2003). Although for most ethnic minority groups the second and third generation have made significant educational progress – especially some ethnic groups such as African Asians, Sikhs and Indians and African-Caribbean women – Caribbean, Pakistani and Bangladeshi boys have made least progress. When social class background is taken into account, Caribbean boys in particular continue to do less well than their white counterparts. Pakistan and Bangladeshi young people are geographically concentrated and segregated in deindustrialised urban areas, disproportionately suffer joblessness and belong to the poorest ethnic groups in British society (Mason 2003; Modood 2003; Owen 2003; Pilkington 2003; Webster 2003). Here, vital class processes interpenetrate with ethnicity to produce enduring structures of disadvantage, but they do not necessarily override the influence of ethnic inequality.

Understanding race, criminal justice and penality

An understanding of race, youth crime and justice cannot rely on surveys alone. Although important in providing 'statistical context', multivariate analysis cannot provide an understanding of the 'community context' in which racism may or may not flourish. Surveys that attempt to measure racism are hampered by their inability to properly 'model' complex processes and contexts of decision-making that exist in the real world because 'social life consists not of events but experience, and thus the same happening can carry totally different meanings for people in different social contexts' (Pawson 1989: 13). Qualitative research into race, crime and justice faces a different set of problems in the reluctance of teachers, police officers and court officials to reveal their attitudes or the underlying reasons they deploy in making decisions (see Shute *et al.* 2005). There are grounds to argue that this lack of close-up understanding is beginning to change as studies switch to more qualitative approaches to studying the work of criminal justice practitioners. Where this has occurred the results seem encouraging in showing considerable satisfaction with the courts (Shute *et al.* 2005) and Probation Service (Lewis *et al.* 2006) among black and minority ethnic suspects and clients. As the next chapter and Chapter 9 show, neighbourhood-based ethnographic studies of minority ethnic youth transitions in Britain and the USA can offer insight, extend understanding and add considerable nuance to the picture painted thus far.

Among other things, these studies show how police and youth justice responses to youth crime can, in effect, criminalise the poor, furthering their disadvantage (Hope 2001; Pitts 2001; Webster 2003; Webster *et al.* 2004). Contrary to popular belief, offender populations living in deindustrialised neighbourhoods strongly share the mainstream values of their societies. If anything, they overidentify with the consumerist values around them. At the same time, these values are difficult to attain because of their racial and social segregation and poverty. It is their 'normality' – whether they are involved in criminality or not – which is most striking. However, rooted for their survival in local social networks, they associate with people like themselves and have few bridges or connections, formally or informally, to wider support in accessing educational aspirations, jobs or other resources. What many seem to share are negative experiences of schooling. In respect of social exclusion at school Muslim, black and white working-class boys in particular can come under the spell of peer-based resistance to teachers and scholasticism.

Finally, as this chapter has begun to argue, there are striking similarities of marginalisation across different domains of transition – from schooling, care, policing, and youth justice to employment – for many white, black, Pakistani and Bangladeshi working-class young people growing up in Britain. Young black men, in particular, disproportionately find themselves under the supervision of a continuum of social control agencies. For these groups, three decades of deindustrialisation and economic restructuring have worsened their social conditions, destabilised their families and neighbourhoods, subjected them to harassment and discrimination by the police, the youth justice, care and schooling systems, and offered them a precarious future at the bottom of a casualised youth labour market. The politicisation and racialisation of youth crime have lent legitimacy to the measures of social control that economic restructuring requires, and the reproduction of racial divisions in society is a part of these linked processes (Keith 1993; Pitts 2001; Solomos 2003; Wacquant 2005). Unless issues of discrimination and reform in schooling, policing, youth justice and the casualised labour market are addressed, rather than concerns about individualised and ethnicised 'deficits', the social and economic processes identified will continue to racialise and criminalise working-class black, Asian *and* white young men and women.

Further reading

The best recent study of whether or not there is racial discrimination in the criminal justice process in England and Wales is Feilzer and Hood (2004). Mhlanga's (1997) earlier study is also useful. Readers should look at Krisberg's (2005) study of the American juvenile justice system. Some of the wider contextual issues for race, youth crime and justice are discussed in Webster (2006). Shute *et al.*'s (2005) qualitative study of ethnic minority perceptions of fairness and equality of treatment in the criminal courts suggests an encouraging picture of improvements in the experiences of black and minority ethnic defendants. Again, the standard text on racism and criminal justice in Britain is Bowling and Phillips (2002) and their summary and development of this text in Phillips and Bowling (2002, 2003).

chapter eight

'Race', class, masculinities and crime: family, schooling and peer groups

Introduction: risk factors

As was seen in the discussion of offending and victimisation in Chapter 4, empirical studies of victims, offenders and offending repeatedly find that offender populations and behaviours are strongly associated with 'risk factors' that are said to emerge in transitions from childhood to young adulthood. To recall, risk factors for offending include being raised in a lone-parent family, poor parental supervision, truancy and school failure, peer influence, living in a poor area, dependent drug use, joblessness and, later, not forming a stable family of one's own. Studies tend to emphasise individual risk factors as proximate causes of delinquency and crime rather than structural background factors such as the effects of poverty on family disruption, school processes and labour market conditions. Writers do not discount social structural factors but suggest that these are insufficient in themselves in accounting for offending and that their effects are at best indirect, although they may provide some of the background conditions which may encourage or discourage individual offending behaviour:

The strongest and most consistent effects on both official and unofficial delinquency flow from the social processes of family, school and peers. Low levels of parental supervision, erratic, threatening, and harsh discipline, and weak parental attachment were strongly and directly related to delinquency ... school attachment had large negative effects on delinquency independent of family processes ... we found that structural background factors have little direct effect on delinquency, but instead are mediated by intervening sources of informal social control ... When the bonds linking youth to society – whether through family or school – are weakened, the probability of delinquency is increased. Negative structural conditions (such as poverty or family disruption) also affect delinquency, but largely through family and school process variables (Sampson and Laub 1993: 247).

This chapter argues that the role of 'background factors' needs to be reassessed in explaining heightened 'risks' of offending among groups as well as individuals. To recall, Chapters 4 and 7 concluded that explanations of crime and of the emergence of factors associated with offending often lack historical, geographical and sociological *context* – of history in terms of the influence of social and economic change on crime rates and crime patterns; of place in terms of neighbourhood influences on crime and fear of crime; of social groups and social structure in terms of age, ethnicity, class and gender; and of institutional processes in terms of family, schooling, training and employment. Chapter 3 discussed place and history, showing how certain places evolve and concentrate 'race and crime' situations over time. This chapter focuses on 'risk factors' in the contexts of age, ethnicity, class and gender – specifically masculinity – and institutional processes of schooling, training and employment.

Race, class and family structure

Some writers have noted a parallel in the development of 'new' family structures among African-Americans and British African-Caribbeans over the recent period. American commentators have suggested that unstable relations between African-American men and women have contributed to welfare dependency and high crime. Smith (2005) has applied a similar argument to British African-Caribbeans. Compared to similarly or more deprived British Pakistanis and Bangladeshis, who have unusually traditional and stable family structures based on cultural and economic self-sufficiency, and the role of family networks in conserving cultural capital, African-Caribbeans have experienced family dissolution to a greater extent. The latter group are said to hold conceptions of masculinity and unstable relations between men and women which contribute to high intergenerational offending rates within this group. Although conceding that

African-Caribbeans have experienced *both* higher rates of offending *and* racial discrimination at several stages of the criminal justice process compared to other minority groups and whites, Smith (2005) essentially discounts disadvantage and neighbourhood segregation as explanations because these are similar or worse in relatively low-offending minority groups. Smith argues that the most important factor explaining high African-Caribbean offending rates is the development of a high prevalence of lone-parent families within this group, and the low proportion of young Caribbeans who live with a partner. The assumptions (see Chapter 4) are that styles of parenting and family functioning influence later offending and crime in the next generation and that lone-parent families are more likely to suffer poverty, and this is detrimental to effective parenting.

Smith concedes that Caribbean migrants who came to Britain in the 1940s and 1950s lived, or were shortly to live, in conventional families. However, radical changes occurred in the African-Caribbean family involving a large rise in lone-parent families. Smith discounts neighbourhood influences of segregation and concentrated deprivation on crime rates in Britain compared with the United States, especially for Caribbeans, as segregation is considerably higher for Bangladeshis and Pakistanis. However, the different identity formation of young African-Caribbeans seems an important basis in explaining high crime rates among this group.

The factual evidence for this thesis in Britain are striking intergenerational changes in family structure between the first generation of Caribbean migrants living in conventional marriages and a situation in the years following migration that saw a dramatic rise in the number of lone-parent households and men and women not living with a partner, with implications of a decline in the effectiveness of parenting and supervision of children and young people. Although these changes affected all groups, they were particularly marked among African-Caribbeans compared to other minorities and whites (Office for National Statistics 2004; Smith 2005). For example, among 25–29-year-olds, 68 per cent of white men and women live with a partner, compared with only 38 per cent of Caribbeans. Among those with a partner, 73 per cent of whites are in a formal marriage, compared with only half of Caribbeans. Among those who have married, Caribbeans are twice as likely to have divorced or separated as whites across all age groups under age 60. A tenth of white women under the age of 35 with children are single, mothers who have never married, compared to a half of their Caribbean mother counterparts. Smith (2005) suggests that a paucity of marriageable African-Caribbean men who are disproportionately unemployed, despite increasingly common mixed partnerships among African-Caribbeans, means that very few Caribbean men and women are married to each other, and 'respectability', marriage and stable partnerships are increasingly unimportant as a means of maintaining and fostering African-Caribbean ethnic identity. According to Smith, young black men in Britain have adopted black American masculine styles and adaptations to the legacy of slavery based on an oppositional culture of protest and hostility to white society.

Parallel arguments are made about the 'crises' in African-American family life as an indirect cause of crime and other social problems. Patterson (1997, 1998) argues that failure to form stable families, illegitimacy and family breakdown are important causes of poverty rather than that poverty and economic insecurity themselves may cause family instability or make it likely. Again, the data appear striking. Around a third of African-Americans are poor and are much more likely to be poor than whites. For African-American children under 18 this rose to 42 per cent in 1995, and according to Patterson, the main reason is that 60 per cent of all African-American children are in female-headed lone-parent households, and 45 per cent of such households are in poverty. Married two-parent African-American households declined from 70 per cent of all African-American families in 1967 to 46 per cent in 1995. When teenage births are taken into account, single women accounted for 70 per cent of African-American births.

Several criticisms can be laid at the door of the above thesis. Some empirical criticisms are mentioned here before the underlying theoretical arguments about emasculation are addressed in the next section. First, there is a problem of cause and effect – whether poverty causes family instability or instability creates poverty. This problem haunts the literature in the context of the complex and rapidly changing dynamics of family structure among all social groups in all Western societies. Because discussions ignore social class, discussions can hide the fact that lone parenthood, separation and divorce are significantly higher among working-class and poor whites than among middle-class whites, so that differences in family structure between whites and African-Caribbeans, although not disappearing, are significantly reduced when blacks and whites of similar socio-economic status are compared. This is developed further below where the significance of family structure in raising crime levels is also questioned. Second, and linked to this first point, commentators can rush to make value judgements and politicise this issue while ignoring the relationship between family structure and social structure. For this reason there is a need to be cautious in interpreting data about family structure. Birth outside marriage has become common among a wide range of social groups in the United States, and teenage pregnancy is much more prevalent among poorly educated and poor men and women, both black *and* white, while class differences in family structure were greater in the 1990s than in the 1970s (Smith 1999). Single-parent families with an employed parent more than doubled among the working class (from 12 to 27 per cent), but grew by only half among the middle class (from 10 to 15 per cent). Non-earning single parents are more common among the working class, thus this group is much more likely to consist of single-parent families than previously (21 per cent in the 1970s compared to 38 per cent in the 1990s), while the middle class has shown only very modest growth in single-parent families

(20 per cent in the 1970s compared to 22 per cent in the 1990s). Although the level of unmarried births among black women is very high compared to whites, the rate of increase has been much greater for whites than for blacks. Third, the data tell us very little about qualitative issues of family stability, quality of parenting or lone-parent and child relationships. In any case, individuals remarry, or marry later, and form reconstituted families (Smith 1999).

Family, masculinity and emasculation

Both Smith (2005), with respect to British African-Caribbeans, and Patterson (1998), with respect to African-Americans, explain the 'crisis' in the black family in terms of these groups' shared ancestry in slavery. This shared ancestry is almost unique to these groups. Smith (2005), following Tonry (1997), notes how although all disproportionately criminalised minority groups in Western countries are disadvantaged, not all disadvantaged minority groups have elevated rates of offending, nor are they disproportionately criminalised. Therefore disadvantage alone cannot explain criminalisation and/or elevated rates of crime. Part of the explanation for consistent patterns of increased crime over the generations (especially among African-Americans and African-Caribbeans in Britain) can be found in the parallel intergenerational family structures of the two groups. This leads to our first encounter with the 'masculinities and crime' thesis, one aspect of which is the claim that when men remain ungoverned and uncontrolled by not having roles as partners, husbands and fathers within stable families, they are more likely to offend.

Both Patterson (1998) and Smith (2005) explain elevated crime rates for these groups in terms of the long-term consequences of slave plantations and post-slavery society in Jamaica and the American South. Baldly put, the argument is that that although family structures within these groups have evolved, they are still influenced by the history of slavery and the resulting patterns of family life have led to higher rates of crime in subsequent generations. This early legacy was embodied in slave codes or laws that enforced a situation whereby slaves could not marry or meet free blacks, marriage between slaves was not legally recognised, and slaves were bought and sold independently of kinship ties, rendering it impossible for slaves to retain family ties (Schaffer 2006). Slavery utterly destroyed the continuity of African family traditions, and this legacy continues to influence African-American and Caribbean family life. Among other legacies of slavery, fatherhood became a marginal role as paternity was not recognised, and in ex-slave societies fathers routinely abandon their families and children. This central theme of the fragmented African-Caribbean family is taken further, based on an analogy with the damaging effects of slavery on relations between African-American men and women and their children. Smith (2005) concludes that a combination of the long-term consequences of slavery, greater integration and contact leading to more encounters with racism, spiralling conflict with the police and the growth of a confrontational and oppositional culture explain rising crime rates in later generations of African-Caribbeans.

The problem with this interpretation is that it reads history backwards from the present to the past, implying that in the era preceding the European Atlantic slave trade, African family traditions were 'stable'. Indigenous slavery, chattel servitude and slave trading, however, were common in Africa both before and during the European slave trade, carried out by Arabs and African chieftains, who to be sure also collaborated and sold slaves to Europeans (Thomas 1997; St Clair 2006). This somewhat abstract although important point does raise doubts about the prior sanctity and subsequent violation of African family traditions. Further, and more concretely, these arguments can verge on moral condemnation of African-American men said to abandon their wives and children not because of their economic inability to support family life but because of a crisis of masculinity arising from their emasculation due to the legacy of slavery. Such speculative arguments can divert us from the recent and present situation of post-slavery racial exclusion, segregation and urban poverty that undermine the possibility of family life. Besides, as the discussion in Chapter 5 shows, emasculation brought by extrajudicial killings and lynching in the Southern post-slavery American states lasted well into the twentieth century.

The masculinity and crime thesis

Much of popular and academic debate about masculinity draws attention to recent associations that have been made between masculinity, boys and disorder – in particular, a supposed crisis of young men's masculinity in the context of more general anxieties about social change and stability. Centred on a growing concern about boys' supposed widespread educational failure relative to girls, their unruly behaviour in the classroom, their lack of interpersonal and employment skills necessary for a service-based economy, that significant numbers of young men are becoming 'unmarriageable' or reject marriage, growing aggressive and violent behaviour, and concerns such as the perceived growing problem of persistent offending by male youth, this list of 'problematic male behaviour' grows incessantly. This supposed crisis in masculinity is seen as emblematic of changes in social values and morality, 'family breakdown' and births outside marriage in the context of widespread divorce and cohabitation that have further undermined traditional ideas of fatherhood and paternity. Changing structures of employment are said by some to have resulted in the emergence of a 'new British underclass' marked by illegitimacy and absent fathers. In each case questions of masculinity have been seen as central to attempts to understand the nature of these social changes. The connection of certain masculine styles and criminality continues the historical centrality of male youth to 'law and order' debates but reframed in terms of problematic masculinities. Collier (1998: vii) identifies the key parameters of the debate as not only that:

> the crimes of *individual* men might be explained through references to their masculinity, but rather the idea that *society* itself is presently experiencing what has been termed a 'crisis' of masculinity, a crisis made manifest in both the changing nature and extent of men's criminality.

What empirical and conceptual purchase do these claims have? Motifs such as 'the trouble with boys', 'the crisis of masculinity' and 'absent fathers, criminal sons', have been recurring themes in discourses about crime and masculinity (Archer 2003), but are these criminological constructions valid? Just as we cannot generalise about race or class, neither can we generalise about 'masculinity'. Like race and class, the concept is also inherently relational in the sense that 'masculinity' does not exist except in contrast with 'femininity'. Masculinity varies and is specific to certain cultures, historical periods and situations. There is no simple or essential quality or universal basis of masculinity. Different 'masculinities' are not fixed and change with individual and social change. As Connell (2005: 71) argues, masculinity is connected to and arises from a system of gender relations – the processes and relations through which men and women conduct gendered lives, and the effects of these practices in bodily experience, personality and culture. Connell's discussion of 'masculinities' suggests that there is an interplay between gender, race and class such that multiple masculinities are produced, but this does not mean that 'there is *a* black masculinity or *a* working-class masculinity' (2005: 76).

According to Connell, the main patterns of masculinity and relations among masculinities are 'dominant' or 'hegemonic', 'subordinate', 'complicit' and 'marginal' masculinity. These describe different dynamic forms of masculinity so that hegemonic masculinity embodies the currently accepted, culturally dominant and 'successful' form, whereas marginal masculinity lacks real power and authority and is usually 'unacceptable'. We have already noted, for example, how the general experiences of black men may have been shaped by certain forms of white hegemonic masculinity seen in attempts to violently emasculate them through post-slavery institutions and lynching, and oppress and control them through segregation, unemployment and urban poverty. Finally, some masculinities are described as having a complicit relationship with hegemonic masculinity in the sense that men benefit from male dominance generally but compromise with rather than dominate women.

This brief discussion of different masculinities provides the basis for going on to examine the relationship between masculinities, race, class and crime. Studies in this area talk of 'exaggerated' or 'hyper-masculinity' as a precursor to anti-social, delinquent and criminal behaviour – terms used by Smith (2005) and Patterson (1998) above. Connell (2005: 93) refers to this when he suggests that one dynamic of masculinity is to 'live fast and die young'. If working-class masculinity was once organised around stable employment and the wage, it has now become more common that some men face intermittent employment and long-term economic marginality. Connell's (2005) biographical case study of young men on the fringe of the labour market found that they had left school early, some had been expelled from school after much truanting and some were illiterate. Disaffection with school and conflict with teachers, arrest and custody marked the group. Connell compared this group with men of a similar age and background who were in employment. The first group saw their criminality (particularly car theft and drug dealing) as excitement and entertainment, but mostly as a kind of work. Violence had been and was central to their lives (in their families, at school and in peer groups). Although their views were divided on violence towards women, they were unanimous in their negative views of state authority, whether of schooling or later, the police and courts. This begins in school: 'They encounter school authority as an alien power and start to define their masculinity against it' (Connell 2005: 100). Although not completely uniform within the group and involving many tensions, Connell described the group in terms of 'compulsory heterosexual masculinity', that masculinity was based in group feelings and collective practices and that there was little indication of emotional investment in women. Their experiences of childhood were ones of powerlessness, yet as they grew older they laid claim to a 'pressured exaggeration' of masculine conventions. This involved a lot of concern with 'face' and 'keeping up a front' and, for some, a kind of 'protest masculinity' (Connell 2005: 111–12): 'Protest masculinity is a marginalized masculinity, which picks up themes of hegemonic masculinity in the society at large but reworks them in a context of poverty' (Connell 2005: 114).

The employed group, although some experienced similar family and school troubles and all were from similar starting points of class deprivation and poverty, presented quite divergent life trajectories to the unemployed group. These men had avoided or rejected protest masculinity and as such were characterised by 'complicit' masculinity. In contrast, the type of masculinity that most characterised the unemployed and (some) offending groups is summarised by Connell (2005: 116) as follows:

> The project of protest masculinity ... develops in a marginal class situation, where the claim to power that is central in hegemonic masculinity is constantly negated by economic and cultural weakness ... By virtue of class situation and practice (e.g., in school), these men have lost most of the patriarchal dividend. For instance, they have missed out on the economic gain over women that accrues to men in employment, the better chances of promotion, the better job

classifications. If they accept this loss they are accepting the justice of their own deprivation. If they try to make it good by direct action, state power stands in their way.

One way to resolve this contradiction is a spectacular display, embracing the marginality and stigma and turning them to account. At the personal level, this translates as a constant concern with front or credibility . . . At the group level, the collective practice of masculinity becomes a performance too . . . the trouble is that the performance is not leading anywhere . . . protest masculinity looks like a cul-de-sac . . . this is a solidarity that divides the group from the rest of the working class.

Protest masculinity, however, and its association with predatory criminality must be understood in relation to, and as an outgrowth of, other dominant masculinities. Connell (2005: 80) argues that 'hegemonic masculinity among whites sustains the institutional oppression and physical terror that have framed the making of masculinities in black communities', amply demonstrated in racist violence towards black men in the USA and elsewhere. Conversely, 'youth gang violence of inner-city streets is a striking example of the assertion of marginalised masculinities against other men, continuous with the assertion of masculinity in sexual violence against women' (Connell 2005: 83).

Messerschmidt (1993), in an American context, has argued for a link between certain forms of masculinity and crime among all social classes, not just the working class or underclass. Accomplishing masculinity is socially situated and intermittent but in the process of constructing masculinity men may simultaneously construct forms of criminality. For some men, crime may serve as an activity for separating them from all that is feminine, especially in situations where men lack other resources to accomplish masculinity. Messerschmidt argues that white working-class opposition masculinity differs from masculinity found among lower-working-class 'racial minority' boys who engage in crime. Because they are less likely to have access to paid employment, attend school, and because of where they live, they are more likely to be involved in youth gangs and street-based culture. For them, hegemonic masculinity (paid work) is almost entirely unobtainable, therefore for some, street crime becomes a collective solution to their predicament of accomplishing masculinity and a lifestyle – see Hallsworth (2005), discussed in Chapter 4, for a not dissimilar argument. Overall, in situations of severe class and race structural disadvantage, gender is held more accountable, augmented, and takes on more salience because more likely to be undermined and threatened. Messerschmidt claims that lower-working-class racial minority young people are more violent in their school opposition because school is seen as unrelated to future success, and are disproportionately involved in such serious property crimes as robbery and in interpersonal group violence, although sustained criminal careers do not usually follow. This 'robbery stage' provides a public ceremony of domination and humiliation of others and therefore a specific type of public masculinity, 'moral superiority' and 'toughness'. Robbery presents the most available opportunity for constructing a type of masculine expression in the short term, although augmented by a defensive territorialism. This ritual rejection of femininity, the offer of a 'competitive arena', and the prestige that accrues with a proven ability to fight, all confer masculine expression, validation, meaning and status. Violent expression, however, is not limited to oppositional masculinity. A study of the life histories of two white working-class adolescent male offenders showed that both oppositional and subordinate masculinity (in Connell's 2005 sense) can produce different kinds of violence (Messerschmidt 1999). Also, Messerschmidt is careful to show that other crimes such as white-collar and corporate crime also originate from (mostly white) men in positions of power just as 'girl sex delinquents' are constructed through other forms of masculinity and so on.

Masculinities, race and schooling

Recent criminological studies continue to confirm the centrality of the school experience and adolescent peer relations in influencing offending (Graham and Bowling 1995; Stephenson 2007). The prevalence of offending and truancy rates can vary dramatically among different schools according to intake, ability and class. Graham and Bowling (1995: 49) found that a low level of parental supervision and truancy from school were the two strongest correlates of starting to offend, and that 'a low level of parental supervision was found to be strongly related to getting on badly with one or both parents, which in turn was found to be more likely in single parent and step families'. However, correlations between parental supervision, truancy and offending are unclear because truancy may be both a cause and a consequence of offending. Also disengagement from school needs to be explained, and not simply causally related to offending, especially when disaffection leads to school exclusion that disproportionately affects black children (Bourne et al. 1994; Parsons et al. 2004; Webster 2006).

Disengagement and disaffection from school, leading to frequent truanting, school exclusion or self-exclusion, are usually explained in terms of individual or parental deficiencies rather than, say, the emergence of certain masculine styles. It is only in more recent scholarship on race, gender and education that an engagement with masculinity and the idea that schools are not gender-neutral has emerged. Connell (2005) argues that masculinities are first made at school. For Messerschmidt (1993), schooling and youth group activities are the chief social settings for the development of youth crime and where 'public' masculine dominance has most salience. Masculinities reflect relative class and race or ethnic positions. In this view, many white middle-class boys develop an 'accommodating masculinity' – a controlled, cooperative and rational strategy to achieve school success – whereas many white working-class boys experience school authority as an 'emasculating' power, and this can lead to 'oppositional masculinity'. For these boys schooling is 'unmanly'. Accordingly, they evolve a counter-school group that carves out an 'acceptable' masculinity that resists the school, celebrates fighting and is group-based. Outside school this public masculinity is expressed through racist and other forms of group and neighbourhood-based hostility and violence, and, among some, intermittent theft.

The subject of black masculinity has come to the fore only relatively recently. At the heart of this literature is a concern with explaining routinely observed conflict between black boys and their teachers. The source of this conflict is different and opposed perspectives between teachers and pupils.

> For most white teachers the primary cause of black youths' 'problems' lies in the black community itself. So, the solution lies in black youth changing and adapting to the schools' demands. For the students, the primary problem is that of racism, including the teachers' racist practices, and the solution lies in the schools changing to meet their needs.
> (Mac an Ghaill 1988: 1)

Mac an Ghaill (1988) compared African-Caribbean and Asian male students' responses to schooling, their labour market destinations, and student–teacher relationships, and drew a number of conclusions about the nature of school processes, teachers' ideologies and practices, and school racism. Despite widely differing groups of teachers – authoritarian, liberal and realist – offering quite different approaches to delivering the schools curriculum and policies, all perceived black young people's 'underachievement' as the primary problem. Pupils did not experience explicit, direct racism from teachers. Rather, racism was mediated through offering different social and technical curricula to different social groups within the school. There was also, however, a system of racist stereotyping of the 'troublesome' African-Caribbeans and the 'passive, cooperative' Asian male student. These and other teacher stereotypes were resisted and survival strategies adopted by both African-Caribbean and Asian boys. Their common experience of racism overshadowed all other social determinants of their lives.

Sewell's (1997) study of a school attended by African-Caribbean boys came to similar conclusions to Mac an Ghaill, that teachers defined the 'problem' of schooling black young people in terms of the students themselves rather than school institutional processes or the wider society. In contrast to Mac an Ghaill, however, he argued that the ways in which some African-Caribbean boys respond to school cannot be understood apart from what happens to them and how they are perceived outside school. Just as the boys brought to school their assumptions and perceptions of

African-Caribbean subculture, so teachers criticised their home background, 'culture' and lifestyle as inherently anti-school and destructive forces in schooling. Although African-Caribbean boys made up only one-third of the pupils in the school studied, they represented 85 per cent of the total exclusions. School exclusions arose directly out of boys' conflicts with teachers. Meanwhile, students responded through various strategies of rejection, resistance, adaptation and accommodation to school mores and expectations. Even when black boys adopted a pragmatic, instrumental but accommodating strategy towards school, the outcomes were still negative. Most boys experienced school as a series of endemic tensions and conflicts and as challenging their ethnicity and masculinity, and African-Caribbean boys received a disproportionate amount of control, discipline and criticism compared to other ethnic groups. The central issue appeared to be that African-Caribbean boys were forced to sacrifice their subcultural affiliations and embrace 'individualism' to succeed, and having rejected their own community and peer group, many found themselves in a 'double bind' between loyalty to parents, peers and surviving at school. Some operated limited resistance to fit in with their peer group while simultaneously attempting to avoid conflict with teachers, while others rejected and resisted school altogether. Generally, most African-Caribbean boys – whether they conformed, retreated or rebelled – could not link academic success with being tough, joining in with the hypermasculine culture of their peer group, nor with power in the labour market.

Some writers (Archer 2003) on schooling and masculinities have questioned whether this debate is not really about class – the collapse of traditional male employment and ensuing identity confusion – rather than an essential crisis in masculinity *per se*. There is evidence, though, that certain masculine styles – whatever their source or influence – sit uncomfortably with the kinds of knowledge and behaviour expected in schools often perceived and felt by boys to be feminised and emasculating.

School disaffection, failure and truancy

When criminologists routinely point to school failure, disaffection, truancy and exclusion as important factors in the development of delinquency, they often take school processes as given and unproblematic so that young people disaffected from school are simply seen as unable or unwilling to avail themselves of educational opportunity, often it is said, because of poor parenting and lack of parental encouragement and supervision. Some writers (M. Phillips 1998) have argued that the distribution of educational rewards must reflect the distribution of 'ability' among pupils, therefore the notion that 'all must have prizes' undermines the credibility of the education system. The reality of schooling in modern Britain is quite the opposite for the 40 per cent who leave school at age 16 or before.

Explanations of school disaffection, school failure and truancy that rely on a pathological or deficit model of poor intelligence and/or poor parenting have been criticised by studies of schooling, masculinities and race. Other studies, while rejecting the deficit model, offer only a minor role, if any, to the masculinities model. In this approach it is the nature and quality of school processes themselves that are to blame for school disaffection, failure and truancy – processes experienced by many working-class black, Asian and white children and young people negatively. Here the focus shifts again from the perceived deficiencies of individual pupils to the perceived deficiencies of schooling for these groups, especially in the areas in which they live. What seems most noticeable is the cross-cutting of race and class in these explanations.

There is plentiful evidence, collected over many years, that most children, of whatever background, start well at school – even if not on a level playing field in terms of pre-school support – yet as their school careers progress some of these groups, particularly black boys, but also British Pakistani, Bangladeshi and white working-class boys and girls, suffer attrition in their performance and engagement with school that may lead to boredom, disaffection, disengagement, truancy and exclusion. This attrition also occurs among some African-American, Hispanic and white working-class children and young people in the USA (MacLeod 1995).

The issue of parental support and aspiration, although important, is less important than parental educational background that can bequeath children the social and cultural capital to succeed at school. For example, among black and minority ethnic groups, the educational progress of second- and third-generation children and young people closely reflects the initial educational backgrounds of their migrant parents (Modood 2003). Of course, parents who themselves may have been educationally disadvantaged nevertheless followed the pattern of many migrants in wanting their children to succeed at school, and some members of relatively disadvantaged groups have overcome their disadvantage (Mason 2003; Modood 2003; Pilkington 2003; Dench *et al.* 2006). Why, then, does attrition take place despite pro-school parental support and aspirations? Part of the answer lies in the schooling process itself, which is not 'neutral' – that schools provide equal opportunities to all pupils to succeed according to individual 'effort' and 'ability' – as many believe. In marked contrast to this belief about opportunities for all, studies have shown that different outcomes between schools reflect pupil intake, and the biggest single indicator of low educational achievement is poverty and class (McKnight *et al.* 2005). Gillborn and Youdell (2000) argue that, contrary to the aforementioned belief that schooling and education offer educational opportunities and progress to all parents and pupils who wish to avail themselves of these opportunities, actual processes of schooling in effect 'ration education'. Education is rationed through school processes of promoting some pupils at the cost of demoting others. One consequence is the often expressed anger and resignation of young people that their efforts have gone so poorly rewarded by teachers (MacDonald and Marsh 2005). Another is the impact such rationing has on minority and white working-class pupils. These processes begin to explain attrition within these groups as pupils become progressively disillusioned and disaffected, or at best wholly instrumental towards their schooling, disliking school but accepting that it is necessary to gain qualifications.

Underlying explanations are found in the nature of modern schooling. In their study of two multiethnic schools in London, Gillborn and Youdell (2000) argue that schools compete under pressure in response to government laid parameters of 'success' in which higher-grade (A–C) General Certificate in Secondary Education (GCSE) passes have become the dominant criterion for measuring success or failure in the British educational system. This has created an 'A-to-C economy' in schools – how many higher-grade passes are achieved and what proportion of pupils meet the benchmark level of at least five such passes. 'Success' becomes synonymous with schools being placed highly in school league tables, 'Ability' is equated with the crudest and most discriminatory definitions of 'intelligence/IQ', and educational outcomes must be predictable from an early stage in a pupils school career. The pressures placed on schools, teachers and pupils by league tables and the ensuing 'A-to-C economy' are an important context for understanding contemporary forms of school disaffection, predicated at least in part on the increased adoption of selection by 'ability'.

As a result of increased pressure on schools and their need to maximise their performance in league tables, there has been a return to selection, especially the adoption of setting and other ways of grouping pupils by 'ability' at an earlier stage in their school career. Such approaches have negative effects for some working-class and ethnic minority pupils, many of whom are disappointed and dissatisfied with their treatment by a selection process that demoralises and demotivates them. Because these processes of selection and differentiation are recognised by the pupils themselves, they feel that peers who attain highly are favoured by teachers in terms of the amount of time and attention they receive. Depersonalised and trapped, both teachers and pupils are constrained by this A-to-C economy regardless of individual needs and interests. While opening up options for some pupils, these processes begin to close down options for others. So far as winners and losers are concerned, Gillborn and Youdell's study found that black and poor pupils were 'without exception' likely to be in the lowest sets and least likely to be in the higher. In one of the two secondary schools studied just 4 per cent of black pupils attained at least five high-grade GCSE passes that included maths, science and English language, and none achieved this in the other school. Setting on the basis of ability and predictions of educational outcomes meant that many black and working-class pupils disproportionately received second-rate teaching in second-rate examination groups, on the basis that the schools invested resources of teacher time and support in pupils expected to show the maximum return (in terms of higher-grade passes). A substantial group designated by teachers as 'without hope' of achieving in the A-to-C economy is thus created at an earlier age (13–15) than in the past. Lower sets were taught different curricula and they were expected to cover less. This placed a ceiling on the maximum grades certain pupils would be allowed to gain – many pupils could not attain the highest grades regardless of how well they performed in the examination. Feelings of being treated unfairly and pupil accounts of inequality in school prominently feature issues of ability, behaviour, social class and 'race'. This sense of injustice can lead to resignation and disaffection.

Perhaps at the heart of the system lies an unquestioned common sense about what constitutes 'ability', its prediction and measurement (see Chapter 2). Gillborn and Youdell (2000: 198) argue that teachers conflate social class, ethnicity and 'ability', such that black and working-class white boys are considerably more likely to be judged as lacking in ability and that this constitutes a 'new IQism' based on hereditary assumptions, coded through the discourse of 'ability' and competition:

> In this way ... elitist and racist assumptions lie at the heart of the processes of selection and differentiation that dominate the system. The gross inequalities that arise from these processes are shielded from scrutiny by a perspective that stresses an *individualized* approach.

In their ethnographic study of young people living in poor white working-class neighbourhoods in the North-East of England, MacDonald and Marsh (2005) concluded that school disengagement was an *effect* of attending 'failed' schools in poor neighbourhoods. We might expect to find a similar relationship between poor areas, poor schools and low educational achievement in ethnically mixed inner-city areas in London and elsewhere. The evidence suggests that the 'poverty penalty' of being brought up in a poor neighbourhood is greatest for white pupils, although black boys have one of the lowest levels of attainment and appear to fall steadily further behind as they go through school (McKnight *et al.* 2005). This suggests that social class as well as ethnicity continue to have salience for school outcomes. It is not difficult to see how young people brought up in poor areas often 'fail' to connect doing well at school with access to decent jobs. MacDonald and Marsh (2005: 66) found that a significant minority of young people believed that having a good education and possessing qualifications would not necessarily enhance their later job prospects, and 'there was little substantial difference between the post-school careers of the most and the least qualified', explained by the paucity of decent, working-class jobs for *all* young adults living in the areas at the time, and that what was available did not require GCSEs:

> That de-industrialised localities like this continue to provide jobs for this age group, albeit now in the form of severely casualised employment that pays no regard to educational credentials, helps to explain

the ready abandonment of formal education by some young people and their often dismissive attitude to it.

Interestingly, they also found that although frequent truancy was a major problem it did not necessarily lead to social exclusion, delinquency and criminality as many criminological studies have suggested. Truancy was driven by frustration, boredom, embarrassment and feelings of failure. For others it was driven by experiences of being bullied, but for most it was driven by a sense of belonging to peer groups having anti-school values. MacDonald and Marsh (2005) and Webster *et al.* (2004) concur that school disaffection and persistent truancy alone are unlikely to lead to delinquency and criminality. Of more importance is with whom and where 'truancy time' is spent. These studies found that involvement with local street-based peer groups was the most significant factor that distinguished those most likely to go on to develop delinquent and criminal careers, while conceding that the link between this form of peer group involvement and offending outcomes is neither necessary nor inevitable.

Finally, in a different national context, MacLeod's (1995) ethnographic study of processes of school disaffection and marginalisation in the USA compared a group of disaffected white Italian-American and Irish-American boys, and a group of conventional and aspirant African-American teenagers. Here, too, success in school did not necessarily translate into success in the labour market, whether attitudes towards education were positive or not. Even pro-school attitudes may not always overcome class and race barriers. Among the white group, most had dropped out of school, been arrested and used drugs on a regular basis. A premium was placed on masculinity, toughness and lower-class street culture, not school authority. Similar to the other findings discussed here, they believed both that school performance was tangential to securing a job and that, in any case, 'decent' or 'good' jobs were out of their reach. The group of black young men, despite their poorer backgrounds, eschewed street culture and rejected drugs. They had worked hard in school, held education in high esteem and were positive about its merits for enhancing employment prospects, but experienced a less than positive return for their adherence to mainstream values – 'dutifully playing by the rules hardly guarantees success . . . aspiration, application, and intelligence often fail to cut through the firm figurations of structural inequality' (MacLeod 1995: 241). If the white group's adherence to an oppositional working-class local street culture enabled them to salvage an alternative form of self-respect while damning them to 'poor work' or possibly prison, the seemingly 'positive' 'choices' of the black group and their work ethic were constrained by the same structural inequalities through which these different choices are played out.

Race, class and peer groups

The issue of friendship-based peer groups runs like a thread throughout this chapter and deserves further focus here. Claire Alexander's (1996) study of African and African-Caribbean young men and women in London claimed that masculinity and gender roles were a primary feature of the construction of the young men's identities, both as individuals and as a group. Focusing on the role of the male peer group, she argued that, contrary to some studies (see above and Chapter 9) that see 'black masculinity' as an alternative or oppositional source of social status and standing apart from wider society, so-called 'Black macho' is an extension of wider gendered power relations within society of which it is a part, and reflects that diversity.

While groups of young black men often display unity to others, the reality of their peer groups is far from harmonious and uniform, and contains 'latent divisions and private hostilities' (Alexander 1996: 144). Here masculinity emphasised the social function of the group – a collective stand – rather than personal friendship or knowledge among group members: 'You don't talk to the guys about your problems' (Alexander 1996: 147). Group relationships were defined in terms of external forces rather than confiding personal problems. This masculine style seems a central characteristic of many of the marginalised peer groups discussed in Chapter 9 and elsewhere in this book. Nevertheless, the oppositional nature of the group, the perceived need to fight others and 'womanise', orientation to the external public arena, and emphasis on public roles and persona – being a good dancer, strong fighter – subordinated and hid one-to-one private interaction that when revealed expressed mostly 'quiet, serious, and reflective' selves. In Alexander's (1996: 149) study 'the boys' achieve significance 'only in opposition to other [primarily white male] groups'. However, the main groups it faced were of similar age and class background, bounded as they were by the same leisure arenas, and only occasionally confronted figures of authority such as the police (and presumably teachers when younger). When within a mainly white environment, these racial boundaries became more rigid in their opposition to other men, and more antagonistic. In these encounters the boys articulated 'race' as a primary marker of the group's self-definition, but not exclusively so. As Alexander (1996: 155) goes on to explain:

> images of 'masculinity' in this arena constituted the yardstick by which success is measured. 'Race' in these encounters becomes a symbol denoting group boundaries. It is employed in relation to other groups, usually, but not exclusively, as a means of opposition. 'Race' is not, however, a sufficient or necessary basis for peer group formation: its meaning may alter according to the situation or be cross-cut by other considerations, such as those based on gender or class constructions.

Alexander's (2000) later study, *The Asian Gang*, offers a useful comparison of the construction of ethnicity, identity and masculinity. In this study of Asian, particularly Muslim and Bengali, young men in South-East London, more emphasis is given to the structural constraints placed on such men by experiences of schooling and encounters with the police than was the case in the earlier study of black young men in London. Both studies challenge the stereotyping of ethnically based, friendship-based peer groups. While Alexander questions the whole basis on which 'the Asian gang' is said to actually exist, myths about the constitution and existence of 'ethnic gangs' have been subject to critical scrutiny in the USA, where 'gang', 'race' and 'crime' are seen as inextricably linked (for a summary of these myths, see Walker *et al.* 2004: 54–9). In her portrayal of the group's relationship to family and friendship, their close relationships to older sisters from whom they sought advice, the complex web of mutual extended family and community ties, obligations and duties in which they are embedded, she challenges 'absolutist notions' of 'the Asian community' and 'racialized constructions of Asian masculinities'. This repositioning of Asian young men as a 'problem' is 'explained' by a breakdown of perceived patriarchal authority and 'crisis in masculinity' within the Asian community.

From several different perspectives writers (Webster 1996, 1997; Goodey 1998, 2001; Macey 2002) have noted a shift from an earlier concern with African-Caribbean to Asian 'hyper-masculinity', with all the incumbent associations of threat, criminality and violence that this implies. However, as Alexander (2000: 17) notes, this shift in popular and academic perceptions of Asian young men joins a long tradition of creating myths of gang behaviour and criminality among working-class young men said to arise from 'masculinity-in-crisis':

> Violence, criminality and hyper-sexuality are posited as the alternatives to the fulfilment of patriarchal responsibilities and control, to 'real' male power. It is no accident, then, that the representation of 'the Asian gang' ... should draw explicit comparisons with African-American 'gang' subculture, with its associations with ghettoes, drugs, black-on-black violence and 'nihilism'.

Similar criticisms are found in Collins *et al.*'s (2000) study of youth crime in Australia in the context of a media-induced moral panic about 'ethnic youth gangs' in Sydney. Goodey's (1998: 251) study of Asian boys in Bradford and Sheffield, Northern England, argued that a new-found assertiveness on the part of Asian young men has resulted in a new-found white fear:

> The interest and apparent 'problem' with Asian youth, for the white majority, arise when an image ... drastically changes from 'passive' to 'aggressive' in combination with the recent ascendancy of Islamophobia on the world stage. The development of a 'tough' identity of and

by Asian youth may assign them a degree of power where there previously existed a sense of powerlessness, but in the eyes of the white population, this can pose a threat against their order and against them. Nowhere is this more the case than when Asian youth are aggressive, violent and apparently racist towards the white population.

The conflation in these accounts of 'Islamist' protest with 'aggressive' or 'hyper-masculinity' is difficult to disentangle from the greatly increased media attention and negative representation of Muslim young men as 'potential terrorists' and of the terrorist attacks themselves.

Understanding 'race', class, masculinities and crime

Accounts of defensive-aggressive displays of 'exaggerated' or 'protest masculinity' seek explanations in the loss of informal and formal controls that have variously accompanied the emergence of a crisis in family structure, intergenerational emasculation and prevention of family formation resulting from slavery, institutionally induced school disaffection, the influence of street- and ethnically-based peer groups, and a crisis in patriarchal authority and belief systems. It can be seen from the discussion that it is difficult to disentangle changing masculinities from changing ethnic and social class structures or from the situations, places and contexts of their enunciation. Overall, ethnic association and 'protest masculinity' may be important within both criminal organisations and peer groups as a source and strategy of friendship ties and loyalty, status and protection, a counter to and compensation for marginalisation, and as an alternative source of cultural and social capital. But it is also likely to be only one of a series of contingent responses to crisis and marginalisation rather than a fixed or essential feature of men's responses to social, economic and cultural humiliation and exclusion brought by social change.

Further reading

One aspect of the 'masculinity thesis' in explaining race and crime is an alleged crisis in family formation among some African-Americans and British Caribbeans. This aspect of the debate is put forward in an argument by Smith (2005), partly based on the work of Patterson (1997, 1998). Readers should refer to the standard theoretical work on 'masculinities' by Connell (2005). In an American context, Messerschmidt (1993) has argued that there is a link between certain forms of masculinity and crime among all social classes, not just the working class or underclass. MacLeod's (1995) is one of the best ethnographic studies that brings together many of the themes discussed in this chapter.

chapter nine

The African-American 'underclass' and the American Dream

Introduction: the existence of an 'underclass'

The key theme of this chapter is the claim that an African-American 'underclass' exists as a distinct social stratum that has become isolated from the rest of society. Some writers claim that there is an identifiably separate group occupying a different moral universe from so-called 'mainstream' America, while others argue that shared values across race and class boundaries make the existence of a separate 'black underclass' unlikely. Whether a separate African-American underclass can be said to exist or not, most studies implicate deindustrialisation and urban economic restructuring in the 1970s and 1980s as a major contributing factor to the worsening conditions of inner-city life, which laid the grounds for the growth of an urban 'underclass'. Other historical studies, however, claim to have identified an African-American urban underclass crime problem going back to the late nineteenth century as a result of the early racist exclusion of African-Americans from the emerging industrial economy. Whatever the continuity or recent growth of a supposed underclass – over

20 per cent of blacks lived in ghettos in 1990, up by over a third since 1980, and the proportion of the black poor who lived in urban ghettos increased from 37 to 45 per cent over the same period (Patterson 1997). Patterson (1997) wishes to remind us, however, that the black underclass is a very small proportion of the African-American population as a whole. Other writers, as we shall see, are less sanguine.

After establishing the historical sequence by which the 'black ghetto' was formed and persists, the chapter reviews studies that emphasise the separate existence of a crime-ridden African-American underclass followed by those studies that question such a clear-cut division between the 'underclass' and the rest of America. However this issue is resolved, it is apparent that ghetto social life is more differentiated and variegated than its depiction in popular images and beliefs as almost exclusively based in joblessness, welfare dependency, drugs and gun crime. Finally, it is argued that ethnographies of the black underclass – whatever their strengths and weaknesses – require for their interpretation an understanding of the wider historical, social and economic context in which they are placed.

The core of the argument about the African-American underclass, whether from the liberal left (Wilson 1987, 1996) or from the conservative right (Murray 1984; Herrnstein and Murray 1994), is the claim that a breakdown of culture has occurred within the urban underclass. Explanations are sought in the absence of positive 'role models' due to the abandonment of the ghetto by the middle and respectable working classes' flight to the suburbs (Wilson) and the discouragement of work due to 'overgenerous' welfare payments leading to dependency (Murray). Whichever explanation is chosen – flight or dependency – inner-city areas are depicted as socially isolated deindustrialised places devoid of skilled, disciplined, employable and 'marriageable' men, which in turn is said to engender the rise of lone mothers. The conclusions, if not the causes, are remarkably similar – that the poor are in some way made morally deficient, resulting in high levels of crime, incivility and disorder.

The American sociologist William Julius Wilson (1987, 1996) famously argued that despite a high rate of poverty in 'ghetto' neighbourhoods throughout the first half of the twentieth century, it was not until the early to mid-1970s that there was a catastrophic explosion of crime, joblessness, single-parent families and welfare dependency in inner-city areas, giving birth to a new African-American black 'underclass' disconnected from, and culturally and behaviourally different from, mainstream American society. However, for Wilson the social problems of urban life in the United States are, in the main, the problems of racial inequality. The worst effects are the disproportionate involvement of African-Americans in violent crime, family dissolution and supposed welfare dependency.

This dislocation of the inner-city and growing inequality are said to have occurred from the impact of economic and demographic changes in the 1970s, particularly deindustrialisation and changed age structure. This period also saw growing expectations among lower-class African-Americans prompted by the successes of the civil rights movement. At the same time the 'poverty drug' crack was introduced into the inner city, with its accompanying violent crime (Patterson 1997). Accompanying these changes were legacies of historic discrimination, a rapid increase in the number of young people belonging to minorities at a time when economic change posed serious problems for unskilled individuals – both in and out of the labour force – and the increased spatial concentration of poverty in larger, mostly Northern and Eastern, urban areas. Change and dislocation encouraged the exodus of middle- and working-class families from many ghetto areas to the suburbs, leaving behind populations, particularly young people, seldom likely to interact on a sustained basis with people who were employed, thus isolating and excluding them from social networks important in learning about jobs in other parts of the city. As joblessness became a way of life, the links between schooling, educational credentials and employment were severed. Unlike his conservative interlocutors, Wilson was careful to argue that it was the growing social isolation of the ghetto from mainstream America, rather than a 'culture of poverty' – a set of inherent values and behaviour – that was set in train by these tumultuous transformations in American society.

Wilson's (1987, 1996) seminal work on the existence of a socially isolated African-American (and we might now say Latino) underclass can be judged in the light of comparatively recent American ethnographic studies of the inner-city 'ghetto' discussed here. Although often unacknowledged within American discussions, this chapter is about the ways in which race, class and crime become embroiled and come to define each other in one of the most racially segregated societies in the world.

The isolation of the black ghetto: a history of segregation

The formation and persistence of the black ghetto are a key aspect of the history of American racism. Ethnographies of the African-American population going back to W.E.B. Du Bois' *The Philadelphia Negro*, written in 1899 (see Du Bois 1996), have consistently shown a history of the segregation of blacks and whites. Depictions of the black ghetto throughout this period reflect their period of writing and therefore should be treated with caution in so far as they inevitably made unfounded generalisations that confirmed stereotypes of the essential nature of 'black folk'. They do, however, reveal change and continuity in the formation of the black ghetto. Drake and Cayton's (1993) *Black Metropolis*, first published in 1945, captured the migration of Southern blacks to Chicago's South Side and the creation of the black ghetto in the late 1930s. Charles Keil's (1966) *Urban Blues* provided a history of African-American music as an expressive form within ghetto life that reached out to and influenced both mainstream

America and Europe. Elliot Liebow's (1967) *Tally's Corner* described the effects of poverty and low-waged precarious work on childhood, family structure and social life among a group of black men in Washington's inner city during the early 1960s, noting how lack of advancement led these men to compensate for their 'failure' through alcohol and serial monogamy. Other studies carried out during the 1960s and 1970s, such as Lee Rainwater's (1970) study of a St Louis housing project, *Behind Ghetto Walls*, and Ulf Hannerz's (1970) *Soulside*, another study of inner-city Washington, were consistent in reporting that ghetto dwellers, despite their poverty, oppression and particular behaviours, essentially subscribed to the mainstream values of American society.

Massey and Denton (1993) described the historical process by which the black ghetto was isolated from 'mainstream' American society (see also Banton 1997). Before 1900 there were very few predominantly black urban neighbourhoods. The black ghetto was primarily created in Northern cities between 1900 and 1940 as a product of industrialisation and the migration of black workers from the South. As the size of the urban black population rose steadily after 1900, white racial views hardened and a relatively tolerant period of race relations in the North drew to a close. As moral panics about black crimes and vice grew, a series of Northern white communal race riots against blacks between 1900 and 1920 further hardened the colour line in employment, education, and especially housing. As a result, blacks previously living in integrated or predominantly white areas fled to the emerging ghettos. As ghettos expanded, white violence escalated to the ghetto periphery. In the making of the black ghetto white violence gave way to institutionalised discrimination in the housing market and white flight to the suburbs. From the very beginning the black ghetto was constructed through whites seeking to contain growing urban black populations. From the early origins of the black ghetto during the nineteenth and twentieth centuries, the manner in which blacks were residentially incorporated into American cities differed fundamentally from the path of spatial assimilation followed by other migrant and ethnic groups. Unlike black ghettos, non-black 'immigrant enclaves' in America proved to be a fleeting transitory stage in the process of immigrant assimilation, whereas the ghetto became a permanent feature of black residential life. Although other groups were progressively integrated into American society, saw their socioeconomic status rise and dispersed to the suburbs, the vast majority of blacks were forced to live in neighbourhoods that were all black, creating an extreme social isolation.

If this historical legacy has to some extent been acknowledged within American society, the continued growth and persistence of black segregation have not. There is a common belief that segregation is declining due to the growth and increased spatial dispersal of a relatively recent black middle class to the suburbs – a belief encouraged by popular TV and film portrayals of an integrated society. Admissions of segregation are rationalised by the supposed voluntary and 'natural' origins of black segregation found in impersonal market forces and choices. Housing is said simply to reflect income and preference, regardless of race or ethnicity. These beliefs are partly responsible for the ineffectiveness of legislation such as the Fair Housing Act 1968 that was supposed to eradicate racial discrimination in housing. The claim that segregation has eased can be contrasted with evidence that racial segregation occurs regardless of income levels, so that poor blacks live under unrivalled spatial concentrations of poverty and affluent blacks live in neighbourhoods that are far less advantageous than those experienced by the middle class of other groups, including other minority groups (Massey and Denton 1993). Evidence supporting increasing segregation rather than integration is found in the extent to which black suburbanisation lagged far behind that of other groups, the fact that blacks are equally highly segregated at all levels of income and in the suburbs, and that this reflects the effects of white prejudice rather than anonymous market forces. Whereas segregation declines steadily for most minority groups as socioeconomic status rises, this has not been the case among African-Americans. If this 'hypersegregation' cannot be accounted for by socioeconomic differences between black and whites then white prejudice must be to blame, despite a strong desire by blacks to live in racially mixed neighbourhoods. Whatever whites might proclaim in principle – that people should be able to live wherever they can afford, regardless of race – they remain prejudiced against black neighbours in practice. As the proportion of blacks in a neighbourhood rises, white demand for homes falls sharply while black demand rises, while in all-white neighbourhoods systematic barriers to black residential mobility are erected through the buying, selling and renting of homes and in the allocation of home mortgages, and through direct discrimination against black home seekers. Massey and Denton (1993: 2) are unequivocal about the unprecedented depth and uniqueness of black segregation in American society: 'racial residential segregation is the principal structural feature of American society responsible for the perpetration of urban poverty and represents a primary cause of racial inequality in the US'.

During the 1970s and 1980s black and Hispanic poverty increased in many urban areas, but underclass communities were created only where increased minority poverty coincided with a high degree of segregation – principally in the older metropolitan areas of Chicago, Detroit, Cleveland and Philadelphia in the Northeast and the Midwest. For example, among Hispanics, only Puerto Ricans developed underclass communities, because only they were highly segregated and this segregation is directly attributable to the fact that a large proportion of Puerto Ricans are of African origin. Segregation creates underclass communities because it builds deprivation into the residential structure of black communities. An increase in poverty of a residentially segregated group leads to the geographic concentration of poverty because all the increase is absorbed by a small number of racially homogeneous neighbourhoods rather than being spread evenly throughout the urban area. During periods of

economic dislocation, a rising concentration of black poverty and segregation results in a self-perpetuating process of lack of investment in and
maintenance of property, housing abandonment, crime and social disorder.
In concentrating poverty, segregation also concentrates drug use, joblessness, and welfare dependency, teenage childbearing and lone parenthood,
producing a social context where these conditions are not only common
but the norm. Segregation perpetuates poverty because, being unable
to move to better neighbourhoods, blacks face barriers to social mobility.
Finally, the isolation that segregation and intense poverty bring sees
the emergence of an 'oppositional culture' at odds with the values of
middle-class society. This in turn creates a 'culture of segregation':

> The conditions of the ghetto . . . make it exceedingly difficult to live up
> to broader societal values with respect to work, marriage, and family
> formation, and poor blacks are thus denied the opportunity to build
> self-esteem and to acquire prestige through channels valued in the
> wider society. As a result, an alternative status system has evolved
> within America's ghettos that is defined *in opposition to* the basic
> ideals and values of American society. It is a culture that explains and
> legitimizes the social and economic shortcomings of ghetto blacks,
> which are built into their lives by segregation rather than by personal
> failings. This culture of segregation attaches value and meaning to a
> way of life that the broader society would label as deviant and
> unworthy. (Massey and Denton 1993: 167)

This African-American oppositional culture had existed since the creation of the black ghetto by white violence before 1920. 'Re-segregation'
(Davis 2002) in the 1970s and 1980s made black street culture powerful
again. Studies conducted during the 1960s and 1970s (Liebow 1967;
Hannerz 1970; Rainwater 1970) show that although the main divergence
of black street culture from the white mainstream occurred during this
period, an emerging black oppositional culture seemed to coexist with
aspirations to mainstream cultural values. Massey and Denton (1993)
argued that pervasive poverty, joblessness and dependency on ghetto social
networks set ghetto blacks apart because of their inability to accomplish
mainstream values. As a consequence of this humiliation, some black men
were led to reject the unskilled and low-waged jobs open to them and seek
compensation and status through alternative means. The authors conclude
that the fact that one-third of all African-Americans live in ghettos
(Patterson 1997 puts this figure at one-fifth) cannot be attributed to class as
discrimination against blacks is widespread and continues at very high
levels in urban housing markets.

The integration of the black ghetto

The somewhat bleak picture of the isolation of the ghetto painted so far can be contrasted with studies of the African-American inner city that provide a more positive and complicated picture. Although conceding most of the negative aspects of inner-city life already outlined, these studies emphasise that the majority of ghetto dwellers are not criminals, are not selling or taking drugs, have complex moral visions, and are often striving for a much more 'mainstream' life (Newman 2002).

This tradition (see Suttles 1968, 1972) warns against the portrayal of neighbourhoods as neatly bounded areas whose residents are said to be of a single mind. Not only does this ignore the interaction and overlap of different, often conflicting, groups and many identities within neighbourhoods, but also such areas are likely to be marked by an intricate organising of moral and social order requiring the same discipline and self-restraint as the moral dictates of the wider society. Conventional norms are not rejected but are given different emphasis according to local conditions, and the range of values found in neighbourhoods are as much the product of wider values as they are of adopting local values and aspirations. Of most importance, the necessary ordering of inner-city social relationships is a way of establishing and maintaining individual and community safety.

Duneier (1992) described the variegated biographies and experiences of older poor working-class 'respectable' black men living at the margins of the ghetto in South Side Chicago who were regular users of a public cafeteria. Their lives were not those of the prevailing negative stereotypes of black men living in the ghetto. Their very location at the margins of the ghetto offered them more interaction with whites, while they also witnessed the deterioration of nearby black areas. The notion of 'respectability' – having moral worth and decent behaviour – pervaded the men's nostalgic accounts. They inveighed against younger middle-class and lower-class blacks, the former for their wastefulness, the latter for their uncommunicativeness, unwillingness to work and lack of authority. By these men's accounts, lack of personal responsibility on the part of other blacks had ruined the ghettos of their youth. They also continued to believe in a political collective responsibility. They had been left with an acute sense of moral and social isolation as their beliefs had increasingly precluded them from wider ghetto sociability. Finally, they regretted 'racial polarisation' and valued interaction with whites.

Duneier (1999) continued this theme in a later study of homeless black book and magazine vendors in the affluent neighbourhood of Greenwich Village, Lower Manhattan. Duneier argued that their entrepreneurial activities engendered informal controls and surveillance on the street that reduced crime, constructed 'moral' behaviour and 'decency' in these men's lives, and maintained them in a positive relationship to society.

In a similar vein of seeking to find some positive aspects of ghetto life,

Newman (1999) studied low-waged workers and unemployed job seekers in Harlem. Newman's (1999) documenting of the experiences of young black and Puerto Rican fast-food workers sought to explore the central tenets of underclass theory – whether 'mainstream' models of behaviour had really disappeared with the exodus of more affluent families, and whether the urban poor were a distinct social stratum that had become isolated from the rest of society as others had claimed (Wilson 1987, 1996). Contrary to underclass theory, Newman found that paid work has been and remains a central and defining activity for many African-American residents of the ghetto, whereas much sociology has emphasised gangs, drugs and hustlers. Over one-third of residents in the poorest neighbourhoods in Chicago were working and over half were either available for work or in school. The absence of the working poor from most literature on the inner city ignores the workplace as a site where the ghetto poor intersect with other groups and low-waged workers are drawn away from street culture.

Newman offers an important account of relationships between schooling, skill and the low-waged labour market in the American inner city that can be compared to the previous discussion in Chapter 8. For inner-city young people getting a job can make the difference between affording to stay in school and dropping out, as well as providing a structure that might enhance school performance, just as the work commitment involved may undermine it. Newman counters conventional claims of the low educational aspirations of young people from poor neighbourhoods – their inability to connect educational credentials and labour market prospects – by pointing to the investment in education of the young people she spoke to and the ways they combined work and school, in many cases supported, it is claimed, by their employer fast-food managers. Balancing the demands of work and school means that the pressure falls on young people themselves to fund their own educational endeavours. Fast-food work, although conventionally disparaged, does, according to Newman, provide entry-level employment, knowledge and experience – memory skills, inventory management, social skills and versatility – that might otherwise be absent. It is, according to Newman, the disparaging and stereotyping of such jobs that is the problem in forming the basis for advancement in the labour market.

Newman (1999: 249) concluded, however, that belonging to the 'right' social networks is key to obtaining work:

> 'Who is making it, who is not?' in the fast food labour market in Harlem comes down to this: African-Americans, young people, native-born applicants, and those who live nearby are less likely to be hired [in fast food outlets] than others. People who lack 'connections' to a network of friends or family members who are already working in the 'target' job are also at a disadvantage. Employers appear to be relying on personal references, which will seriously disadvantage anyone who does not have a network of working friends or family.

In this context Newman compares the American system of supporting school-to-work transitions unfavourably with the German and Japanese training systems, such that the former leaves considerable room for the floundering, churning period that is typical among American young people entering the labour market. Rather than managing transitions, the American system relies on a free-market approach in which it is assumed that educational credentials 'naturally' carry over into work, whereas other systems link school and work through job placement.

The notion of 'decency', central to Duneier's (1999) account of scavengers and vendors in Lower Manhattan, recurs in Elijah Anderson's (1999) study of the inner-city ghetto in Philadelphia. According to Anderson, 'decency' embodies peculiarly American mainstream values that, contrary to popular stereotypes, are widespread in the inner-city ghetto. However, 'decent' values contend with opposed 'street' values in a series of complex interactions and negotiations among ghetto residents and families. Those who claim 'decency' and those whom the 'decent' socially place in the 'street' status emerge during interaction:

> Almost everyone residing in poor inner-city neighborhoods is struggling financially and therefore feels a certain distance from the rest of America, but there are degrees of alienation, captured by the terms 'decent' and 'street' or 'ghetto,' . . . suggesting social types. The decent family and the street family in a real sense represent two poles of value orientation, two contrasting conceptual categories. The labels 'decent' and 'street,' which the residents themselves use, amount to evaluative judgments that confer status on local residents. The labeling is often the result of a social contest among individuals and families of the neighborhood. Individuals of either orientation may coexist in the same extended family. Moreover, decent residents may judge themselves to be so while judging others to be of the street, and street individuals often present themselves as decent, while drawing distinctions between themselves and still other people. There is also quite a bit of circumstantial behavior – that is, one person may at different times exhibit both decent and street orientations, depending on the circumstances. Although these designations result from much social jockeying, there do exist concrete features that define each conceptual category, forming a social typology. (Anderson 1999: 35)

Over the course of his Chicago and Philadelphia studies, the thrust of Anderson's (2002: 1533; see 1990, 1999, 2003) argument has been as follows:

> As a result of the breakdown or weakness of civil law in the most distressed inner-city communities, a survival strategy with implications for local public order has emerged – a 'code of the street' that relies on 'street justice', whose transactions involve a currency of reputation, respect, retribution, and retaliation. Because civil law has been so

compromised and eroded locally, people often rely on themselves and their reputations for protection, a situation that leads to high rates of urban violence. A legacy of institutionalized racism, joblessness, and alienation suffuses distressed inner-city neighborhoods and exacerbates these conditions.

Just as decent values contend with street values, so respectability contends with 'respect'. The governance and regulation of violence through an informal, unwritten set of rules – the code of the street – reflects a desperate search for respect and survival. Paradoxically, because it attempts to maintain some semblance of order, and fills the vacuum left by the ineffectiveness of inner-city policing, the 'code of the street' further isolates ghetto street culture and places it in opposition to mainstream American values. The 'code of the street' emerges where the influence of the police ends leading to street-based 'justice' – an individual's credible reputation for vengeance. In a social context of persistent poverty and deprivation, alienation from the broader society's institutions is widespread. Nevertheless, most people in the inner-city neighbourhoods studied identified themselves as decent and aligned themselves with mainstream institutions and conventions. Being 'decent' compensates for racism.

The studies reviewed in this section suggest at least a *partial* integration of *some* ghetto residents into more mainstream values and labour markets. They address the variety of responses to economic deprivation and blocked opportunity evident among the ghetto poor, ranging from the felt moral isolation of 'respectable' citizens living within the ghetto to redemption and integration through poor work. In effect, Duneier argues that the popularly perceived dichotomy between stereotypes – the black underclass and the black middle class, those who have made it and those who have not, those who work and those who do not – invites an overriding stereotype of the black population that ignores and makes irrelevant the experiences of the vast majority of ordinary working-class blacks who remain in the ghetto and the role they might play in processes of informal control. This challenges Wilson's (1987) argument that the exodus of working and black middle-class 'positive role models' from the ghetto left in its wake socially isolated poor blacks. Wilson never really spelt out in precisely what ways black middle-class people who left the inner city had been significant to urban neighbourhoods in the first place, or whether they really had been 'role models' or were likely to provide entry into relevant work networks. From the turn of the last century, Du Bois (1996) had shown that middle-class and working- and lower-class blacks may have had little contact.

Anderson (1990, 1999) attempted to understand what had been lost by this abandonment of the ghetto and argued that the majority of those who remained and who worked in low-waged jobs did not somehow lack the 'moral integrity' of those who were able to leave. As Duneier (1992: 127) argued:

What distinguishes the poor from other members of society is not that they are isolated from mainstream values, but that they do not have the standard of living to buffer them from the destructive effects of the permissiveness, freedom, and spontaneity of American life. Many pathological social trends in the ghetto are more concentrated reflections of life in the wider society.

Clearly, teenage sex, illegitimacy, adultery, divorce and other concerns of a peculiarly American moral discourse are prevalent in the wider society, and in any case 'middle-class morality is all very well if you can afford it'. Duneier demonstrates a more nuanced account of the influence, or lack of influence, of middle-class role models in the African-American ghetto than Wilson, that ghetto masculinities are varied and that, to the extent that ghetto criminality departs from the supposed traditional institutions of the ghetto, it is difficult to see how middle-class status offers much charisma or influence on these relatively new cultures, compared to say, the celebrity culture of rap. In presenting a one-sided image of the black male, earlier ethnographers have made demeaning assertions about the nature of black men and a ghetto-specific masculinity, whilst 'The aspiration to respectability within the black population is largely ignored or misrepresented' (Duneier 1992: 155).

The paradox of the black ghetto

In arguing that many pathological social trends in the ghetto are more concentrated reflections of life in the wider society, Duneier (1992) draws attention to the paradoxical nature of ghetto life. This paradox lies in the fact that, although marginalised and excluded economically, ghetto dwellers are included in so far as they share the values and aspirations of the wider society. Some writers take this further by arguing that this paradox defines the relationship of the ghetto to wider society and creates much resentment on both sides of this divide (Young 2002).

In contrast to the studies reviewed so far, which sought to show that majority *elements* of the ghetto-dwelling population aspire to 'respectability' and mainstream American values through low-waged work and a sense of 'moral worth', other writers such as Nightingale (1993), Bourgois (1995) and Young (1999, 2002) argue that it is precisely aspirations to mainstream values among *core* ghetto members – often those involved in criminality – that are the problem. Previous studies argued that people living in the black ghetto are divided between the majority – those who belong to the 'respectable' working poor – and a minority core who identify with 'unrespectable' street culture.

Nightingale's (1993) study of inner-city African-American young people in Philadelphia asks why, although these young people strongly share

'American values' – particularly patriotism in strongly revering, for example, the army and marines – they are perceived and treated as un-American and vilified in derogatory terms. His answer is that young people share American values and are alienated from them at the same time. Although they would prefer to move out to 'decent' houses in suburbia to realise and sustain their American dreams, the means – the better jobs and decent schools – by which this might be possible have disappeared from their neighbourhoods. Their schools are segregated by race and class. They fear crime and homicide in the context of the entry of crack cocaine related violence in the 1980s. This visceral portrayal of the black ghetto, based on the reconstruction of the biographies of a group of young people and their parents, traces the crisis of the black family and a surge of fatal violence from 1955 onwards as an *exceptional* experience of community erosion and historical memory in American society.

Poverty and job loss are a necessary but not sufficient explanation of why black people's experiences of frustration, disappointment, humili-ation and shame has been so much more drastic than those of other groups of the urban poor, including poor whites. Although clearly, as most studies concur, the deindustrialisation of American cities was a contributory factor that excluded African-American children and young people from meaning-ful participation in economic and social life, this does not explain their subsequent collective adaptations to earlier economic dislocation. A more comprehensive explanation, according to Nightingale, lies in the responses of mainstream culture to the felt distress of African-American young people. Parenting, policing, juvenile justice and prisons have centred on the idea that control of aggressive or community-threatening behaviour demands the use of violence or incarceration. Both mainstream *and* inner-city America use a racial imagery drawing on contradictory American values and traditions of consumerism, violence, forceful parenting and law and order. But the main explanation is recent racial exclusion and resur-gence of the idea that black men are inherently violent, although some ghetto residents defiantly glorify this caricature as compensation in the face of racial humiliation. Compensation takes other forms as young African-Americans have embraced American consumer culture and portrayals of violence. Paradoxically, '[it] is the increasing presence of mainstream American cultural forms in inner-city life that offers the best explanation for why urban African Americans' experience of poverty, joblessness, and racial exclusion has become so filled with violence' (Nightingale 1993: 11). Economic marginalisation is accompanied by inclusion in mainstream American culture. Very high levels of joblessness result in marital separ-ation or delay of marriage, while lone-parent or reconstituted but unstable families are characterised by erratic, neglectful, harsh and aggressive parenting which further encourages violent responses.

One kind of inner-city response to economic marginalisation has been drug trafficking. In his study of Latino-Americans in El Barrio, East Harlem, Bourgois (1995) describes the underground crack cocaine economy that allows people to generate alternative income. Here a range of alternative income-generating strategies are employed to subsidise meagre welfare payments (among those in receipt of these) or as sole income. However, since the 1980s, dealing in cocaine, crack and heroin, has been the fastest-growing source of employment for men in Harlem. Very public, visible and widespread retail drug sales easily came to outcompete other – legal or illegal – income-generating opportunities. Ghetto members' proximity to a multi-million-dollar business within their own neighbourhood – where 40 per cent of households have no wage or salary – easily overrode any attractions found in the surrounding low-waged economy.

It is unlikely that rapid deindustrialisation and the mushrooming of a low-wage service economy in themselves laid the foundations for this new illegal economy – Harlem has a long history of illegal responses to economic marginalisation. However, there can be little doubt that drug trafficking has become the most important and lucrative aspect of global criminal networks. East Harlem's long and disruptive heritage of a substance abuse-driven underground economy has seen a wave of ethnic successions in which some Puerto Ricans have filled the vacuum left by the Italian Mafia's 'upward mobility'. In 1994 it was estimated that the global trade in drugs amounted to $500 billion a year, larger than the global trade in oil. A substantial proportion of 'narcodollar' profits is laundered, and about half of the laundered money is reinvested in legitimate activities influencing the legal economy. Economic globalisation and new communications and transportation technologies have greatly facilitated the supply of illicit drugs (Castells 2000). Although the risks are considerable, so too are the rewards. There was no shortage of budding inner-city entrepreneurs who were only too eager to establish high-profit, high-risk crack businesses, despite drug arrests being the single most important cause of a very rapid rise in the incarceration of inner-city African-Americans (see the discussion in Chapter 7).

Bourgois' uncompromising and visceral account of this illegal enterprise in Harlem describes how most of its participants become embroiled in lifestyles of violence, substance abuse and 'internalised rage':

> Contradictorily, therefore, the street culture of resistance is predicated on the destruction of its participants and the community harboring them. In other words, although street culture emerges out of a personal search for dignity and a rejection of racism and subjugation, it ultimately becomes an active agent in personal degradation and community ruin. (Bourgois 1995: 9)

Although crack dealers were only a small minority of East Harlem residents, they offer a persuasive, even if violent and self-destructive, alternative lifestyle to other young people around them, and they come to dominate public space and induce fear in other residents.

Again, a complex inner-city street culture emerges in opposition to exclusion from mainstream society, offering 'an alternative forum for autonomous personal dignity' for those growing up poor in the richest city in the world. Bourgois' subjects were almost exclusively composed of second-generation, New York-born Puerto Ricans, and most were explicitly hostile to African-Americans despite their emulation of African-American street culture, which had an almost complete dominance over style in the underground economy. Paradoxically, El Barrio youths often face vilification when they venture out of their neighbourhood, while inner-city street culture is recuperated and commercialised by mainstream society, recycled as pop culture which reinforces and affirms the culture by flattering and seducing its members, rendering it even more powerfully appealing than it had been in previous generations. This entrapment inside the ghetto is both self-enforced and enforced from without by pervasive racism. Thus inner-city apartheid was enforced not only by the police (police brutality was routine) but also because it was too dangerous for El Barrio youths to venture into other poor African-American and Latino neighbourhoods. Ghetto members become trapped inside the cocoon of El Barrio's streets, unable to operate outside their neighbourhood also because of their illiteracy and very low educational levels. The isolation of the ghetto comes from within and without. Virtually all the violence is confined to a small subgroup of individuals who are directly involved in substance abuse and the underground economy. However, street culture generates a dynamic of violence which can terrorise locals, involves rivals from within the area or from immediate adjoining neighbourhoods, and conjoins with the violence experienced from the police.

Bourgois' ethnography stands out from comparable studies in wanting to contextualise what he witnesses in the effects of the colonial legacy of the United States' subjugation of Puerto Rico and its inhabitants and the subsequent history and pattern of Puerto Rican immigration to the United States – a history born of American slavery and racist segregation (Thomas 1997; Smith 2005). In particular, he focuses on the effects of the economic and cultural precariousness of Puerto Rican entry to East Harlem, and the overwhelming economic and social changes imposed so rapidly on the formerly rural-based Puerto Rican population in the United States. The street history of El Barrio is intimately implicated in these wider histories, particularly the economic imperatives shaping the lives of Puerto Ricans, and the US 'cultural assault' on Puerto Rican rural-based culture. Of course, these historical and structural factors do not translate directly on the street – Bourgois' subjects were unaware of them, and for the most part they attribute their marginal living conditions to their own psychological or moral failings rather than blaming society – but are indirectly present in street culture to form the characteristic brutally self-destructive features of this culture.

There is not space to delve into Bourgois' richly textured account of how crack houses manage addiction and maintain discipline and dignity and the effects of spiralling drug arrests and the toughening of drug-sentencing rules, as well as familiar inner-city themes of humiliation in low-waged work, the dissolution of patriarchal authority and its effects on children, and masculinity and vulnerable fathers. Bourgois' (1995: 326) conclusion about the relationship between the Immigrant's Dream and the American Dream is clear enough:

> Like most other people in the United States, drug dealers and street criminals are scrambling to obtain their piece of the pie as fast as possible. In fact, in their pursuit of success they are even following the minute details of the classical Yankee model for upward mobility. They are aggressively pursuing careers as private entrepreneurs; they take risks, work hard, and pray for good luck. They are the ultimate rugged individualists braving an unpredictable frontier where fortune, fame, and destruction are all just around the corner, and where the enemy is ruthlessly hunted down and shot.

In the end Bourgois, like Nightingale, argues that the oppositional culture found in East Harlem is on closer inspection nothing of the sort. The assertion of and pride in street culture, found, for example, in a specifically Puerto Rican appropriation of 'hyper-urban' hip-hop, seems to rest ultimately on an overidentification, surfeit and exaggeration of mainstream values embodied in the American Dream. The material base for this search for cultural respect is, however, 'tragically' confined to the street economy.

Support for this view is found in the writings of Jock Young (2002) who, using the current British term 'social exclusion', rejects simplistic accounts that contrast the contented and secure 'included' with the 'excluded' who are said to lack these positives and live in a different moral universe. Instead he suggests that the heightened resentment of the excluded is propelled by the similarity of values and 'crossing of borders' between the excluded and included. Keeping in mind the themes of the earlier studies reviewed here that drew lines between the 'respectable' and 'disreputable' within the black ghetto, Young's argument is worth recalling. The division between a mainstream, 'respectable', included majority and despondent excluded ghetto minority is exaggerated because these divisions and boundaries are blurred and regularly crossed. They can overemphasise the differences in morality, mores and values between the included and excluded, while at the same time leaving the 'normality' of the majority unquestioned.

These dichotomies reinforce views of the ascribed deficits of a presumed underclass as 'dysfunctional' and 'the problem' – deficits of disorganisation, worklessness, welfare dependency, lone parenthood and unstable family structures, immigration, drug use and criminality – contrasted with the virtuous qualities of the included majority. They assume that the deficits of the underclass are virtually absent in the rest of society and that what is required is to move ghetto members into work in the precarious low-wage economy – which has extended far beyond a minority of the population – with its own pressures and precarious conditions, as if entry into this secondary labour market is a meaningful way of mainstreaming the excluded minority. The implication of Young's analysis, to which we will return in the concluding section, is that the mainstream values to which many ghetto residents aspire – whether through legal or illegal means – are themselves precarious and possibly unsustainable.

Understanding the ghetto

So far in this chapter, much has been made of the American Dream, which is an umbrella term for much that passes for legitimate aspiration and moral, cultural and economic goals within American society. What basis does this dream have in reality as a realisable possibility for many Americans, including those who reside in the ghetto? After all, as we have seen, the inner city incorporates *both* adherence to American cultural values embodied in the American Dream *and* a black oppositional culture. An important aspect of the American Dream is that through their own efforts the poor will eventually avail themselves of opportunities to move out of poverty through upward social mobility. The essence of the idea is that through hard work and endeavour, conservative values and appropriate behaviour and taking up the many opportunities available, individuals can better their situation through moving up the class structure (social mobility) into the suburbs and beyond (spatial mobility). These social and spatial dimensions of mobility are supposed to lead to highly sought-after American affluence, income and wealth, as well as the status that goes with this. An important test of the realistic possibilities of individuals and groups acquiring and then improving their employment, income and wealth positions commensurate with mainstream values is the extent to which America is a meritocratic society that distributes social and economic rewards equitably.

Some writers have expressed a guarded optimism about the extent to which African-Americans have benefited from longer-term rises in prosperity encouraging integration, while noting high levels of social and economic polarisation within the African-American population (Patterson 1997, 1998). To see whether this optimism is justified we need to turn to some detailed data about poverty and class structure in the USA. There was a sustained period of somewhat reducing inequalities after the Second World War up to the early 1970s, largely because of improved social security and welfare benefits for the poor. Since then US society generally has seen a startling increase in inequality as the incomes of poor Americans have shrunk while the incomes of the richest families have continued to grow. The average income of the poorest Americans remains well below where it was at the end of the 1970s (Burtless 1999; Appelbaum *et al.* 2003; Gilbert and Kahl 2003). Thirty-seven million Americans live below the poverty line, and this group has grown by 5.4 million since 2001. Between a fifth and a quarter of all black and Hispanic Americans live below the poverty line, while for whites the figure is just 8.6 per cent. Many are the 'working poor' and are forced to take two or three jobs simply to survive because the minimum wage (at time of writing) of $5.15 per hour has not risen since 1997, and, adjusted for inflation, is at its lowest since 1956. However, African-American teenage official unemployment was 33 per cent in 2003, rising to 45 per cent in the inner city. If we include the teenage under-employed and those not at school, not at work and not looking for a job, this climbs to 90 per cent in inner-city areas (Schaffer 2006). In the 1990s American capitalism boomed, but increases in average wages were modest while social inequality and polarisation between richer and poorer families grew. Indeed, between the mid-1970s and 1999 the poorest 20 per cent of families saw their income plunge. As well as increasing inequality and polarisation between the better off and the worse off, poverty has also increased. Gilbert and Kahl (2003) concluded that the American class structure has seen a shift from falling class inequalities and shared prosper-ity in the 1950s and 1960s to growing class inequality today. This turn-around is marked by occupational and income polarisation between well-paid, well-educated managers and professionals and other workers (especially among men). The benefits of change have been unevenly dis-tributed among African-Americans and polarisation is greater. The occu-pational shifts associated with the postindustrial economy have had an especially negative effect on black workers. In 1995, the proportion of black professionals and managers was five times what it had been in 1940, but low-paid 'service occupations' remained the largest single black occu-pational category, as they had been 50 years earlier, and have been increas-ing since the late 1960s. In the 1990s many black workers had no job at all (Gilbert and Kahl 2003).

Although important, the existence of poverty – even increasing poverty – itself is not the sole indicator of whether meritocracy is a realistic ideal. Poverty might be an unfortunate but temporary condition for some groups. Rather, we need to ask whether people stay in poverty or move out of it. Despite the fact that there has been a *general* rising prosperity in the USA, this not only has failed to close income gaps, but also seems to have had a negative effect on upward mobility – the very essence of the American Dream. The overall trend is that relative mobility – the share of Americans changing their income group in either direction, up or down – rose until the 1970s then stopped or declined during the 1980s and 1990s (Gilbert and Kahl 2003). The number of people who stayed in the same income bracket – at the bottom or at the top – over the course of a decade increased in the 1990s. Half of families who started the 1970s in poverty were still stuck there at the end of the decade, and that figure increased during the 1990s. In recent decades American inequality and poverty increased while mobility, especially among the poor, declined. Relatively secure, relatively skilled middle-ranking jobs disappeared, especially in the older industrial cities and in public sector employment, and low-waged part-time and temporary service sector jobs have increased, making it far harder for those at the bottom to pull themselves up into higher socio-economic groups. Increasing inequality and reducing social mobility generally hit African-American inner-city populations hardest. Although Gilbert and Kahl (2003) have shown that upward social mobility among African-American men changed remarkably over a relatively short period between 1962 and 1973, partly due to civil rights legislation, it still lagged behind that of whites. However, in recent years there is evidence of stagnating opportunities for younger men, white and black, although upward mobility among middle-class African-Americans continues to improve. The most recent reliable data about the intergenerational economic mobility of black families in the United States shows an especially low rate of upward mobility from the bottom of the income distribution (Hertz 2005). While only 17 per cent of whites born to the bottom tenth of family income remained there as adults, for blacks the figure was 42 per cent. This white–black mobility gap in the probability of upward mobility and therefore expectation of income exists irrelevant of parents' level of education. Hertz (2005: 187) concludes that 'much of the current measurable persistence of poverty in the United States is due to the significantly higher rate of persistence among poor African-Americans as opposed to poor white households'. Bowles et al. (2005: 1) are unequivocal that 'children from the least well-off families do not have a fair chance at attaining the level of economic security most other families manage to attain'. The success of some families and the 'failure' of others' cannot be accounted for – as is often assumed – by parents passing superior IQ on to their children, as much as it can to parents passing their material wealth to their children, at least for those at the top of the income distribution (Bowles et al. 2005). Although children may well inherit certain genetically and culturally transmitted cognitive skills and behavioural characteristics that strongly affect their labour market success, the major role of the environmental influences of family, neighbourhood, and schooling is beyond doubt (Bowles et al. 2005). Not only do conventional measures of schooling attainment not capture this transmission process (see Chapter 8), the inheritance of general cognitive skill (IQ) as a determinant of earnings is much less than more and better-quality schooling, health, wealth and race.

The key development in labour market opportunities, however, is the emergence of new strata of service-orientated menial workers. Appelbaum et al. (2003) offer a series of close-up case studies of low-wage service and manufacturing industries in the USA, ranging from hotel, hospital and catering services to call centres, auto suppliers and the hosiery industry. The 'working poor' were a quarter of the US labour force in 2001. The majority of low-wage workers in the USA have no educational credentials beyond a high school diploma. The average real wage of these workers has declined rapidly since 1973. Paradoxically, this has occurred in the context of rapid economic growth and the lowest unemployment rates in 30 years in the 1990s. Technological change, deregulation, changes in financial markets and globalisation have put pressures on employers to reduce wages and labour costs. Again, this has disproportionately affected African-American workers.

These trends have led some writers to refer to a 40:30:30 society in which 40 per cent of the population are in tenured secure employment, 30 per cent are in insecure employment and 30 per cent are economically marginalized, idle or working for poverty wages (Hutton 1995). As we have seen, a third of African-Americans live in ghettos (Gilbert and Kahl 2003). Ghetto and poor neighbourhoods concentrate and trap poverty (Bowles *et al.* 2006). The growth of inequality since the early 1970s has taken place in the context of a shrinking primary labour market offering relatively secure, full-time work and career advancement contrasted with a growing secondary labour market of poor job security, where career structures are absent and where life is experienced as precarious (Young 1999). Castells (2000), referring to 'Dual America', locates these changes in an increasing disparity in wages between the 'new informational economy' requiring a high level of education and the traditional industrial and service sectors. Further polarisation of the US labour market takes place as higher-level, high-skilled jobs, requiring high levels of education, increase. Meanwhile, in traditional sectors wages have been driven down by the inducing of deindustrialisation through the impact of global competition, the incorporation of women into paid labour and growing racial discrimination in the context of growing immigration. Furthermore, there is a systematic relationship between these structural transformations and the growing dereliction of the inner-city black ghetto. The particular requirements of the new 'knowledge economy' for higher education and verbal/relational skills are rarely provided in inner-city public schools, yet the key to upward mobility in the USA is a university education. Although college enrolment has soared for higher-income students, more children from poor families can only afford to go to community colleges, which typically do not offer bachelor's degrees. The small number of poor students who get a degree has barely increased in 30 years (Burtless 1999; MoneyWeek 2003; Harris 2006). Without education, black male ghetto dwellers are also discriminated against in the low-wage service economy (Newman 1999). To factors that have had a particularly negative effect on the underlying poverty of black inner-city populations, such as a 40 per cent cut in the real value of the minimum wage and state welfare benefit between 1970 and the late 1980s, must be added political inertia, federal disinvestment in America's big cities, rapid falls in public sector employment, a fall in military employment and expenditures diverted to the war on drugs (Davis 2002).

Economic and social exclusion has its corollary in spatial exclusion of the poor (Gilbert and Kahl 2003). Various 'anti-urban' policies that in effect subsidised white flight and 'resegregation' in every American metropolitan area during the 1980s have resulted in a 30 per cent loss of the employment base in inner cities and a concomitant rise in suburban employment and income. For example, in Los Angeles, almost the entire white working class of the older southeast industrial belt – some 250,000 people – moved to the job-rich suburban fringe during the 1970s and early 1980s. They were replaced by Mexican immigrants, whose second and third generation have themselves experienced mobility to the suburbs, while African-Americans, on the whole, have remained trapped in inner-city Los Angeles (Davis 2002). The inner-city black population is facing new forms of spatial exclusion seen in the growth of affluent and mostly white 'gated communities' (Blakely and Snyder 1997; Low 2004). The contrast could not be greater between poor African-Americans corralled into racially segregated ghettos or prisons and those able to choose to live in 'gated communities'. Gated residential communities represent a new version of the middle-class American Dream beyond suburban solutions to fear of crime. They further intensify social and racial segregation because they mirror the ghetto. Gated communities are affluent ghettos in reverse, except that black ghetto residents have little choice where they live while gated residents choose and pay a premium to be segregated. This cordoning off of poor and affluent 'ghettos' with physical urban barriers, suburban-isation, high security walls, fences and closed-circuit television, confuses 'the vicissitudes of class with those of race' (Young 1999: 20).

The scale and intensity of spatial and social exclusion in the USA compared to Europe, and the exceptionally exclusionary nature of the American Dream are precisely because it is based on the ideal of equality of opportunity and meritocracy (Young 1999). If all are supposed to get a chance to compete according to merit, then individuals who lose in this meritocratic race have only themselves to blame because the distribution of reward is simply held to be a reflection of the distribution of effort within a given society. The missing link in this equation of reward and effort, however, is race and class, because individuals do not begin the race from the same starting points. Young (1999: 23) is surely right when he says that Europe's much lower levels of urban segregation and suburbanisation have made it more difficult 'to give spatial bearings to a distinct underclass', making it more difficult to cordon off crime and anti-social behaviour.

In understanding the ghetto and its supposed housing of an African-American 'underclass' characterised by some as embodying poor work discipline, unstable family structures, excessive masculinity and an abundance of crime and violence, others have argued that despite the alienation of black young people, paradoxically there is a high degree of inclusion of such people in American culture. Still others have argued that the ghetto is not a repository of alternative values, but that it has a *surfeit* of American values that blur morally dichotomous myths of difference and separate-ness: criminal and non-criminal, good guy and bad guy, oppositional sub-cultures and mainstream culture (Young 1999: 86). The absorption of African-American culture in the American mainstream points to *both* social exclusion *and* cultural inclusion, and this is the main source of resentment and fear between ghetto and mainstream. As compensation for their humiliation many inner-city young people create identities that select and exaggerate wider cultural values, creating essential notions of masculinity, and rigid distinctions that even play upon racial stereotypes. In other words, the ghetto is fully immersed in the American Dream of consumerism, television, materialism, obsession with violence, and even sharing in a perverse way the racism of the wider society. Rather than there being a deficit or difference in core values, there is variation in their accentuation. Access to global media messages and travel to work outside the ghetto further integrate the underclass in cosmopolitan values and the larger burgeoning service economy while also heightening their sense of relative deprivation. The poor are not excluded morally, and they are far from socially isolated (Young 2002).

An important theme running through most commentaries about the African-American underclass is the absence or presence of work and, more importantly, work values. As we have seen, urban ethnographers such as Anderson, Duneier and Newman have emphasised the role that work – any work – plays as a redeeming aspect of the efforts of African-Americans in the inner city to gain and maintain 'respectability'. The problem here is not so much the 'disappearance of work' (Wilson 1996) as it is the disappearance of decent work. The poor work on offer to African-American inner-city residents is often repetitive, demeaning and characterised by low pay for long anti-social hours, and therefore can undermine those very values and activities it is supposed to bolster – family relations, childrearing and the capacity of communities to maintain order and networks of mutual support and care (Currie 1996). When writers such as Anderson and Duneier speak of redemptive values of 'decency' and 'decent families' predicated on the availability of work, they can downplay the nature of the kind of work that is on offer.

The feared and resented ghetto: beyond urban ethnography

Clearly, as the previous section suggests, we cannot rely solely on urban ethnographic accounts of the African-American inner city to understand its emergence and persistence in the context of American 'apartheid' and inequality. Neither can we take the views and understandings of either ghetto residents or those outside the ghetto at face value – views that seemingly rationalise the apparent randomness, chaos and unfairness of the competition for education, housing and jobs in terms of racial and ethnic favouritism and discrimination. Instead we need to ask some further questions that take us away from sole empirical scrutiny of the African-American inner city towards an understanding, found elsewhere in this book, that 'race' and racism arise from social relationships governed by both interaction and segregation of minority and majority groups over time in particular places. For example, studies of race relations in deindustrialised Detroit – one of the most segregated cities in the United States –

have shown that the construction and persistence of the black ghetto is as much a consequence of the formation of white working-class identity and responses of whites to the black ghetto as it is to do with social relationships inside the ghetto (Sugrue 1997; Hartigan 1999; Welch *et al.* 2001). Ethnographies of the American white working class (MacLeod 1995; Hartigan 1999; Welch *et al.* 2001; Linkon and Russo 2002), discussed in Chapter 3, appear to show that poor whites living in deindustrialised places may experience similar processes of social exclusion, isolation and economic marginalisation as poor blacks.

Relationships between the included mainstream and the excluded underclass, and the responses and perceptions of the former towards the latter, are perhaps closer and more interdependent than the thesis of an African-American underclass isolated from the rest of society would suggest. In his discussion of how boundaries between the ghetto and mainstream America are regularly crossed, Young (2002) argues that both hostility towards and discontent amongst African-American inner-city residents is exacerbated by the very similarity of aspiration which the underclass has to the mainstream. On one side of this boundary, as wider values of consumerism and hedonism are absorbed and converge with the values of wider society, some inner-city residents, especially the young, adopt an exaggerated version of these values that can encourage crime. The criminality, violence and drug use of the underclass are not only acquisitive but also transgressive, driven by humiliation arising from a combination of acceptance of mainstream values followed by rejection of mainstream society which generates intense resentment. The culture of the underclass, with its compensatory masculinity, while resorting to violence and rampant individualism, overaccentuates the wider culture which it is influenced by and influences.

On the other side of the boundary, amongst the mainstream included, there is resentment and vindictiveness towards the underclass because it is claimed that they are reluctant to work and are a disproportionate source of social problems. In a society based on instant gratification, where consumption replaces work as the central cultural value, and reward is valued more than effort, the underclass come to stand in as a proxy for mainstream insecurities, fears and resentment. Young (2002) argues they are both feared and desired as much as they are resented – feared as predators, desired because unrestrained and resented because seemingly unwilling to defer gratification. 'Our' decency, restraint and hard work are measured against 'their' absence of these qualities, projecting all 'our' problems of constraint onto them. Yet this polarisation of attitudes requires qualification. As Patterson (1997) reminds us, the significance of the kinds of 'hypersegregation' or 'apartheid' described by Massey and Denton above may have been exaggerated and in any case may be changing. Patterson points to very substantial declines in crime rates among African-Americans since *American Apartheid* was published (1993), and although the spatial isolation of the African-American poor has increased, whites have become more tolerant about living in 'moderately' mixed neighbourhoods – from a white perspective those not having more than 25 per cent African-Americans, that is, not having *too* many blacks! – and there is more social integration in work and leisure spheres, even in places such as hypersegregated Detroit (Sigelman and Welch 1991; Farley *et al*. 1994; Sigelman *et al*. 1996; Patterson 1997).

Understanding the African-American 'underclass': the 'balance sheet' of segregation?

Are there grounds for being hopeful about the current and future fortunes of the African-American underclass? Certainly recent economic data in respect of growing income poverty and inequality, stagnation or decline in social mobility and the growth of low-waged work have increasingly polarised the American class structure, hitting the African-American 'underclass' particularly hard. There is some evidence, though, that American society is not as immutably segregated by 'race' or ethnicity as is sometimes argued and that a balance needs to be struck between evidence of high levels of segregation and contradictory, paradoxical and complicating forms of integration. The main historical source of segregation is the legacy of humiliation and exploitation of African-Americans by white supremacists. Patterson (1997, 1998) in particular draws out grounds both for optimism and pessimism about the position of inner-city African-Americans, attesting on the one hand to what he sees as a deep and continuing crisis in African-American family relations and masculinities, and on the other to popular cultural and educational progress and the relative growth of the 'new' African-American middle class.

There has been a seemingly long-term decline from the early 1990s in victimisation and crime, especially violent crime, in urban areas most associated with the African-American underclass. On some accounts desegregation appears to have stalled or reversed. On the other side of the balance sheet, poverty within the underclass has worsened relative to the past and compared to poor whites, partly because of continuing high levels of joblessness, but mostly because of the proliferation of low-waged work. Those whose situation has improved most over time are African-American women. At a more abstract level, we might say that if racialised *attitudes* have, in general, declined, the socioeconomic *position* of the African-American 'underclass' continues to be parlous. A lack of local opportunity and access to wider opportunities will continue to be linked, for some, to delinquent and criminal 'solutions'. To conclude, the ghetto is redolent of the embracing and some would argue, overaccentuation, of mainstream American values by ghetto dwellers. Some see defiance of poverty and racism in this embracing of American consumerism. The main thrust of ethnographic studies, in celebrating the virtues and dignity of 'hard work' and respectability as alternatives to welfare, drug dealing and criminality, risks moralising and ignoring the ways in which ghetto residents are *objectively* degraded and exploited in insecure, low-waged employment (Wacquant 2002).

Further reading

The main lines of debate about the alleged existence of an African-American 'underclass' based on very high levels of residential and other sorts of racial segregation can be represented by Patterson's (1997) argument that racial segregation is declining and racial integration is increasing (also see Young 1999, 2002), and Massey and Denton's (1993) argument that segregation defines and causes black poverty and is worsening. Close-up studies of the 'black ghetto', however, suggest considerable nuance in how we might understand life there, of which two good examples are Nightingale (1993) and Bourgois (1995).

chapter ten

State crime: the racial state and genocide

Introduction: criminology's neglect of mass killing

Until very recently criminology has mostly ignored mass killing, crimes against humanity, the conduct of war and the crime of genocide (but see Morrison 2006, Nikolic-Ristanovic 2000, and Jamieson 1998, for examples of criminological attention to these issues). It is not completely clear why this is the case. Although the tradition of analysing state crime has been, in general, of low priority in criminology's main concerns (Green and Ward 2004), this chapter draws on a wide range of non-criminological literature to focus on the crime of genocide. Genocide is by definition the most heinous racial crime imaginable, uniquely perpetrated on a scale and level of planning and organisation without precedent for any other crime.

Rather than being seen as an aberrant or even 'unique' event (in the case of the Nazi genocide and Jewish Holocaust), genocide seems to have been a not uncommon feature of human history to the present (Diamond 1991, 2005; Morrison 2006). Diamond (1991: 256–8) lists the following alleged and recognised genocides. From the slaughter of over a million Caribbean Indians by the Spaniards in the West Indies between 1492 and 1600, to the slaughter of over 10,000 Muslims and Christians in the Lebanon that ended in 1990, Diamond argues that there have been 37 recorded genocides, of which 17 occurred relatively recently (between 1950 and 1990). This does not include alleged genocide in Bosnia-Herzegovina in 1992–4, and the genocide in Rwanda in 1994 in which over 800,000 mostly Tutsi were murdered by Hutu. Of these 37 genocides, eight involved over a million victims: Caribbean Indians killed by Spaniards as already mentioned; Indians killed by Americans in the USA between 1620 and 1890; Indians killed by Spaniards in Central and South America; Armenians killed by Turks in Armenia in 1915; Russian political opponents killed by Russians between 1929 and 1939; Jews, Gypsies, Poles and Russians killed by Nazis in Europe between 1939 and 1945; Bengalis killed by the Pakistan army in Bangladesh in 1971; and Cambodians killed by the Khmer Rouge in Cambodia between 1975 and 1979.

The problem with such 'lists' is that they risk inflating the concept to apply to all or most instances of mass killings judged in retrospect to have been genocides. Yet the legal definition limits the term to specific events, aims, intentions and actions, and only came into existence in the 1948 United Nations Convention on the Prevention and Punishment of the Crime of Genocide. Retrospectively designating many instances of mass killing as 'genocide' loses the specificity of the meaning of genocide as a usually (some might argue fundamentally) racial crime. Morrison (2006: 93–4) lists 20 'major genocidal acts' committed between 1885 (Belgians victimising Congolese) and 1994 (Hutu victimising Tutsi in Rwanda), of which nine were retrospectively recognised as genocides by the United Nations. This is not to limit the meaning of genocide to a narrow legal definition but to be clear what constitutes genocide. If there is no internationally agreed definition and understanding of what constitutes the specific crime of genocide then the term risks being used for political reasons rather than humanitarian reasons of prevention, protection and punishment.

The definition included in the 1948 Convention stipulates (Article 2):

In the present Convention, genocide means any of the following acts committed with intent to destroy, in whole or in part, a national, ethnical, racial or religious group, as such:

(a) Killing members of the group;

   (b) Causing serious bodily or mental harm to members of the group;

   (c) Deliberately inflicting on the group conditions of life calculated to bring about its physical destruction in whole or in part;

   (d) Imposing measures intended to prevent births within the group;

   (e) Forcibly transferring children of the group to another group.

And, as confirmed in Article 1, 'genocide, whether committed in time of peace or in time of war, is a crime under international law which [the Contracting Parties to the Convention] undertake to prevent and to punish'.

Leaving aside controversies over definitional issues – for example, the definition does not include the destruction of 'political' opponents by a totalitarian state (see Horowitz 1997; Overy 2004) – it is important to recognise the distinction implied in the convention between direct (killing) and indirect means (preventing births through sterilisation), both aimed at the *biological destruction* of the group, the first universally illegal, the second having been legal in some jurisdictions. In this sense the Nazi 'euthanasia' and forced sterilisation programmes described in Chapter 2 can be understood as integral aspects of the Nazi genocide (see Fein 1979). To the above legal definition can be added subsequent historical and sociological understandings that: genocide is a *process* that involves staged escalation; involves the *biological* destruction of a group (usually, but not always, racially or ethnically defined by the perpetrators); and is nearly always perpetrated by, encouraged or condoned by a *state* (and only the state can prevent it).

The accounts given in this chapter focus on the processes leading to the paradigmatic German genocide of 1939–45 and those leading to the Rwandan genocide of 1994, and on the genocides themselves, and does not consider the immediate aftermaths of either, the resulting refugee crises, international interventions during and subsequent to the genocides, nor legal and prosecution processes. For treatments of these in respect of Rwanda, see Prunier (1997), Melvern (2000), Neuffer (2000), Dallaire (2003) and Polman (2004). The analysis also limits itself to a main focus on the perpetrators and their knowing and unknowing supporters. These restrictions and choices hopefully allow a deeper and more thorough analysis of the contexts, processes, causes and conduct of the crimes. Finally, the chapter does not attempt to chronicle the horror of these crimes as found in the first-hand accounts of the victims, witnesses and sometimes the perpetrators and bystanders. There is an extensive close-up literature that does so, and readers might wish to look at Gilbert (1986), Hilberg (1992), Goldhagen (1996), Browning (1998), Rees (2005) and Steinbacher (2005) on the German genocide; and Keane (1995), African Rights (1995), Gourevitch (1998) and Human Rights Watch (1999) on the Rwandan genocide. The Nazi and Rwandan genocides are not compared and should be seen as separate phenomena, having wholly different causes and courses. Nevertheless, their discussion in the same chapter is instructive as they raise in different ways the question of the role of the past in creating the present. For example, some analysts have given more weight to national legacies of intrinsic and pervasive racist ideology as a factor determining these genocides, while others give much more weight to contingent, incremental and situational processes and factors.

The Nazi genocide

'Ordinary' perpetrators

On 30 January 1939, speaking to the Reichstag on the sixth anniversary of his appointment as Reich Chancellor, Hitler said:

> I have often been a prophet in my life and I was mostly laughed at. In the time of my struggle for power it was in the first place the Jewish people who received with nothing but laughter my prophecy that one day I would take over the leadership of the state and with it the whole people and then among many other things bring the Jewish problem to its solution. I believe that the roars of laughter of those days may well have suffocated in the throats of the Jews in the meantime.
>
> I want to be a prophet again today: if international finance Jewry in Europe and beyond should succeed once more in plunging the peoples into a world war, then the result will not be Bolshevization of the earth and thus the victory of Jewry, but the annihilation of the Jewish race in Europe. (Cited in Evans 2005: 604)

This still abstract threat, born of the Nazis' paranoid racist ideology, had been expressed in many guises previously – including Hitler's early political biography, *Mein Kampf*, of 1926 – but never so explicitly and publicly – the speech was broadcast on the weekly newsreel in its entirety. The threat was to be cited on numerous subsequent occasions, and even found its way, in late December 1941, into the training journal of the German Order Police (given responsibility for a solution to the Jewish question in Eastern Europe, i.e. killing Jews there):

> The word of the Führer [in his speech of January 1939] that a new war, instigated by Jewry, will not bring about the destruction of anti-Semitic Germany but rather the end of Jewry, is now being carried out. The gigantic spaces in the east, which Germany and Europe have now at their disposition for colonization, also facilitate the definitive solution of the Jewish problem in the near future. This means not only removing the race of parasites from power, but its elimination from the family of European peoples. What seemed impossible only two years ago, now step-by-step is becoming reality: the end of the war will see a Europe free of Jews. (Cited in Browning 2004: 300)

By 1941, Hitler's abstract threat to 'annihilate the Jewish Race in Europe' had indeed become reality.

The review of the literature on the Nazi genocide in this chapter should be read in unison with the discussion in Chapter 2 of earlier ideas found in German 'racial science' and the German eugenics and 'euthanasia' programmes that laid some of the grounds for Nazi race thinking. In his study *Hitler's Willing Executioners: Ordinary Germans and the Holocaust*, Goldhagen (1996) spectacularly argued that the Holocaust[1] originated from a peculiarly pervasive and uniquely *German* form of historical racist anti-Semitism, that ordinary Germans were the perpetrators, and focused on their willing complicity rooted in German cultural history rather than the role of the Nazi racial state. According to this account the 'personalised brutality and cruelty' and 'pleasure' that the killers took in their work made the German (rather than Nazi) genocide 'distinctive' and 'unprecedented' in the 'long annals' of barbarism (cited in Morrison 2006: 258). This argument sought explanations in a pre-determined deep-rooted German cultural history rather than contingency and choice:

> anti-Semitism moved many thousands of 'ordinary' Germans – and would have moved millions more, had they been appropriately positioned – to slaughter Jews. Not economic hardship, not the coercive means of a totalitarian state, not social psychological pressure, not invariable psychological propensities, but ideas about Jews that were pervasive in Germany, and had been for decades, induced ordinary Germans to kill unarmed, defenceless Jewish men, women and children by the thousands, systematically and without pity. (Cited in Morrison 2006: 258)

Although correct to implicate the role of ordinary people in the genocide (Browning 1998; Johnson 1999; Gellately 2001; Johnson and Reuband 2005), Goldhagen's account of the flawed racist German national character is itself deeply flawed in identifying a unique national racist ideology as the cause rather than the coming and rise of the National Socialist racial state, and the particular men it brought with it (Kershaw 1998; Finkelstein and Birn 1998; Eley 2000; Evans 2003, 2005). Nevertheless, the question of the motivations and intentions of the perpetrators remains a pressing one.

We know that in Nazi Germany, as Bauman (1989: 20) asserts, that the 'people enlisted into the organisations most directly involved in the business of mass murder were neither abnormally sadistic nor abnormally fanatical. We can assume that they shared in the well-nigh instinctual human aversion to the affliction of physical suffering, and even more universal inhibition against taking life.' Hannah Arendt famously used the phrase 'the banality of evil' in her report of the post-war trial of Adolf Eichmann, one of the initiators of the 'final solution to the Jewish problem'. This phrase was meant to convey the ordinariness of Eichmann and the other men and women who perpetrated the Holocaust. As Arendt

(1994: 106) suggested, the most difficult problem that the initiators of the 'final solution' encountered (and resolved!) was 'how to overcome ... the animal pity by which all normal men are affected in the presence of physical suffering'. It was not even that small numbers of well-trained, disciplined people who were persuaded to overcome their scruples did the killing. The sheer scale of the enterprise (the killing of over 10 million Jews, Poles, Russians and Gypsies) directly involved tens of thousands at various stages of the operation, from ordinary clerks to professionals and the special killing squads themselves. This, like all genocides, was not the work of relatively small numbers of vengeful and murderous individuals.

Beginning with Hitler, he too was an 'ordinary man', not German but Austrian. There was little in his early background that could have predicted his later course. Born in the provincial Austrian city of Linz, Hitler suffered, like many of his place, time and generation, from a tyrannical father, and benefited from a loving and loved mother. Hitler was later to be driven by a particular sort of politics, not pathology, engendered by his upbringing. In his youth he was surrounded and influenced by the turbulent conservative nationalist politics that dominated Austria and many European countries at the time. Although the 'young Hitler diligently studied the alleged differences between races' (Hamann 1999: 17), anti-Semitism hardly played a major role in his thinking. It was when he moved to Vienna that he first encountered and began to draw on a widespread racist anti-Semitism ('The Jews form a state within a state'), which was also an aspect of the nationalist opposition to the Austro-Hungarian multi-national state before its collapse after the First World War. At the time, Hitler's hatred of communists was more significant than any hatred of Jews (Hamann 1999). What Hitler's sojourn in Vienna taught him was that racist anti-Semitism was normal in public discourse, but also, more importantly, how it might be used as a political tactic and strategy (Hamann 1999). And as Kershaw's (1998) magisterial biography of Hitler convincingly shows, the single most influential event on his life was Germany's defeat in the First World War, in which he fought in the German army. Hitler's elation at fighting in the war was followed by an extraordinary embittered feeling about defeat. Writing about his feelings at the end of the First World War in *Mein Kampf*, he said (cited in Kershaw 1998: 72):

> And so it had all been in vain ... Did all this happen only so that a gang of wretched criminals could lay hands on the fatherland? ... In these nights hatred grew in me, hatred for those responsible for this deed.

Kershaw (1998: 73) is unequivocal:

> The First World War made Hitler possible. Without the experience of war, the humiliation of defeat, and the upheaval of revolution the failed artist and social drop-out would not have discovered what to do with his life by entering politics and finding his metier as a

propagandist and beerhall demagogue. And without the trauma of war, defeat and revolution, without the political radicalization of German society that this trauma brought about, the demagogue would have been without an audience for his raucous, hate-filled message. The legacy of the lost war provided the conditions in which the paths of Hitler and the German people began to cross. Without the war, a Hitler on the Chancellor's seat that had been occupied by Bismarck would have been unthinkable.

Völkisch or popular nationalist ideology too was a minority taste before the war, but its influence grew in the last two years of the war and after the defeat. The essential strands of *völkisch* ideology were extreme nationalism, racist anti-Semitism, and mystical notions of a uniquely German social order, with roots in a Teutonic past, resting on order, harmony, and social hierarchy. It is important to note again, as Chapter 2 demonstrated, that racist anti-Semitism, and the notion of the quest for racial purity through eugenics by sterilising or removing the degenerate and the unfit were popular and widespread in Germany and elsewhere. But it was the application of the word 'degenerate' to Jews that began to distinguish different national versions of biological racism and eugenics. If Hitler's all-devouring obsession with the Jews was not observable before 1919, and never absent thereafter, he was doing no more than reflect sentiments which were widespread at the time. Hitler's first public statement about the Jews came in his letter to a supporter in which he stated that Jewry was a race, not a religion; that anti-Semitism should be based on 'reason', and lead to the systematic removal of the rights of Jews; and that 'its final aim', he concluded, 'must unshakably be the removal of the Jews altogether' (Kershaw 1998: 125). As Kershaw pointed out, from then on these views remained unaltered to the last days in the Berlin bunker in 1945. He lashed out at the Jews in speech after speech. In 1920, thirteen years before eventually coming to power in 1933, he demanded internment in concentration camps to prevent 'Jewish undermining of our people' and the Jews' removal from Germany. As with some much earlier pre-war anti-Semites, the language itself was implicitly genocidal in its biological similes – the Jews were 'parasites' and 'bacilli', and were to be as 'quickly and fully as possible destroyed' (Paul De Lagarde, 1887, cited in Kershaw 1998: 151). The underlying source of Hitler's racist anti-Semitism (as alluded to in his 1939 speech) was his paranoid fantasy that foreign Jews (so-called 'international Jewry' and their domination of 'finance capital') had somehow manipulated the First World War into being, and that German Jewry had 'betrayed' Germany into surrender and defeat. Hitler was quite explicit about this. He told the Czechoslovakian Foreign Minister on 21 January 1939: 'The Jews have not brought about the 9 November 1918 [the end of the World War] for nothing. This day will be avenged' (cited in Kershaw 2000a: 128). Like most racists, he was able in his own mind to appropriate the mantle of being the 'victim' as a justification for victimising others. Horrific though as their treatment was after 1939, no genocidal programme immediately followed. But the language and the 'genocidal mentality' behind it were all too apparent (Kershaw 2000a: 152):

> The germ of a possible genocidal outcome, however vaguely conceived, was taking shape, destruction and annihilation, not just emigration, of the Jews was in the air.

Already on 24 November 1939 the SS publication *Das Schwarze Korps* portrayed the Jews as sinking ever more to the status of pauperised parasites and criminals, and had concluded (cited in Kershaw 2000a: 152):

> In the stage of such a development we should therefore be faced with the hard necessity of eradicating the Jewish underworld just as we are accustomed in our ordered state to eradicate criminals: with fire and sword! The result would be the actual and final end of Jewry in Germany, its complete annihilation.

Thus was Jewishness elided with criminality, and not for the first time.

Adolf Eichmann, with Himmler and others, was Hitler's organiser of the genocide. He was also Austrian by birth and similarly unremarkable. Eichmann, like Hitler, was socialised and politicised in an environment in which Jews were routinely denigrated (Cesarani 2004: 32–3):

> Austria had a long tradition of anti-Jewish political movements and a popular culture that was saturated with negative stereotypes of Jews ... They were perceived as foreign by origin, dubious as to their allegiance, and alien in both religion and culture. Jews and non-Jews did not mingle much socially, even if they maintained cordial business and commercial relations ... conversely, German nationalist sentiments were cultivated to extreme levels. In the discourse of German nationalism Jews were implicitly the inferior inassimilable and threatening 'Other', excluded by virtue of not sharing the blood or the soil of the Germanic people.

Nevertheless, for Eichmann, like millions of Austrians and Germans (and others elsewhere), dislike of Jews was quite unremarkable, but that is to miss the point, which is that (Cesarani 2004: 367):

> To the fully indoctrinated Eichmann the Jews had no intrinsic claim to life. Even more radically, according to his doctrinaire view of the Jews as 'the enemy' they *had* to be destroyed. Jews and Aryans were engaged in a war to the death ... to eliminate a racial-biological threat to the Aryan people. This threat was inherent in every Jew, no matter how feeble they seemed. Behind the danger of racial degeneration stood the political and military might of the USA, and the British Empire and the Soviet Union, which were Jewish-controlled ... his final 'memoirs' are shot through with self-justifications and reference

to the power of world Jewry. Eichmann had learned to hate and he taught himself to be a practitioner of genocide. He learned so well that he was never able to understand that he acted wrongly . . . The key to understanding Adolf Eichmann lies not in the man, but in the ideas that possessed him, the society in which they flowed freely, the political system that purveyed them, and the circumstances that made them acceptable.

These and other men in the Nazi elite were motivated by ideas – a particularly virulent and brutal utopian racist political ideology. But what of the killers themselves, what were they motivated by? Browning's (1998) remarkable study based on documents from their trial in the 1960s, *Ordinary Men: Reserve Police Battalion 101 and the Final Solution in Poland*, asked how the men of this unit – grass-roots perpetrators – became 'professional killers'. The context in which they carried out their share of the genocide was that in mid-March 1942 some 75–80 per cent of all victims of the Holocaust were still alive, while 20–25 per cent had perished. A mere 11 months later, in mid-February 1943, the percentages were exactly reversed. As Browning (1998: xv) reminds us, at the core of the genocide was a short, intense wave of mass murder, centred in Poland.

The ranks of the Order Police were filled with older drafted reservists rather than fanatical members of the SS. These 'ordinary' German policemen were sent with their unit to Poland in May 1940 and were assigned to guard the Łódź ghetto in November 1940. Men from Reserve Police Battalion 101 were involved in various phases of the deportation of Jews from Hamburg and other German cities to Poland. On 20 June 1942, the battalion received orders for a 'special action' in Poland – the orders did not specify the true nature of the duties that awaited them (Browning 1998: 53). Most of this work was collecting and moving Jews from smaller settlements to larger ghettos and camps. The local Nazi authorities lost patience with this consolidation process and decided to experiment with renewed killing (there had been a lull in the genocide). As deportation to the extermination camps was not possible at the time, mass execution through firing squad was the available alternative. Reserve Police Battalion 101 was the unit to be assigned for this task. The battalion rounded up 1800 Jews in a village – the men of working age were to be sent to one of the camps, the women, children, and elderly were simply to be shot on the spot. While the reluctant commander explained the battalion's murderous assignment, he offered that any of the older men who did not feel up to the task could step out. Some dozen men stepped forward. While the commander complained of his orders and wept, his men proceeded to carry out the battalion's task (Browning 1998: 57–9). Some men dropped out during the course of the action. Alcohol was made available to those who stayed and continued shooting. Afterwards, 'When the men arrived at the barracks . . . they were depressed, angered, embittered, and shaken. They ate little but drank heavily . . . Major Trapp made the rounds, trying to console and reassure them, and again placing the responsibility on higher authorities' (Browning 1998: 69).

Browning (1998: 72) noted the 'surprise' and lack of time for reflection, the pressure for conformity to the group, even though at this time the men did not know each other very well and were not bonded, the sense that those who had refused felt themselves to be 'too weak' or 'cowardly', and had 'lost face'. Overall, there was little evidence of overt anti-Semitism, only of an 'enemy' and 'us' and 'them'. It would appear that the men of Reserve Police Battalion 101 had not consciously adopted the racist anti-Semitic ideas of the regime, but they had 'at least accepted the assimilation of the Jews into the image of the enemy' (Browning 1998: 73). Although the vast majority of the battalion carried out their duties, even 25 years later the men who did not stop shooting along the way cited sheer physical revulsion against what they were doing. The resentment and bitterness in the battalion over what they had been asked to do was shared by virtually everyone, even those who had shot the entire day (Browning 1998: 76). By September 1942 Police Battalion 101 had participated in the shooting of 4600 Jews and had helped deport 15,000 Jews to the extermination camp at Treblinka. These and other subsequent actions, including their participation in the single largest German killing operation against the Jews – the Lublin massacre of 42,000 Jews – charted their descent into becoming professional mass killers. How do we explain this? In particular, why did most men in Reserve Police Battalion 101 become killers, while only a minority of 10–20 per cent did not (either they refused or stopped shooting – and, amazingly, were given the choice)?

Browning's (1998: 160–89) explanation lies in the context and in the notion and nature of choice. The 'race war' was conducted under cover of the extraordinarily brutal wider 'war of annihilation' against the Russians (Beevor 1998; Burleigh 2000; Kershaw 2000a; Browning 2004; Overy 2004). But the men of Reserve Battalion 101 had not seen battle or encountered a deadly enemy. Brutalisation was not the cause but the effect of these men's behaviour: 'Distancing, not frenzy or brutalization, is one of the keys to the behavior of Reserve Police Battalion 101. War and negative racial stereotyping were two mutually reinforcing factors in this distancing' (Browning 1998: 162). Other scholars noted how the bureaucratic and administrative aspects of the genocide process distanced the 'desk murders' from their victims (Hilberg 1992), but this cannot explain the behaviour of the direct killing by the men of Battalion 101. After ruling out a number of other alternative explanations – careerism, self-interest, self-selection on the basis of personality traits, fear of punishment, obedience to orders, Nazi brainwashing, etc. – Browning (1998: 216) concluded that a complex combination of situational factors, an ideological overlap with Nazism that conferred enemy status on the victims, peer group pressure – conformity to the group – and yes, choice, had turned ordinary men into 'willing executioners'. For, even among them, despite group pressure, the group was multilayered, and some refused to kill and others stopped killing, taking individual responsibility for their actions.

The Nazi genocide

The immediate origins and course of the genocide are by now well known (see, for example, Burleigh 2000; Kershaw 2000a, 2000b; Roseman 2002; Browning 2004). The Nazis' long-planned war was a means of achieving 'living space' (*Lebensraum*) and the racial 'purification' of Europe, and involved both relocating entire populations and killing every Jewish man, woman and child they could capture. Although the comprehensiveness of the onslaught against the Jews differentiated it from Nazi violence towards such categories as communists, Poles, Gypsies or homosexuals, persecution of whom did not routinely extend to killing every family member, the 'Final Solution' was the central element of a broader racial-biological framework (Burleigh 2000: 571). As was seen in Chapter 2, the Nazi 'euthanasia' programme drew on discourses other than anti-Semitism. The genocide of the Jews evolved, not in a simple, linear way, but in an incremental, halting way, as each of the problems the process created for, and by, the Nazis was solved in new more radical ways. This 'radicalization of the regime' (Kershaw 2000a, 2000b) began with the notion of expelling German Jews from Germany, but with the German military victories in Europe more and more 'foreign Jews', especially impoverished 'Eastern' (Polish and Russian) Jews, came into the orbit and reach of the Nazi authorities. For how long would the Nazis tolerate the existence of impoverished Jews, whose dependency was entirely a result of their own racist policies of disqualifying Jews from working, welfare, property and housing (Burleigh 2000: 580)? Initial Nazi policy towards the Jews involved expropriation and extortion of their possessions and labour, concentrating, controlling, exploiting, and of course isolating them. Ghettoisation in particular was a cheaper option than the ever burgeoning concentration camps, and the ultimate logic behind the use of ghettos was to make them diminish and vanish (Burleigh 2000: 588). The turn eastwards to Poland and Russia changed the Nazis' thoughts on a territorial solution of the 'Jewish Question'.

A strategy of forced slave labour in the ghettos vied with the policy of attrition through disease and deliberate starvation. The vision of 'resettlement in the East' vied with a 'war of racial extermination'. After the killings in the East had already began, on the coattails of the invasion of Russia, and on the basis of local initiatives, and even after the first extermination camps were selected, the genocide of the Jews was agreed at a high-ranking Nazi meeting at Wansee on 20 January 1942 where it had become 'official' policy (Roseman 2002). What had begun as 'extermination through labour' was now to be industrial-level extermination through the use of gas chambers, methods inaugurated by the euthanasia programme, methods now to be massively expanded and refined, to accommodate the whole of European Jewry.

The decision-making process in Nazi Jewish policy

The search for a Final Solution through expulsion during 1939–41 and then the conception and implementation of the genocide from October 1941 to March 1942 involved a decision-making process that did not possess those features of inevitability towards genocide sometimes ascribed it. The role of Hitler in the supposedly 'fateful' evolution of a process of radicalisation, culminating in 1941 in the ultimate Final Solution of systematic mass murder, is sometimes discussed as an academic question of Hitler's 'intentions' relative to the 'structural' conditions and circumstances – the nature of German ideology, the nature of the Nazi totalitarian state, the pressures that the onset of war brought, political and economic conditions, etc. – that may in a wider sense have encouraged the move to a genocidal solution to the 'Jewish Question' (see Kershaw 2000b). Browning (2004: 424) correctly states that 'The commitment to some kind of final solution to the Jewish question had been inherent in Nazi ideology from the beginning'. What is less clear are the precise mechanisms and decisions by which the search for a solution to this self-imposed problem, 'one way or another', were arrived at and progressed. As Browning (2004: 425) argues, 'No leading Nazi could prosper who did not appear to take the Jewish question as seriously as Hitler himself'. Kershaw (2000a) characterised this as 'working towards the Fuehrer' – anticipating his wishes and intentions, and thereby coming up with solutions he would approve of without him actually ordering them to take specific actions (which served the dual purpose of Hitler being able to distance himself from murderous acts conducted in his name while progressing the careers of the organisers and perpetrators, of whom he approved). His deliberately vague and inexplicit statements, exhortations and prophecies were taken up with gusto by others, especially Himmler (head of the SS), bringing to Hitler more specific guidelines for his approval.

Browning (2004) offers an admirably clear and accurate account of the Nazi decision-making process in Nazi Jewish policy. The 'true believers' completely identified with Hitler's racist convictions. The eugenicists and planning experts saw an opportunity to realise an agenda of their own that overlapped with that of Hitler. For others, it was a cynical exercise in political careerism, opportunism and accommodation. Finally, much of the wider public seemed to accept the Nazis' giving priority to Jewish policy (Browning 2004: 425). Hitler's role in the decision-making process was immediate, active and continuing. According to Browning (2004: 427), the radicalisation of Jewish policy coincided with periods and peaks of elation and euphoria as a result of military successes, 'as the euphoria of victory emboldened and tempted an elated Hitler to dare ever more drastic policies'. The steady realisation of Hitler's twin obsessions of

Lebensraum and Final Solution through victory gained an unstoppable momentum. As the tide of war turned, this momentum doggedly continued in defeat.

The Rwandan genocide

The massacres started during the night of 6–7 April 1994 in most of the *préfectures* in Rwanda, with the exception of Butare where things remained relatively safe until 20 April when the authorities were replaced by genocidal extremists. All that could stop the killings were UN troops already stationed in Rwanda, but they were too few, too ill equipped, and, crucially, their mandate prevented them from intervening (Dallaire 2003). The killings, organised and endorsed by the Rwandan state, lasted only six weeks, and led to 800,000 deaths – 'the daily killing rate was at least five times that of the Nazi death camps' (Prunier 1997: 261). The main target of the genocide – the Tutsi social and 'ethnic' group – lost approximately 80 per cent of their members living in the country. Furthermore, between 10,000 and 30,000 Hutu opponents of the Rwandan regime were murdered (Prunier 1997: 264–5; African Rights 1995; Human Rights Watch 1999). The Rwandan genocide was a classical genocide, with the systematic massacre of an allegedly racial population, and partly political, with the systematic killing of political opponents.

The legacy of racism: pre-colonial and colonial 'beginnings'

Some writers have argued that Rwanda's distinctive very high density of human occupation and population, resulting from a favourable climate, rich soils and prosperous agriculture, as well as it being relatively free from disease – aspects unusual among African countries (Reader 1998) – has also been a source of conflict, particularly around land disputes. For example, Diamond (2005: 327) has stated that 'population pressure was *one* of the important factors behind the Rwandan genocide'. Others have challenged what they see as this 'myth' of overpopulation (Human Rights Watch 1999). The essential argument, though, is that there were and are too many people making claims on resources that could not and cannot support them. A connected argument is that landholdings are small, and social interactions are constant, intense and value-laden in the context of this high population density. Other seemingly mitigating factors are that the two main supposedly 'ethnic' groups – Tutsi and Hutu – live side by side in compounds on the same hilly slopes and intermarry, so there is no segregation; and the very success of agriculture created an agricultural surplus facilitating early, sophisticated, but very centralised forms of political authority that led to a high degree of social control, which has endured to this day. This last factor is said to have been a major one in the 1994 genocide (Prunier 1997: 4). Agreeing with Diamond (2005), Prunier (1997) in particular has argued that the decision to kill was made by politicians for political and ultimately racist reasons, but at least part of the reason for 1994 was population density – a feeling among ordinary peasants that there were too many people on too little land, and that, with a reduction in numbers, there would be more for survivors. This would seem to confuse a proximate cause – a common-sense perception, and possibly myth, of overpopulation among ordinary people – with ultimate causes of history, racism and power. There is no necessary or direct Malthusian relationship between the fact of high population density and competition or conflict over resources, only particular ways of organising economies, which are political and social choices, influenced by forces both within and outside a country's territory.

Much of what follows relies on Prunier's (1997) definitive and authoritative account, *The Rwandan Crisis: History of a Genocide*. What, according to this account, were the other factors (assuming we accept the overpopulation explanation as one among other factors for now)? The impact of first German and then Belgian colonialism between 1849 and 1959 in the 'making of a cultural mythology' seems key to explaining the legacy of racism within Rwanda. The country is made up of three seemingly distinct groups: the Tutsi, the Hutu and the Twa (the latter being only 1 per cent of the population). These groups are *not* tribes, as some popularly imagine, but neither are they nor were they, strictly speaking, distinct ethnic groups. They shared the same Bantu language, religion, lived together, and often intermarried. Prunier (1997: 5) states: 'But they were neither similar nor equal. Each group had an average dominant somatic type, even if not every one of its individual members automatically conformed to it.' These different social (one might say social class or caste) groups reflected an early division of labour between the Twa who were pygmies living as hunter-gatherers in forested areas or served high-ranking individuals, the majority Hutu who were mostly peasants who cultivated the soil, and the Tutsi who were cattle-herders. Prunier (1997: 5) seems to accept as given that these groups belonged to different 'racial stock', suggesting that the Hutu had 'a standard Bantu physical aspect, rather resembling the populations of neighbouring Uganda or Tanganyika', stocky and small, and the Tutsi were tall and thin, with more angular features. To the extent that this was the case, it is probably better explained by differences in diet linked to different sorts of work between the groups.

The colonial context in the nineteenth century was that the colonisers made much of the assumed physical features of the three groups in heavy pseudo-scientific terms and in ways that defined the Tutsi as racially and socially superior (see Chapter 2 for an account of this general European legacy of race thinking). Nineteenth-century Europeans theorised their origins as variously Ethiopian, descendants from Ancient Egyptians, Semitic, and so on. These ideas conditioned deeply durable European views and attitudes regarding the Rwandan social groups they were dealing with. They governed decisions made by German and even more so later by the Belgian colonial authorities. At the same time they had a massive impact on the subjective feelings of superiority and inferiority of Rwandans themselves.

Colonial impositions of a belief in racial hierarchies, though in themselves important, were not the sole reason for the racialisation of Rwandan society from early on. In pre-colonial Rwandan society class and caste hierarchies were such that the system of kingdom institutions beneath which were the three chiefs (of land holdings, taxation and 'chief of men') were dominated by Tutsi. In addition, a new form of compulsory work was imposed in the late nineteen century and abused by the Belgian colonisers, and was perceived by Hutu as disadvantaging them. The Belgian colonisers had already introduced their own brutal and murderous form of compulsory labour in the neighbouring Belgian Congo by the late nineteenth century under the personal tutelage of the Belgian King Leopold to devastating effect on the population of Congo (Hochschild 1998). It should be noted that the Belgian colonisers were not unique in the methods they used, and colonisation generally was often a brutal and highly exploitative affair, not least among the British (Elkins 2005). Whatever the role of the Belgian colonisers in whipping up racial and ethnic hatreds, their role in reinforcing already existing class and caste resentments was palpable.

Indigenous *beliefs* about the Tutsi's early origin as an invading, conquering group were reinforced by the Europeans because of their preconceived cultural and racial notions. This myth of origin was reinforced in *fact* as Tutsi dominated Rwandan systems of lineage and patronage in respect of land holding, political and class power, through the chieftainship system. By the end of the nineteenth century the vast majority of Hutu were a quasi-rural waged working class in the centralised state system. First the German and then the Belgian colonisers arriving in 1916 reinforced growing Tutsi domination and used this to rule indirectly, strengthening ethnic feelings at the top and at the bottom of the class system. As a result, by the end of the Belgian presence in 1959, the consolidation of the Tutsi domination of the Rwandan chieftainship system was complete. At the other end of the system, the Belgians brutally generalised and extended the hated forced labour system, transferring this burden and obligation from lineages and families to every single male. As Rwandans became individualised, grazing lands privatised, the money economy extended to replace the old clientship system, social cohesion and tradition disrupted, the Belgians continued to sponsor and advantage Tutsi at the expense of Hutu.

Racism and 'Rwandan ideology'

All the above strands came together in an administratively expedient vision of Tutsi racial superiority reinforced by European race ideas, despite in reality many Tutsi not benefiting from the system in any way, and there being little trace of pre-colonial history of systematic violence between Tutsi and Hutu as such. However, the race idea had been implanted by elites and colonisers alike, and it was to become central to 'Rwandan ideology'. As Prunier (1997: 39) explains:

> the Hutu, deprived of all political power and materially exploited by both the whites and the Tutsi, were told by everyone that they were inferiors who deserved their fate and also came to believe it. As a consequence they began to hate *all* Tutsi, even those who were just as poor as they, since *all* Tutsi were members of the 'superior race', something which was to translate itself in the post-Second World War vocabulary as 'feudal exploiters'. . . . The time-bomb had been set and it was now only a question of when it would go off.

This rather deterministic reading – that somehow the Rwandan genocide was inevitable, given the history of the country – neglects the many intervening factors that could have prevented the genocide, and makes the error of reading history backwards from the present (with the benefit of hindsight).

The end of colonialism and the advent of the Hutu republic, 1959–90

Throughout the colonial period traditional structures and collective relations of social subordination increasingly were transformed to serve the ends of individual relations of economic exploitation and the coffee and cash economy. Paradoxically, this had increasingly meant that the average economic power of Hutu and Tutsi had become more similar. However, by 1959 widespread fighting had broken out between Hutu and Tutsi, sparked by the beating of a Hutu sub-chief. Amidst growing chaos and Tutsi flight to neighbouring Burundi and Uganda, the colonial authorities organised communal and then legislative elections. Hutu political parties were quickly created using explicit references to race. The main Hutu party, PARMEHUTU, overwhelmingly won the 1961 elections. Rwanda became a formally independent republic in 1962. In 1963 an attack by Tutsi refugees from Burundi was beaten off, an estimated 10,000 Tutsi were slaughtered in Rwanda, and all surviving Tutsi politicians living in Rwanda were executed. The inauguration of independent Rwanda was from the beginning mired in a proto-genocide. Violence in Rwanda forced many Tutsi into exile between 1959 and 1964, then again during 1972–3, amounting to approximately 600,000–700,000 people (Prunier 1997: 63).

A coup in 1973 established an essentially single-party totalitarian state run by President Habyarimana and his MRND Hutu party (see the glossary at the end of this chapter for all acronyms and Rwandan names). Nevertheless the economy prospered, and although Tutsi were discriminated against they were not persecuted. In the 1980s a major source of revenues collapsed with the fall in the price of coffee. This was connected to various political crises over the apportioning of land, perceived overpopulation and an increasingly marginal food supply. By 1990 the political system was in deep pervasive crisis. It was at this point that the Tutsi refugee movement – the Rwandan Patriotic Front (RPF) – was spurred into preparing for war. The Rwandan Patriotic Army forces (the military wing of the RPF) invaded from Uganda but were driven back. This limited-scale civil war (the regime faked an attack on Kigali) sparked intervention by French and Belgian troops to protect their large expatriate communities in Rwanda. The French, however, eventually backed the 'Francophone' Habyarimana regime against the RPF, which the French somehow (and perversely) associated with 'Anglophone' forces.

Preparation for genocide

As with the National Socialists in Germany, a growing war culture served as an important backdrop (and rationalisation) which drove radicalisation. Using the faked attack on Kigali as a pretext, the regime launched a massive wave of arrests against educated Tutsi, opposition-minded Hutu and foreign African residents. On national radio the Minister of Defence asked the population to 'track down and arrest the infiltrators', which resulted in the massacre of some Tutsi civilians. At the same time, opposition parties began to appear and a new multi-party constitution was declared under internal and international pressure, and also 'to please the French' (Prunier 1997: 127). This apparent move towards democracy in the context of an RPF hit-and-run guerrilla war and further rounds of massacres against Tutsi in 1992 provided the essential grounds for the April–May 1994 genocide. Official sanction to kill came from the Kigali state, but the massacres were carried out by ordinary peasants rather than militias, organised on the spot by their local authorities.

Why were ordinary people prepared to kill? There is no general or single answer to this question. Political mobilisation processes are quite different according to time and place and each depends on the culture, history, geography and traditions of the country. Again, Prunier's (1997: 140–1) answer is found in the manipulation of group identification through shared guilt and material advantage, not tribalism:

> In a world where illiteracy is still the rule, where most of the population has horizons which are limited to their parochial world, where ideologies are bizarre foreign gadgets reserved for intellectuals, solidarity is best understood in terms of close community. In turn, these positive (or negative) group feelings are manipulated by the élite in their struggles for controlling scarce and even shrinking financial, cultural and political resources.

The most important reasons, however, were a cultural tradition of obedience to authority, a belief that the Tutsi were a real threat as evidenced by Tutsi RPF incursions, as well as a spontaneous popular hatred for the RPF, and what people were told by those in authority, material spoils of land

and cattle from the victims, and the routine use of a common-sense dehumanising and brutalising language. The latter came into play as gardening metaphors carrying horrible double meaning. Killing people was made banal: 'chopping up men was "bush clearing" and slaughtering women and children was "pulling out the roots of the bad weeds" ' (Prunier 1997: 142; see Bauman 1989). Most important of all, the official racist state political ideology – 'the democratic majority ideology' – decreed that the state was exclusively identical with the dominant ethnic group.

A more positive note might have been struck with the moves towards democracy and peace during 1992–3. Relenting to pressure from a united opposition, a new multi-party government was established and opened peace negotiations with the RPF on 14 April 1992 at Arusha, in Tanzania. The Arusha peace negotiations dragged on from 1992 to 1993, and the systematic dominance of the Hutu in all spheres of life and their monopolistic grip on the economy worked against the negotiations. Conducted in a climate of increasing tensions, the negotiations fed the rise of the extremist ultra-racist Hutu parties who were becoming increasingly defiant and critical of the way the peace process was being negotiated, while pretending to act in support of President Habyarimana. Instead of softening conflict, the peace negotiations seemed to be hardening the divides, particularly within the government itself. For example, the Coalition for the Defence of the Republic (CDR), critical of the president, thought the French backed them – after all, the French trained the MRND(D) and CDR militiamen (the notorious *Interahamwe* and *Impuzamugambi* who were later to organise and lead the April–May 1994 genocide). As the peace negotiations dragged on, it is likely that CDR extremists first put together the genocide plan in the late months of 1992. According to Prunier (1997: 169) the 'preparation' for the genocide was complete by late 1992 (again, it is important to realise there was nothing inevitable, even at this stage, that genocide would occur):

> By late 1992, the protagonists in the future genocide had all found their places as shadowy counterparts of the official institutions. The FAR had its secret society, the extremists parties their militia, the secret service its killer squads. But all were still doing little more than flex their muscles, killing on a small scale and hoping that their sporadic murders and massacres would somehow lead to a change of policy inflexion and that the opposition parties would be terrorised into submission.

All that was left was to gain the total support of the Hutu peasant masses.

From late 1992 to early 1993 there were frequent demonstrations, clashes and fighting and killing between pro- and anti-Arusha supporters. Violence engulfed the whole North-West and on 8 February RPF forces decided to break the ceasefire and attack, for the first time committing some atrocities, even though the massacres had stopped. The RPF offensive was immediately successful, arriving 30 kilometres north of Kigali, upon which the RPF proclaimed a unilateral ceasefire. Once again French troops intervened against the RPF. The French seemed wilfully ignorant of the racial situation they were in, and the RPF had inadvertently brought together the Hutu opposition and the Rwandan government in an anti-Tutsi alliance. This all provided the needed opportunity the extremist CDR and *Interahamwe* militia wing of the MRND(D) had been waiting for, with the CDR now positioning itself as a 'new opposition'. The new movement immediately proved enormously popular with a public opinion tired of the old regime and wary of the RPF and its opposition 'allies'. As the economy further collapsed, and amidst a high-profile political assassination, the 'new opposition' informally restructured itself to create what it called 'Hutu Power'. Meanwhile, a new CDR-inspired radio station began broadcasting in July 1993 – Radio Télévision Libre des Mille Collines (RTLMC). Its popular street-based racist message was to become a key factor in encouraging and guiding the genocide, in a country totally reliant on radio broadcasting.

Brief lull before the storm

On 4 August 1993 the peace agreement was signed in Arusha amidst general political acrimony and exhaustion, if only to buy time and look good in the eyes of foreign donors (Prunier 1997: 194–5). Part of the agreement was that a UN force (UNAMIR) was to replace French troops to monitor the agreement. As UNAMIR troops arrived in Kigali, the fact that weapons had been distributed to the extremist militia had become public knowledge, which UNAMIR was quite incapable of stopping under its weak mandate. At the same time the assassination of President Melchior Ndadaye, a Hutu, in neighbouring Burundi, helped the Hutu supremacists in Rwanda exploit hatreds and destroyed the last vestiges of moderation. After all, Ndadaye had been a moderate. Virtually every political faction was now obstructing or postponing the transfer of power to the newly constituted Broad Based Transitional Government. The hiatus between the Arusha agreements and the genocide was filled with (to Westerners) seemingly obscure cultural allusions and hate radio. The RTLMC kept reminding its listeners – through its particular style of Hutu popular culture and slang, that soon 'one would have to reach for the top part of the house' (kill tall people), that the Tutsi were evil and that 'we have learnt about it at school' (Prunier 1997: 211).

On 6 April 1994, coming in to land at Kigali airport from talks in Burundi, the presidential jet carrying Habyarimana and the President of Burundi (who was hitching a lift to somewhere else), was shot down by two missiles, killing all on board. It is not known to this day who was responsible or why Habyarimana was killed. Various theories have since been put forward. Prunier (1997: 223–9) argued that the assassination triggered and was linked to the immediately following genocide and the most likely assassins were Hutu Power extremists.

The genocide

As soon as the president's plane crashed, militia roadblocks appeared all over the streets of Kigali. Begun by the Presidential Guard and militiamen, some elements of the Rwandan army tried to stop the killing but bowed to majority feelings, and the army leadership was replaced by a Hutu extremist army commander-in-chief. As the slaughter spread to the interior of the country from 7 April, the UNAMIR General Roméo Dallaire tried to broker a ceasefire between the RPF and the Rwandan army, to no effect. The 2519 Canadian-led UNAMIR troops in Rwanda could not protect themselves or stop the massacres while they had neither a mandate nor equipment enabling them to do anything (Dallaire 2003). French and Belgian troops arrived to rescue their white nationals, stood by while Tutsi were slaughtered before their eyes, and hurriedly left. On 8 April the RPF decided to renew hostilities and moved south the next day.

Who were the actors? Organisers, killers, victims and bystanders

The people who actually carried out the organisation of the murder squads, distributed weapons and gave or relayed instructions at a high level were high-ranking members of the army, the Presidential Guard, the police, the governing political party MRND(D) and CDR militia, as well as businessmen (African Rights 1995; Human Rights Watch 1999). Teachers and administrators helped identify Tutsi individuals for slaughter. These figures – political and military elites within the Rwandan state, and in the economy – as was found in the Nazi genocide, followed a pattern of thinking that verbally attacked the victims while denying (despite all the evidence to the contrary) that any physical violence is taking place or has taken place; fudging their responsibility and remaining vague about the identities of the killers; never claiming any 'credit' for what they were actually doing when talking to supporters, while hinting at the great benefits derived from the unmentionable thing that was being done, and sharing complicity in the 'unspoken secret' of the genocide (Prunier 1997: 241). The 'states of denial' – involving lies and self-deception, thinking errors, knowing and not knowing, rhetorical devices, collusion and cover-up, official and perpetrator accounts as denial, and appeals – seem enduring psychological features in the perpetration of genocide and other atrocities (Cohen 2001).

The efficiency of the killings and the obvious planning were not enough without fairly large moral support and the recruitment of people as actual killers – possibly a majority of the population (Prunier 1997: 242). Beginning in the capital, Kigali, the Presidential Guard targeted opposition figures, calling for help from the *Interahamwe* and *Impuzamugambi* militias. These militias were composed predominantly of young lower-class men (although many women took part in the killings, too). Armed with grenades and machetes, and some with AK-47 assault rifles, they looted as well as killed, often drunk. They were controlled and directed by almost the entire civil service in central government (most of whom were MRND(D) members) and local politicians, at least until the later part of the war the government was simultaneously conducting against the Tutsi-led RPF (see above), when the administration of genocide fell apart. Here, Prunier (1997: 245) argues that a good part of the explanation for the centralised and ordered nature of the killings was a strong state authoritarian tradition going back to the roots of Rwandan culture, and an equally strong acceptance of group identification. Other actors in the genocide, such as the rural police and army, followed a predictable pattern, as seen in the German genocide. Nevertheless, the main agents of the genocide were the ordinary peasants themselves. This was partly out of material interest, but mainly because of a shared belief in Hutu racist ideology and obedience to the political authority of the state.

The vast majority of victims were people belonging to the Tutsi social group, all of whom 'were slated to die' (Prunier 1997: 248). The aim of the killing was the physical elimination of the whole racialised social group, without exception, and therefore their biological ability to reproduce in the future. Because of this the killing was absolutely thorough – the killers did not spare women, old people, children or babies. People knew each other well, there was the Belgian colonial legacy that everyone had to carry a card identifying their ethnicity, Tutsi households were usually surrounded by several Hutu families, all making escape or concealment almost impossible. *Interahamwe* roadblocks and searches could easily overcome the relative anonymity of the towns and the capital, since either having a Tutsi ethnic card or not carrying a card meant certain death. Carrying a Hutu card was not automatically a guarantee of safety if the person was suspected of supporting the political opposition to the government, and even Hutu who 'looked' Tutsi were killed (accused of carrying a false card), as on occasion were Hutu perceived as educated or affluent.

According to Prunier (1997), the main bystanders were the church. Despite the killing of some priests and nuns – mostly liberal Hutu and Tutsi priests – the native Hutu clergy did little to protect their charges. With a few courageous exceptions, neither the Catholic nor the Protestant churches acted with moral impunity. Only the very small Muslim community protected each other.

Killing patterns

The geographical features of Rwanda also limited the possibilities of escape from the genocide. The dense population and virtual absence of wild country meant there were few places to hide. In any case many hiding-places were betrayed by neighbours, while neighbours protected and hid many others. Many grouped in churches in hope of collective protection, but for most the local or larger churches proved to be death traps. Perhaps most poignantly of all, extraordinary moral complexities were introduced among those in mixed marriages and those of mixed parentage, not in the killers' eyes – they killed anyway – but between husbands and wives, parents and children. There were also heroes: in many cases Christians, but also some of no faith, risked their lives to protect victims.

According to African Rights' (1995) meticulous documentation of the genocide, the primary quarry were Tutsi men and boys, followed by women and girls, then children and the elderly. Before being killed, women and girls were often raped and abducted as sexual slaves. As well as churches, hospitals were attacked and patients, medical staff, visitors and refugees were killed. Rape is omnipresent in genocides. The mass rape, abduction, torture and sexual humiliation of women seem a particular feature of genocides, almost as a continuation of the project to disrupt the biological existence of the group targeted (Nikolic-Ristanovic 2000).

Understanding the racial state and genocide

The question of how in three short years (1939–42) 'ordinary' Germans had been transformed from 'bystanders' into mass murderers can be answered in terms of a change in time and place. The changed situation was one of a crusade against Bolshevism and 'war of destruction' in the East, the geographical opportunities this presented as a site for various policies of racial imperialism, and a readiness after years of racist propaganda and exhortation to identify certain social and national categories as 'racial enemies'. Each increment in the ratcheting up of racial policy – disfranchisement, dependence, concentration, expulsion, deportation, ghettoisation – created self-made problems for the Nazis that then had to be solved by further actions. According to Browning (2004: 431), it was in the Soviet Union that 'The decisive leap from disappearance through expulsion to disappearance through systematic mass murder' was first taken. The decision to kill *all* Soviet Jews was then extended to *all* European Jews in the context of the murderous 'war of destruction' against Bolshevism.

Rwanda was unusual among African countries (perhaps with the exception of South Africa) in the extent to which an (imaginary) *ethnic* domination had been concentrated in a highly centralised political system, and in the ways that the long-standing class system had been mirrored in an extremely hierarchical ethnic system. The political and economic domination of the majority Hutu by the minority Tutsi, consolidated and reinforced by the racist preconceptions of the German and then Belgium colonisers, gave way to the 'Democratic Revolution' of 1959 and the ending of colonialism, and Tutsi rule. In effect, one totalitarian regime had been replaced by another. The built-in 'majority principle' of Hutu rule and Tutsi persecution engendered the flight of Tutsi to bordering countries from where they eventually embarked on an intermittent guerrilla war against the Hutu regime. The period of relative stability and peace in the

1970s and early 1980s was associated with relative prosperity. As world commodity prices plunged in the 1980s, Rwanda's economy became vulnerable. By 1990 the political system was in deep crisis, and as external Tutsi forces attempted unsuccessfully to exploit the situation, the Hutu state became more and more racialised and extremist as it began to fracture into different explicitly racist and supremacist political parties.

Crucially, and as in most totalitarian states, political parties in Rwanda were permitted to posses their own militias, and it was the militias that subsequently took part in the genocide (Griffin 1996). This development towards a multi-party system that seemed, on the face of it, a development towards democracy, was anything but. From 1992 to the Arusha 'peace' agreement, sectarian racist parties, opposed to the agreement because of the Hutu–Tutsi power sharing it allowed, turned against the old regime and planned genocide, to consolidate 'Hutu Power' once and for all through mass murder. Once again, the turn to war (by the Tutsi RPF) and assassinations of Hutu leaders triggered genocide, although it is likely that the assassination of the Hutu President was the work of Hutu extremists.

In both cases – National Socialist Germany and Hutu Rwanda – the incremental evolution and wide acceptance of exterminationist racist political ideologies embodied in totalitarian states, and the notion of extending 'living space', eventually found their expression in opportunistic genocides.

Glossary of Rwandan acronyms and names

CDR Coalition for the Defence of the Republic: extremist party which supported President Habyarimana, then went into opposition when it found him too moderate. Later, CDR members were among the main organisers of the genocide.

FAR Forces Armées Rwaindaises, Rwandan armed forces of the Habyarimana and interim governments. Within 10 days of the start of the genocide, the army became heavily involved in the genocide.

Impuzamugambi 'Those with a single purpose': the CDR youth wing and militia.

Interahamwe 'Those who work together'. This was described by the government as the 'MRND youth movement'. It was the first civilian militia, officially created for tasks of 'voluntary work'. Its members started to take part in the killings as early as 1992 and were later the main perpetrators of the genocide. Their name is a reminder of *both* virtuous cooperation *and* of the slogan of the 1959 massacres, 'Let us go and do the work'.

MDR Democratic Movement Republican: the main opposition party, which became the main coalition partner in the July 1994 government.

MRND(D) Revolutionary Movement of National Development (Democratic): President Habyarimana's party, later revamped by the addition of a second 'democratic' D. Many of its leaders were among the main organisers of the genocide.

Further reading

One of the main issues to come out of the discussion in this chapter, but not developed here, is that of international intervention to prevent genocide, or to pursue and punish the perpetrators, as well as supporting survivors. Lebor's (2006) study of the role of United Nations officials and the apparent ineffectiveness of the United Nations in preventing genocide and pursuing perpetrators carefully documents the seemingly intractable political problems. Simms (2001) covers the role of the British in the Bosnian crisis. The best chronicling of the Rwandan genocide and its aftermath is to be found in two comprehensive documents: African Rights (1995) and Human Rights Watch (1999). Burleigh's (2000) highly original historical overview of the Third Reich and its genocidal tendencies and character convincingly argued that the regime was mostly driven by a utopian racist political ideology. The best demonstration of the thesis that 'ordinary men and women' were transformed into mass killers is Browning's (1998) study of men in a police battalion who, among others, carried out the killings, while Browning's (2004) recent excellent, if somewhat 'technical', study of the decision-making processes that led to genocide can be contrasted with Burleigh's more iconoclastic perspective. An interesting criminological perspective on genocide is found in Morrison (2006).

Note

1 The term's original meaning was 'burnt offering that is completely consumed' (Edelheit and Edelheit 1994: 257).

chapter eleven

Understanding race and crime: some concluding thoughts

Race, criminality, normalcy and visibility
Racialised geography of fear
Disproportionality of offending and victimisation
Racist violence
Policing black and minority ethnic communities
Disproportionality in the criminal justice system
Race, class, masculinities and crime
Race and the American Dream
The racial state
The myth of 'race'

Race, criminality, normalcy and visibility

The association of crime with race became popular in the nineteenth century, reflecting the pseudo-scientific and common-sense knowledge claims at the time. The new discipline of criminology emerged from and reinforced these prejudices. Embracing new social scientific methods aimed at measuring the distribution of 'normality' and 'deviance' in populations, criminology proved useful to the emerging forms of governance, based on morally classifying and socially controlling individuals and populations deemed potentially threatening in the move from a traditional-hierarchical to a modern-democratising social order. The threat or actuality of mass enfranchisement across European societies and America raised the spectre of previously excluded groups 'joining' the polity. Groups previously unknown, unseen and unheard were clamouring at the gates of 'mass' society. Proper governance required they be selected, identified, known and classified as to their social and political loyalties and 'racial fitness'.

The traditional 'problem of the poor and unfit', particularly their cost, became heightened amidst perceived threats of liberal, social democratic and socialist agitation against traditionally highly hierarchical societies (see Byrne 2005).

Increasingly, as the nineteenth century wore on, an earlier idea of the existence of 'races' became pervasive. At the height of European colonisation, American slavery and post-Civil War emancipation, and strong nationalist sentiment, the idea of the superiority of the 'white races' insinuated itself into governing discourses. 'Race' became a term denoting the 'fitness' and superiority of the nation and its mental and physical capacities. Based in notions of inherited biology and physicalism, a person's inner character and moral worth were now to be judged by his or her outward appearance. The assigning of individuals and groups to a hierarchy of visible 'races' and classes according to their 'worth' relegated the lower classes, the poor, the 'unfit', the 'degenerate', the criminal, and social deviants in general to inferior and potentially dispensable moral categories. Widespread concerns about the physical, mental and moral 'degeneration of the race' (and nation), were translated into concerns about the fecundity and progeny of the 'unfit' compared to lower fertility rates among the middle and upper classes. If nations were not to be weakened and were (ominously) to be made strong, then racial population policies discouraging or preventing the reproduction of the dubious and the weak were necessary to improve the 'fitness' of the nation. Of course, such policies varied in their application according to national context, and their advocates were more 'successful' in some places than others.

Early criminology – the new 'science' of criminality – helped found and develop these ideas, notably a certain sort of binary thinking that posited and identified physical and mental characteristics and attributes of the 'criminal type' compared to the 'normal' citizen. The criminal was categorised and classified as inferior and a 'race apart', and his or her outward appearance, physiognomy and stigmata were signs (and sins) of criminality. This method was extended to a rag-bag of 'the unfit', not only the morally unfit, but also the behaviourally, physically and mentally unfit, as well as to visible racial groups. Attempts to 'improve the race' through highly popular eugenic population policy and programmes ranging from segregation to forced sterilisation eventually found their apotheosis in the National Socialist sterilisation programme and the mass killing of 'the unfit' in the 'euthanasia' programme – their elimination.

In Britain, eugenic demands, although displaced and insinuated into segregationist penal policy and criminological discourse, remained unrealised with regard to sterilisation. Pioneered in Britain, implemented in the United States and Scandinavia, and mostly abandoned after the Second World War, a weaker sort of eugenics lingered on in various hereditary notions of intelligence, criminality and of course race. This sorry history of the association of race, 'the unfit' and crime – both in the identification of criminality and in racist crimes against those deemed unfit – serves to remind us of some of the thinking and dangers inherited by contemporary criminology.

Racialised geography of fear

Fear of crime tends to vary according to place. One aspect of how fear arises is found in processes of social and economic change that can disrupt and destabilise communities, creating amorphous anxieties. In certain circumstances anxieties are projected onto those who are proximate and fear becomes spatially concentrated, particularly in poor neighbourhoods. If wider social, cultural and economic changes are accompanied by perceived changes in the demographic or ethnic composition of neighbourhoods, in competition over, and access to, neighbourhood and other resources, and in employment, fear is heightened, especially when destabilisation processes cause rises in crime. Such fears are felt at the local level and can be projected onto race and ethnicity in complex ways to create 'racial situations'. We have seen how this works in various places and contexts, and raises the spectre of segregation or integration of groups at the local level. The extent to which interethnic conviviality or hostility can be said to exist in urban metropolitan settings is an empirical question and must be settled according to the specific dynamics and history of different places. Most neighbourhoods that become stressed due to social change are particularly affected by perceptions of 'outsiders', seen as not 'established' residents, as an unwelcome and new presence often blamed for this unwelcome change, particularly through alleging the criminality of their young people. In many cases, however, the outsider group eventually becomes accommodated and themselves become the 'established'. Local 'narratives of decline' seem the preserve of older members of neighbourhoods, while younger people may more readily come to an accommodation with ethnic diversity. Nevertheless, evidence of racialised fear of crime among young people suggests a different story in some places, 'policed' by young people according to their 'colour-coding' of areas as either safe or threatening.

Disproportionality of offending and victimisation

It would appear that among suspects, offenders and victims known to the police and among those who end up in the criminal justice system and prison, black and minority ethnic groups have a disproportionate presence compared to their numbers in the population. This would appear to be the case in all Western societies having significant ethnic minorities, although the data are less clear regarding European societies. In this sense we can speak of a 'convergence' of the race and crime problem across a wide variety of countries (Newburn and Sparks 2004). Generally speaking, minority ethnic groups are disproportionately victimised, in part because of where they tend to live – in poorer urban areas – and partly because they tend to be a younger population. They may also suffer from less police concern and protection. The obverse is that *some* ethnic groups appear to be disproportionately involved in *some* kinds of offending. Their disproportionate victimisation and offending may be linked for the same reasons – being younger, poorer and living in high-crime areas where there are more victimisation and offending opportunities. In larger cities the proximity of suitable (young and/or affluent) victims may be a factor, as is the formation of sometimes ethnically based local criminal networks and markets. Most offending and victimisation, however, is intra-ethnic, and in Britain, and especially in the United States, there is a particular concern regarding the homicide rate within some black and minority ethnic groups.

The real offending and victimisation rates of black and minority compared to white groups cannot be known. To infer these from known offenders and victims is to ignore the possibility that some groups may receive disproportionate attention from the police. For example, the American 'war on drugs' disproportionately affected the arrest and prosecution of inner-city African-Americans. In both Britain and the USA some minority groups are disproportionately harassed, stopped and searched by the police. Self-report offending and victimisation surveys can show very different patterns from those found among known offenders and victims in the criminal justice system in that many ethnic differences in offending and victimisation reduce or disappear. These differences similarly reduce or disappear when age, area and social class are taken into account. This is not to discount that some differences remain for some sorts of offending, for example street robbery, and some sorts of victimisation, notably racist violence, but this may still in part be accounted for by police activity. The reporting, recording and actions taken (or not taken) towards offences and victimisation are subject to factors and biases that may mean they are not a true picture of reality. Those who end up in prison or under the supervision of the criminal justice system do so after a protracted criminal justice process that may involve at least some racial and/or class discrimination, so it is unwise to draw too many inferences from the ethnic or class profile of the prison population. Finally, black and minority ethnic and working-class groups face greater risks of factors likely to lead to offending behaviour and being victimised. These groups also tend to be more 'available' in situations and places where offending and victimisation are more likely to occur, and to be detected by the police.

Racist violence

Changes in the ways in which racist violence is policed in Britain have arguably reduced the dissatisfaction and disaffection victims and their families have felt towards the police in this respect. Like other sorts of victimisation, racist violence is patterned by age, area, gender, social class, and recording and reporting biases. Unlike most other sorts of victimisation, racist violence is disproportionately felt and experienced by black and minority ethnic groups. This recognition has led to unprecedented recent changes in English law that now define racist violence and related offences as offences against a *group*, and, as such, aggravated – considered a worse criminal offence than some other sorts of violent offence.

Perpetrators tend to be involved in other sorts of criminality and violence and are often motivated, encouraged and feel condoned by local racism that, although not violent itself, nevertheless is complicit in tolerating feelings and attitudes that may lead to violence. Racist violence is also often a group phenomenon in the sense that it is expressed or discouraged by changing dynamics of race relations and power between minority and majority groups.

Policing black and minority ethnic communities

If policing is defined first and foremost as a public order function, then historically the mere presence of visible and invisible minority groups, indigenous people, foreigners and immigrants in Western societies has often presented a challenge to 'authority' in the eyes of the police. Contact involving conflict between the police and some minority groups has seemed ubiquitous and striking, especially in the USA, Australia and Britain, although this is also likely to have been the case in Europe. That there is police racism there is little doubt. But police racism is not static (nor is it universal) and its intensity and targets change over time and vary both within and between countries. Neither is it wholly one-sided in the sense that in contact and conflict with the police, alleged suspects and victims enter into a social relationship that has interaction effects. This relationship over time may reflect mutual hostility based on conclusions drawn from previous experience, however false or stereotyped they may be. Crucially, though, the relationship is of very unequal power, and that is why some countries have sought to influence the ways that police officers go about their business. Whether this has been successful – in terms of the police reforming themselves or being reformed – it remains the case that officers have a great deal of discretion and power in the ways they enforce the law.

One of the fundamental problems of policing is that the police reserve a disproportionate attention for what they believe are 'suspect populations' – young men in general, and black and minority ethnic, working-class and poor young men in particular. Whether it is because they believe these groups are more likely to be involved in law-breaking or whether it is because of their racism or moral judgement about the worth of individuals of lower status than themselves, such stereotypes become a self-fulfilling prophecy. We cannot, of course, assume that all, or even most, encounters involving police officers and individuals from these groups will involve unwarranted suspicion or generalisations on the part of police officers. Police officers are just as likely to pursue a suspect without fear or favour when they have genuine grounds to do so. The problem of race and policing is that the police often do not have intelligence or evidence that an individual has broken the law so they trawl for suspects and can select individuals because of their supposed membership of a group deemed suspicious, and individuals who are available to them in public places. Once having stopped someone, they may treat them differently or more harshly at later stages in the police process on grounds of racial and social ascriptions. The question of whether police racism continues at previous levels or has subsided is difficult to answer.

It is the case that particular individuals or groups become disaffected, detached and alienated from authority for reasons that the police can do little about, and at certain times these same individuals may pose a threat to public order, but it must also be asked what contribution the police themselves make to this disaffection in the ways they have routinely policed relatively powerless groups and communities.

Disproportionality in the criminal justice system

Overrepresentation of black and some minority ethnic groups in the criminal justice process and prisons seems a feature of most Western jurisdictions. The explanation for this is usually given in terms of racial bias in the criminal justice system versus heightened rates of offending among some minority groups. Less seldom given is the explanation that there is *both* some racial bias *and* some heightened offending among some minority groups of the sort that is pursued and prosecuted.

Evidence of racial bias at different stages of the criminal justice process, from pre-trial processes to sentencing, is available from a number of countries, most reliably Britain and the USA. We cannot easily know the real extent of bias because studies do not have close-up access to the detailed basis of criminal justice officials' decision-making. Also, racial discrimination in sentencing and other criminal justice decisions seems to vary by area, so that some courts and jurisdictions are more racially biased than others, creating justice by geography. The evidence of bias is less equivocal at some stages of the criminal justice process than others. For example, in the USA there is clear evidence that the pre-trial stage greatly disadvantages poorer African-Americans, who are denied proper access to defence lawyers. The harsher treatment of African-American men is most evident in their hugely disproportionate presence on death row, usually because their victim was white. Their similarly disproportionate presence in US prisons has led writers to conclude that there is a 'symbiosis between the prison and the ghetto', and that the American system of justice systematically 'penalises poverty'.

For these and other reasons, it is necessary to place racialised criminal justice processes in their social and economic context, and note the roles that the criminal justice system plays in a complex and continuum of social control institutions and practices. These include families, neighbourhoods, schools, care systems and the regulation of the poor and jobless, especially poor children and the young poor and jobless (Webster 2006).

Race, class, masculinities and crime

The strongest correlations with crime found within criminology are age and gender. Particular sorts of expressive masculinity, it is argued, are most likely to be associated with crime and violence, and other sorts of anti-social behaviour such as school disaffection and exclusion. A linked version of this argument, found particularly in American writing but also some British accounts, is the claim of a loss of informal controls on delinquency and criminality engendered by a breakdown in family structure among some groups, especially African-Americans and African-Caribbeans. Although said to have arisen through a legacy of slavery and from the post-slavery experience, the consequence has been an intergenerational emasculation and prevention of family formation, particularly prevalent in these groups. A similar argument might be made with regard to indigenous peoples in Australia, although for somewhat different reasons.

The masculinity argument can be extended to apply to school disaffection, the influence of street- and ethnically based peer groups, and notions of a crisis in patriarchal authority and belief systems that particularly affects boys. An important criticism of these kinds of argument is that they essentialise 'masculinity' as an almost fixed, immutable psychological state. Another is that these arguments are more to do with a moral discourse about the supposed breakdown of family life, especially among some minority groups, than that they provide evidence about any direct effects of family structure on behaviour. There is plentiful evidence that being brought up in a lone-parent family does not in itself predict later anti-social or criminal behaviour, and in any case, especially in America, studies may be confusing being brought up by a lone parent with being brought up poor in high-crime areas, which often go together.

Race and the American Dream

There is a long-standing claim that a crime-ridden African-American 'underclass' has existed in inner-city or 'ghetto' areas as a distinct social stratum that had become isolated from the rest of society. In its mores and behaviour this group is said to occupy a different moral universe from 'respectable', 'law-abiding', 'mainstream' America. Others argue that this vision is a racialised misnomer and that the large majority of the African-American poor are the 'respectable' working poor, trapped in the burgeoning American low-wage economy, but otherwise sharing the same aspirations, consumerist and cultural values of individualism, and conformity encapsulated in the American Dream.

The subtext to these arguments is the nature and extent of racial segregation found in urban metropolitan areas; whether segregation is decreasing or increasing; the effects on race relations; and whether white fear and resentment of the black ghetto drive exaggerated fear of black crime while continuing to trap ghetto members in poverty; and, in particular, whether 'racial residential segregation is the principal structural feature of American society responsible for the perpetuation of urban poverty and represents a primary cause of racial inequality in the US' (Massey and Denton 1993: 2).

The evidence seems to suggest that shared values, friendships and work relations across complex race and class boundaries make the existence of a separate 'black underclass' unlikely. Although housing a significant but diminishing criminal minority, inner-city urban areas in large US cities are most noticeable as a major source of America's exploitative low-wage service economy. They are also, however, a major recent historical source of America's prison population. What *is* undeniable, though, are striking and continuing levels of residential segregation based on race and class and the ways segregation traps people in poverty and among risks not faced by other Americans. In this sense, whichever argument is followed about the existence of a separate African-American underclass, deindustrialisation and urban economic restructuring in the 1970s and 1980s were a major contributing factor to the worsening conditions of inner-city life, giving rise to relative poverty levels in the richest society in the world analogous to urban Third World relative poverty rates (Burton 2005; Davis 2006).

The racial state

Mostly ignored by criminology, mass killing has been and continues to be prevalent in the recent and current period, from Bosnia and Kosovo to Darfur. The Nazi and Rwandan genocides were the mass murder of groups assumed to be biological 'races'. These crimes were carried out by totalitarian but internationally legally recognised and constituted states. Examination of the perpetrators reveals them to have been 'ordinary' members of those societies transformed into mass murders either directly themselves or as 'desk murderers' – organisers and administrators of the genocides.

Although having their own causes and conditions, both genocides were incremental and opportunistic in their evolution, and were motivated by pervasive and popular beliefs turned into a particularly virulent aggressive racism. Each was conducted under the guise of an actual or pending racial 'war of destruction' in which all members of the target groups, without exception, were designated 'racial enemies'. In both cases – National Socialist Germany and Hutu Rwanda – the incremental evolution and wide acceptance of exterminationist racist political ideologies embodied in totalitarian states, and the notion of extending 'living space', eventually found their expression in opportunistic genocides.

The myth of 'race'

It is now easier to understand how 'race' – whether visible or not – becomes insinuated into 'crime' and 'criminality', whether to justify or rationalise crimes against others, to criminalise others, or treat them differently and more suspiciously, or to segregate or even eliminate. Whether the idea of 'race', and by extension 'ethnicity', will continue to influence such practices, where and when these occur in the twenty-first century, and their enlargement or reduction, will depend on material and political events and choices. If these practices and false reasoning are foreseen and understood, then the myth of race and some of its consequences – both intended and unintended – might be better identified and dealt with, so that the myth of race loses its power to influence.

References

African Rights (1995) *Rwanda, Death, Despair and Defiance*. London: African Rights.

Albrecht, H.-J. (1997a) Minorities, crime and criminal justice in the Federal Republic of Germany. In I.H. Marshall (ed.) *Minorities, Migrants, and Crime: Diversity and Similarity Across Europe and the United States*. Thousand Oaks, CA: Sage.

Albrecht, H.-J. (1997b) Ethnic minorities, crime, and criminal justice in Germany. In M. Tonry (ed.) *Ethnicity, Crime, and Immigration: Comparative and Cross-National Perspectives*. Chicago: University of Chicago Press.

Alexander, C. (1996) *The Art of Being Black*. Oxford: Clarendon Press.

Alexander, C. (2000) *The Asian Gang: Ethnicity, Identity, Masculinity*. Oxford: Berg.

Aly, G. (1999) *'Final Solution': Nazi Population Policy and the Murder of the European Jews*. London: Arnold.

Anderson, E. (1990) *Streetwise: Race, Class and Change in an Urban Community*. Chicago: University of Chicago Press.

Anderson, E. (1999) *Code of the Street: Decency, Violence, and Moral Life of the Inner City*. New York: W. W. Norton.

Anderson, E. (2002) The ideologically driven critique. *American Journal of Sociology*, 107: 1533–50.

Anderson, E. (2003) *A Place on the Corner*, 2nd edition. Chicago: University of Chicago Press. First published in 1976.

Anderson, S., Kinsey, R., Loader, I. and Smith, C. (1994) *Cautionary Tales: Young People, Crime and Policing in Edinburgh*. Aldershot: Avebury.

Appelbaum, E., Bernhardt, A. and Murnane, R.J. (eds) (2003) *Low Wage America: How Employers Are Reshaping Opportunity in the Workplace*. New York: Russell Sage Foundation.

Archer, L. (2003) *Race, Masculinity and Schooling: Muslim Boys and Education*. Maidenhead: Open University Press.

Arendt, H. (1994) *Eichman in Jerusalem: A Report on the Banality of Evil*. London: Penguin. First published in 1964.

Association of Chief Police Officers (1985) *Guiding Principles Concerning Racial Attacks*. London: ACPO.

Aye Maung, N. (1995) *Young People, Victimisation and the Police: British Crime Survey Findings on the Experiences and Attitudes of 12–15 Year Olds*, Research Study 140. London: Home Office.

Back, L. (1996) *New Ethnicities and Urban Culture: Racisms and Multiculture in Young Lives*. London: UCL Press.

Back, L. and Solomos, J. (eds) (2000) *Theories of Race and Racism: A Reader*. London: Routledge.

Banton, M. (1997) *Ethnic and Racial Consciousness*, 2nd edition. London: Longman.

Barkan, E. (1992) *The Retreat of Scientific Racism*. Cambridge: Cambridge University Press.

Barkan, S.E. (2006) *Criminology: A Sociological Understanding*, 3rd edition. Upper Saddle River, NJ: Pearson Prentice Hall.

Barker, M. (1981) *The New Racism*. London: Junction Books.

Bauman, Z. (1989) *Modernity and the Holocaust*. Cambridge: Polity.

Becker, P. and Wetzell, R.F. (eds) (2006) *Criminals and Their Scientists: The History of Criminology in International Perspective*. Cambridge: Cambridge University Press.

Bedau, H.A. (2004) *Killing as Punishment: Reflections on The Death Penalty in America*. Boston: Northeastern University Press.

Bedau, H.A. (ed.) (1997) *The Death Penalty in America: Current Controversies*. Oxford: Oxford University Press.

Beevor, A. (1998) *Stalingrad*. London: Penquin.

Bentley, T. and Gurumurthy, R. (1999) *Destination Unknown: Engaging with the problems of marginalized youth*. London: Demos.

Benyon, J. and Solomos, J. (eds) (1987) *The Roots of Urban Unrest*. Oxford: Pergamon.

Black, E. (2003) *War against the Weak: Eugenics and America's Campaign to Create a Master Race*. New York: Thunder's Mouth Press.

Blakely, E.J. and Snyder, M. (1997) *Fortress America: Gated Communities in the United States*. Washington, DC: Brookings Institution Press.

Blee, K.M. (2005) Racial violence in the United States. *Ethnic and Racial Studies*, 28: 599–619.

Bottomley, K. and Pease, K. (1986) *Crime and Punishment: Interpreting the Data*. Milton Keynes: Open University Press.

Bourgois, P. (1995) *In Search of Respect: Selling Crack in El Barrio*. Cambridge: Cambridge University Press.

Bourne, J., Bridges, L. and Searle, C. (1994) *Outcast England: How Schools Exclude Black Children*. London: Institute of Race Relations.

Bowles, S., Gintis, H. and Osborne Groves, M. (eds) (2005) *Unequal Chances: Family Background and Economic Success*. Oxford: Princeton University Press.

Bowles, S., Durlauf, S.N. and Hoff, K. (eds) (2006) *Poverty Traps*. Oxford: Princeton University Press.

Bowling, B. (1990) Conceptual and methodological problems in measuring 'Race' differences in delinquency: A reply to Marianne Junger. *British Journal of Criminology*, 30: 483–92.

Bowling, B. (1999) *Violent Racism: Victimization, Policing and Social Context.* Oxford: Clarendon Press.

Bowling, B. and Phillips, C. (2002) *Racism, Crime and Justice.* Harlow: Longman.

Box, S. (1987) *Recession, Crime and Punishment.* London: Macmillan.

Bradford Congress (1996) *The Bradford Commission Report: The Report of an Inquiry into the Wider Implications of Public Disorders in Bradford which Occurred on 9, 10 and 11 June 1995.* London: Stationery Office.

Britton, L., Chatrik, B., Coles, B., Craig, G., Hylton, C. and Mumtaz, S. (2002) *Missing Connexions: The Career Dynamics and Welfare Needs of Black and Minority Ethnic Young People at the Margins.* Bristol: Policy Press.

Brogden, M., Jefferson, T. and Walklate, S. (1988) *Introducing Policework.* London: Allen & Unwin.

Browning, C. (1998) *Ordinary Men: Reserve Police Battalion 101 and the Final Solution in Poland.* New York: HarperCollins.

Browning, C. (2004) *The Origins of the Final Solution: The Evolution of Nazi Jewish Policy 1939–1942.* London: Heinemann.

Bruinius, H. (2006) *Better for All the World: The Secret History of Forced Sterilization and America's Quest for Racial Purity.* New York: Alfred A. Knopf.

Bureau of Justice Statistics (2005) *National Crime Victimization Survey, 1992–2004.* Washington, DC: US Department of Justice

Burgess, S., Wilson, D. and Lupton, R. (2005) Parallel lives? Ethnic segregation in schools and neighbourhoods. *Urban Studies,* 42: 1027–56.

Burleigh, M. (1994) *Death and Deliverance: 'Euthanasia' in Germany 1900–1945.* Cambridge: Cambridge University Press.

Burleigh, M. (2000) *The Third Reich: A New History.* London: Macmillan.

Burnett, J. (2004) Community, cohesion and the state. *Race and Class,* 45(3): 1–18.

Burney, E. (1990) *Putting Street Crime in its Place.* London: Goldsmiths' College.

Burtless, G. (1999) Growing American inequality: sources and remedies. *Brookings Review,* 17(1): 31–5.

Burton, A. (2005) *African Underclass: Urbanisation, Crime & Colonial Order in Dar es Salaam.* Athens: Ohio University Press.

Byrne, D. (2005) *Social Exclusion,* 2nd edition. Maidenhead: Open University Press.

Cantle, T. (2002) *Community Cohesion: A Report of the Independent Review Team.* London: Home Office.

CARF/Southall Rights (1981) *Southall – The Birth of a Black Community.* London: Institute of Race Relations.

Cashmore, E. (1996) *Dictionary of Race and Ethnic Relations,* 4th edition. London: Routledge.

Cashmore, E. and McLaughlin, E. (1991) *Out of Order? Policing Black People.* London: Routledge.

Cashmore, E.E. and Troyna, B. (eds) (1982) *Black Youth in Crisis.* London: Allen & Unwin.

Castells, M. (2000) *End of Millennium,* 2nd edition. Oxford: Blackwell Publishing.

Cavalli-Sforza, L. (2001) *Genes, Peoples and Languages.* London: Penguin.

Cesarani, D. (2004) *Eichmann: His Life and Crimes.* London: Heinemann.

Chahal, K. and Julienne, L. (1999) *'We Can't All Be White!': Racist Victimisation in the UK.* York: York Publishing Services.

Chan, J. (1997) *Changing Police Culture: Policing in a Multicultural Society.* Cambridge: Cambridge University Press.

Choongh, S. (1997) *Policing as Social Discipline*. Oxford: Oxford University Press.

Clancy, A., Hough, M., Aust, R. and Kershaw, C. (2001) *Crime, Policing and Justice: The Experience of Ethnic Minorities. Findings from the 2000 British Crime Survey*, Home Office Research Study 223. London: Home Office.

Clark, I. and Moody, S. (2002) *Racist Crime and Victimisation in Scotland*, Crime and Criminal Justice Research Findings No. 58. Edinburgh: Scottish Executive Central Research Unit.

Clarke, A. (2001) *Burnley Task Force*. Burnley: Burnley Borough Council.

Coard, B. (1971) *How the West Indian Child is Made Educationally Subnormal in the British School System*. London: New Beacon Books.

Cohen, P. (1988) The perversions of inheritance. In P. Cohen and H.S. Bains (eds) *Multi-racist Britain*. Macmillan: Basingstoke.

Cohen, S. (2001) *States of Denial: Knowing about Atrocities and Suffering*. Cambridge: Polity Press.

Coleman, C. and Moynihan, J. (1996) *Understanding Crime Data*. Buckingham: Open University Press.

Coles, B., Rugg, J. and England, J. (1998) *Young People on Estates*. Coventry: Chartered Institute of Housing.

Colley, L. (1992) *Britons: Forging the Nation 1707–1837*. London: Yale University Press.

Collier, R. (ed.) (1998) *Masculinities, Crime and Criminology*. London: Sage.

Collins, J., Noble, G., Poynting, S. and Tabar, P. (2000) *Kebabs, Kids, Cops and Crime: Youth, Ethnicity and Crime*. Annandale, NSW: Pluto Press.

Collins, M. (2004) *The Likes of Us: A Biography of the White Working Class*. London: Granta Books.

Collison, M. (1996) In search of the high life. *British Journal of Criminology*, 36: 428–43.

Commission for Racial Equality (2005) *The Police Service in England and Wales*. London: CRE.

Connell, R.W. (2005) *Masculinities*, 2nd edition. Cambridge: Polity Press.

Cook, D. (2006) *Criminal and Social Justice*. London: Sage.

Corrigan, P. and Sayer, D. (1985) *The Great Arch: English State Formation as Cultural Revolution*. Oxford: Blackwell.

Crawford, A., Jones, T., Woodhouse, T. and Young, J. (1990) *The Second Islington Crime Survey*. London: Middlesex Polytechnic Centre for Criminology.

Crutfield, R., Bridges, G.S. and Pitchford, S. (1994) Analytical and aggregation biases in analyses of imprisonment: Reconciling discrepancies in studies of racial disparity. *Journal of Research in Crime and Delinquency*, 31(2): 166–92.

Cunneen, C. (2001) *Conflict, Politics and Crime: Aboriginal Communities and the Police*. Crows Nest, NSW: Allen & Unwin.

Currie, E. (1996) *Crime and Punishment in America*. New York: Metropolitan Books.

Dallaire, R. (2003) *Shake Hands with the Devil: The Failure of Humanity in Rwanda*. London: Arrow Books.

Davis, M. (2002) *Dead Cities*. New York: New Press.

Davis, M. (2006) *Planet of Slums*. London: Verso.

Dench, G., Gavron, K. and Young, M. (2006) *The New East End: Kinship, Race and Conflict*. London: Profile Books.

Denham, J. (2002) *Building Cohesive Communities: A Report of the Ministerial Group on Public Order and Community Cohesion*. London: Home Office.

Devlin, B., Fienberg, S.E., Resnick, D.P. and Roeder, K. (1997) *Intelligence, Genes, and Success: Scientists Respond to 'The Bell Curve'*. New York: Springer-Verlag.

Diamond, J. (1991) *The Rise and Fall of the Third Chimpanzee: How Our Animal Heritage Affects the Way We Live*. London: Vintage.

Diamond, J. (1999) *Guns, Germs and Steel*. London: Vintage.

Diamond, J. (2005) *Collapse: How Societies Choose to Fail or Survive*. London: Penguin.

Docking, M. and Tuffin, R. (2005) *Racist Incidents: Progress since the Lawrence Inquiry*, Home Office Online Report No. 42. London: Home Office.

Dodd, V. and Travis, A. (2005) Muslims face increased stop and search. *The Guardian*, 2 March.

Dorling, D. and Thomas, B. (2004) *People and Places: A 2001 Census Atlas of the UK*. Bristol: Policy Press.

Drake, St. Clair and Cayton, H.R. (1993) *Black Metropolis*. Chicago: University of Chicago Press. First published in 1945.

Du Bois, W.E.B. (1996) *The Philadelphia Negro: A Social Study*, with an introduction by Elijah Anderson. Philadelphia: University of Pennsylvania Press. First published in 1899.

Dugdale, R. (1910) *The Jukes: A Study in Crime, Pauperism, Disease and Heredity*. New York: Putnam.

Duneier, M. (1992) *Slim's Table: Race, Respectability and Masculinity*. Chicago: University of Chicago Press.

Duneier, M. (1999) *Sidewalk*. New York: Farrar, Straus and Giroux.

Dyer, R. (1997) *White: Essays on Race and Culture*. London: Routledge.

Economist (2006) The forgotten underclass. *The Economist*, 26 October.

Edelheit, A.J. and Edelheit, H. (1994) *History of the Holocaust: A Handbook and Dictionary*. Oxford: Westview Press.

Eley, G. (ed.) (2000) *The 'Goldhagen Effect': History, Memory, Nazism – Facing the German Past*. Ann Arbor: University of Michigan Press.

Elias, N. and Scotson, J.L. (1994) *The Established and the Outsiders*. London: Sage.

Elkins, C. (2005) *Britain's Gulag: The Brutal End of Empire in Kenya*. London: Jonathan Cape.

Evans, R.J. (2003) *The Coming of The Third Reich*. London: Penguin Books.

Evans, R.J. (2005) *The Third Reich in Power 1933–1939*. London: Penguin Books.

Farley, R., Steeh, C., Krysan, M., Jackson, T. and Reeves, K. (1994) Stereotypes and segregation: Neighbourhoods in the Detroit area. *American Journal of Sociology*, 100(3): 750–80.

Farrington, D.P. (2002) Developmental criminology and risk focussed prevention. In M. Maguire, R. Morgan and R. Reiner (eds) *The Oxford Handbook of Criminology*, 3rd edition. Oxford: Oxford University Press.

Fedo, M. (2000) *The Lynchings in Duluth*. St Paul: Minnesota Historical Society Press.

Feeley, M. and Simon, J. (1994) Actuarial justice: The emerging new criminal law. In D. Nelken (ed.) *The Futures of Criminology*. London: Sage.

Feilzer, M. and Hood, R. (2004) *Difference or Discrimination? Minority Ethnic People in the Youth Justice System*. London: Youth Justice Board.

Fein, H. (1979) *Accounting for Genocide: National Response and Jewish Victimization during the Holocaust*. New York: Free Press.

Fergusson, R. (2002) Rethinking youth transitions: Policy transfer and new exclusions in New Labour's New Deal. *Policy Studies*, 23(3/4): 173–90.

Fevre, R. (1984) *The Woollen Textile Industry in Bradford*. London: Routledge.

Field, J. (2003) *Social Capital*. London: Routledge.

Finkelstein, N.G. and Birn, R.B. (1998) *A Nation on Trial: The Goldhagen Thesis and Historical Truth*. New York: Henry Holt & Co.

Fischer, C.S., Hout, M., Janowski, M.S., Lucas, S.R., Swidler, A. and Voss, K. (1996) *Inequality by Design: Cracking the Bell Curve Myth*. Princeton, NJ: Princeton University Press.

FitzGerald, M. (1999) *Final Report into Stop and Search*. London: Metropolitan Police.

FitzGerald, M. (2001) Ethnic minorities and community safety. In R. Matthews and J. Pitts (eds) *Crime, Disorder and Community Safety*. New York: Routledge.

FitzGerald, M. and Hale, C. (1996) *Ethnic Minorities: Victimisation and Racial Harassment: Findings from the 1988 and 1992 British Crime Surveys*, Home Office Research Study 154. London: Home Office.

FitzGerald, M., Hough, M., Joseph, I. and Qureshi, T. (2002a) *Policing for London*. Cullompton: Willan.

FitzGerald, M., Stockdale, J. and Hale, C. (2002b) *Young People and Street Crime*. London: Youth Justice Board.

Flood Page, C., Campbell, S., Harrington, V. and Miller, J. (2000) *Youth Crime: Findings from the 1998/99 Youth Lifestyle Survey*, Home Office Research Study 209. London: Home Office.

Friedlander, H. (1995) *The Origins of Nazi Genocide: From Euthanasia to the Final Solution*. Chapel Hill: University of North Caroline Press.

Furlong, A. (2005) Maintaining middle class advantage, *British Journal of Sociology of Education*, 26(5): 683–5.

Furlong, A. and Cartmel, F. (1997) *Young People and Social Change: Individualization and Risk in Late Modernity*. Buckingham: Open University Press.

Gardner, H. (1993) *Frames of Mind: The Theory of Multiple Intelligences*. London: Fontana Press.

Garland, D. (1985) *Punishment and Welfare: A History of Penal Strategies*. Aldershot: Gower.

Garland, D. (2001) *Culture and Control: Crime and Social Order in Contemporary Society*. Oxford: Oxford University Press.

Garland, D. (2002) Of crimes and criminals: The development of criminology in Britain. In M. Maguire, R. Morgan and R. Reiner (eds) *The Oxford Handbook of Criminology*, 3rd edition. Oxford: Oxford University Press.

Gellately, R. (2001) *Backing Hitler: Consent and Coercion in Nazi Germany*. Oxford: Oxford University Press.

Gibson, M. (2002) *Born to Crime: Cesare Lombroso and the Origins of Biological Criminology*. Westport, CT: Praeger.

Gilbert, D. and Kahl, J.A. (2003) *The American Class Structure in an Age of Growing Inequality*, 6th edition. Belmont, CA: Wadsworth.

Gilbert, M. (1986) *The Holocaust: The Jewish Tragedy*. London: HarperCollins.

Gillborn, D. and Youdell, D. (2000) *Rationing Education*. Buckingham: Open University Press.

Gilroy, P. (1987) *There Ain't No Black in the Union Jack: The Cultural Politics of Race and Nation*. London: Hutchinson.

Gilroy, P. (2000) *Between Camps: Nations, Cultures and the Allure of Race*. London: Allen Lane.

Ginzburg, R. (1988) *100 years of Lynching*. Baltimore, MD: Black Classic Press.

Glass, R. (1960) *Newcomers: The West Indians in London*. London: George Allen & Unwin.

Goddard, H. (1927) *The Kallikak Family: A Study in the Heredity of Feeblemindedness*. London: Macmillan.

Goldberg, D.T. (1993) *Racist Culture: Philosophy and the Politics of Meaning*. Oxford: Blackwell.

Goldhagen, D.J. (1996) *Hitler's Willing Executioners: Ordinary Germans and the Holocaust*. London: Little, Brown.

Goodey, J. (1998) Examining the 'white racist/black victim' stereotype. *International Review of Victimology*, 5: 235–56.

Goodey, J. (2001) The criminalization of British Asian youth, *Journal of Youth Studies*, 4(4): 429–50.

Goodey, J. (2005) *Victims and Victimology: Research, Policy and Practice*. Harlow: Longman.

Gordon, P. (1983) *White Law*. London: Pluto Press.

Gould, S.J. (1996) *The Mismeasure of Man*, revised edition. Harmondsworth: Penguin Books.

Gourevitch, P. (1998) *We Wish to Inform You That Tomorrow We Will Be Killed With Our Families*. Basingstoke: Picador.

Graef, R. (1989) *Talking Blues: The Police in Their Own Words*. London: Collins Harvill.

Graham, J. and Bowling, B. (1995) *Crime and Young People*. London: Home Office.

Greater London Council (1984) *Racial Harassment in London: Report of a Panel of Inquiry Set up by the GLC Police Committee*. London: GLC.

Greater London Council (1985) *Report by Head of Housing Services* (TH192). London: GLC.

Green, P. and Ward, T. (2004) *State Crime; Governments, Violence and Corruption*. London: Pluto.

Griffin, R. (1996) *The Nature of Fascism*. London: Routledge.

Hall, S., Critcher, C., Jefferson, T., Clarke, J. and Roberts, B. (1978) *Policing the Crisis: Mugging, the State, and Law and Order*. London: Macmillan.

Hallsworth, S. (2005) *Street Crime*. Cullompton: Willan.

Hamann, B. (1999) *Hitler's Vienna: A Dictator's Apprenticeship*. Oxford: Oxford University Press.

Hannerz, U. (1970) *Soulside: Inquiries into Ghetto Culture and Community*. New York: Columbia University Press.

Harris, P. (2006) 37 million poor hidden in land of plenty. *The Observer*, 19 February.

Hartigan, J. (1999) *Racial Situations: Class Predicaments of Whiteness in Detroit*. Princeton, NJ: Princeton University Press.

Hartless, J.M., Ditton, J., Nair, G. and Phillips, S. (1995) More sinned against than sinning: A study of young teenagers' experience of crime. *British Journal of Criminology*, 35(1): 114–33.

Hawkins, D.F. (ed.) (1995) *Ethnicity, Race, and Crime: Perspectives across Time and Space*. Albany: State University of New York Press.

Herrnstein, R.J. and Murray, C. (1994) *The Bell Curve: Intelligence and Class Structure in American Life*. New York: Free Press.

Hertz, T. (2005) Rags, riches, and race: The intergenerational economic mobilty of black and white families in the United States. In S. Bowles, H. Gintis and M. Osborne Groves (eds) *Unequal Chances: Family Background and Economic Success*. Oxford: Princeton University Press.

Hesse B., Rai D.K., Bennett, C. and McGilchrist, P. (1992) *Beneath the Surface: Racial Harassment*. Aldershot: Avebury.

Hilberg, R. (1992) *Perpetrators, Victims, Bystanders: The Jewish Catastrophe 1933–1945*. New York: Aaron Asher.

Hiro, D. (1991) *Black British White British: A History of Race Relations in Britain*. London: Grafton.

Hochschild, A. (1998) *King Leopold's Ghost: A Story of Greed, Terror, and Heroism in Colonial Africa*. New York: Marina Books.

Holdaway, S. (1997) Some recent approaches to the study of race in criminological research. *British Journal of Criminology*, 37: 383–400.

Holmes, C. (1988) *John Bull's Island*. Basingstoke: Macmillan.

Home Affairs Committee (1986) *Racial Attacks and Harassment*. London: HMSO.

Home Affairs Committee (1989) *Third Report from the Home Affairs Committee, Session 1986–88: Racial Attacks and Harassment*. London: HMSO.

Home Office (1981) *Racial Attacks*. London: Home Office.

Home Office (1989) *The Response to Racial Attacks and Harassment: Guidance for the Statutory Agencies*. London: Home Office.

Home Office (2000a) *Prison Statistics England and Wales 1999*, Cm. 4805. London: Home Office.

Home Office (2000b) *Statistics on Race and the Criminal Justice System 2000*. London: Home Office.

Home Office (2004) *Race and the Criminal Justice System: An Overview to the Complete Statistics 2002–2003*. London: Home Office.

Home Office (2005) *Statistics on Race and the Criminal Justice System*. London: Home Office.

Home Office (2006) *Statistics on Race and the Criminal Justice System*. London: Home Office.

Home Office Affairs Committee (1982) *Racial Attacks: Second Report from Session 1981–82*. London: HMSO.

Hood, R. (1992) *Race and Sentencing*. Oxford: Clarendon Press.

Hope, T. (2001) Crime victimisation and inequality in risk society. In R. Matthews and J. Pitts (eds) *Crime, Disorder and Community Safety*. London: Routledge.

Hopkins Burke, R. (2005) *An Introduction to Criminological Theory*. Cullompton: Willan Publishing.

Horowitz, I.L. (1997) *Taking Lives: Genocide and State Power*. London: Transaction.

Hudson, B. (ed.) (1996) *Race, Crime and Justice*. Aldershot: Ashgate.

Human Rights Watch/Federation Internationale des Ligues des Droits de l'Homme (1999) *Leave None to Tell the Story: Genocide in Rwanda*. Paris: International Federation of Human Rights.

Husband, C. (1982) The East End racism 1900–1980: Geographical continuities in vigilantist and extreme right-wing political behaviour. *London Journal*, 8(1): 3–26.

Hussain, Y. and Bagguley, P. (2005) Citizenship, ethnicity and identity: British Pakistanis after the 2001 'riots'. *Sociology*, 39(3): 404–25.

Hutton, W. (1995) *The State We're In*. London: Cape.

Jackson, J.L. (2001) *Harlem World: Doing Race and Class in Contemporary Black America*. Chicago: University of Chicago Press.

Jamieson, R. (1998) Towards a criminology of war in Europe. In V. Ruggiero, N. South and I. Taylor (eds) *The New European Criminology: Crime and Social Order in Europe*. London: Routledge.

Jarman, N. (2002) *Overview Analysis of Racist Incidents Recorded in Northern Ireland by the RUC 1996–1999*. Belfast: Office of the First Minister and Deputy First Minister, Research Branch.

Jefferson, T. (1988) Race, crime and policing: Empirical, theoretical and methodological issues. *International Journal of the Sociology of Law*, 16: 521–39.

Jenkinson, J. (1993) The 1919 riots. In P. Panayi (ed.) *Racial Violence in Britain 1840–1950*. Leicester: Leicester University Press.

Johnson, E. (1999) *The Nazi Terror: Gestapo, Jews & Ordinary Germans*. London: John Murray.

Johnson, E. and Reuband, K.-H. (2005) *What We Knew: Terror, Mass Murder and Everyday Life in Nazi Germany*. London: John Murray.

Johnston, L. (2000) *Policing Britain: Risk, Security and Governance*. London: Longman.

Johnston, L., MacDonald, R., Mason, P., Ridley, L. and Webster, C. (2000) *Snakes & Ladders: Young People, Transitions and Social Exclusion*. Bristol: Policy Press.

Johnston, R., Poulsen, M. and Forrest, M. (2005) On the measurement and meaning of residential segregation: A response to Simpson. *Urban Studies*, 42(7): 1221–7.

Jones, S. (1980) *Social Darwinism and English Thought*. Brighton: Harvester Press.

Jones, S. (2000) *The Language of the Genes*, revised edition. London: Flamingo.

Junger, M. (1989) Discrepancies between police and self-report data for Dutch racial minorities. *British Journal of Criminology*, 30(3): 273–84.

Junger, M. (1990) Studying ethnic minorities in relation to crime and police discrimination: Answer to Bowling. *British Journal of Criminology*, 30(4): 493–502.

Junger-Tas, J. (1994) The International Self-Report Delinquency Study: some methodological and theoretical issues. In J. Junger-Tas, G.-J. Terlouw and M.W. Klein (eds) *Delinquent Behavior among Young People in the Western World: First Results of the International Self-Report Delinquency Study*. Amsterdam: Kugler.

Junger-Tas, J., Terlouw, G.-J. and Klein, M.W. (eds) (1994) *Delinquent Behavior among Young People in the Western World: First Results of the International Self-Report Delinquency Study*. Amsterdam: Kugler.

Kalra, V.S. (2000) *From Textile Mills to Taxi Ranks: Experiences of Migration, Labour and Social Change*. Aldershot: Ashgate.

Kalra, V.S. (2003) Police lore and community disorder: Diversity in the criminal justice system. In D. Mason (ed.) *Explaining Ethnic Differences: Changing Patterns of Disadvantage in Britain*. Bristol: Policy Press.

Katz, J. (1988) *Seductions of Crime: Moral and Sensual Attractions in Doing Evil*. New York: Basic Books.

Keane, F. (1995) *Season of Blood: A Rwandan Journey*. London: Penguin.

Kefalas, M. (2003) *Working-Class Heroes: Protecting Home, Community, and Nation in a Chicago Neighborhood*. Berkeley: University of California Press.

Keil, C. (1966) *Urban Blues*. Chicago: University of Chicago Press.

Keith, M. (1993) *Race, Riots and Policing: Lore and Disorder in a Multi-racist Society*. London: UCL Press.

Kershaw, C., Budd, T., Kinshott, G., Mattinson, J., Mayhew, P. and Myhill, A. (2000) *The 2000 British Crime Survey*. London: Home Office.

Kershaw, I. (1998) *Hitler: 1989–1936 Hubris*. London: Allen Lane.

Kershaw, I. (2000a) *Hitler: 1936–1945 Nemesis*. London: Allen Lane.

Kershaw, I. (2000b) *The Nazi Dictatorship: Problems and Perspectives of Interpretation*, 4th edition. London: Arnold.

King, D. (1999) *In the Name of Liberalism*. Oxford: Oxford University Press.

Kleck, G. (1981) Racial discrimination in criminal sentencing: A critical evaluation of the evidence with additional evidence on the death penalty. *American Sociological Review*, 46: 783–805.

Krisberg, B. (2005) *Juvenile Justice: Redeeming Our Children*. London: Sage.

Kuhl, S. (1994) *The Nazi Connection: Eugenics, American Racism, and German National Socialism*. New York: Oxford University Press.

Kundnani, A. (2001) From Oldham to Bradford: The violence of the violated. *Race and Class*, 43(2): 105–10.

Laub, J. and Sampson, R. (2003) *Shared Beginnings, Divergent Lives: Delinquent Boys to Age 70*. Cambridge, MA: Harvard University Press.

Layton-Henry, Z. (1984) *The Politics of Race in Britain*. London: Allen & Unwin.

Lea, J. (1986) Police racism: Some theories and their policy implications. In R. Matthews and J. Young (eds) *Confronting Crime*. London: Sage.

Lea, J. (2000) The Macpherson report and the question of institutional racism. *Howard Journal of Criminal Justice*, 39(3): 219–33.

Lea, J. (2002) *Crime & Modernity*. London: Sage.

Lea, J. and Young, J. (1993) *What Is to Be Done about Law and Order?*, revised edition. London: Pluto.

Lebor, A. (2006) '*Complicity with Evil': The United Nations in The Age of Modern Genocide*. London: Yale University Press.

Lewis, S., Raynor, P., Smith, D. and Wardak, A. (2006) *Race and Probation*. Cullompton: Willan Publishing.

Lewontin, R. (2000) *It Ain't Necessarily So: The Dream of The Human Genome and Other Illusions*. London: Granta Books.

Lewy, G. (2000) *The Nazi Persecution of the Gypsies*. Oxford: Oxford University Press.

Liebow, E. (1967) *Tally's Corner: A Study of Negro Street Corner Men*. Boston: Little, Brown.

Linkon, S.L. and Russo, J. (2002) *Steeltown U.S.A.: Work and Memory in Youngstown*. Lawrence: University Press of Kansas.

Lizotte, A.J., Thornbury, T.P., Krohn, M.D., Chard-Wierschem, D.J. and McDowall, D. (1994) Neighborhood context and delinquency. In E. Weitkamp and H. Kerner (eds) *Cross-National Longitudinal Research on Human Development and Human Behaviour*. Dordrecht: Kluwer.

Loader, I. (1996) *Youth, Policing and Democracy*. London: Macmillan.

Lombroso, C. (2006) *Criminal Man*. Durham, NC: Duke University Press. First published in 1876.

Lombroso, C. and Ferrero, G. (2004) *Criminal Woman, the Prostitute, and the Normal Woman*. Durham, NC: Duke University Press. First published in 1893.

Low, S. (2004) *Behind the Gates: Life, Security, and the Pursuit of Happiness in Fortress America*. London: Routledge.

Lupton, R. (2003) 'Neighbourhood effects': Can we measure them and does it matter?' Centre for Analysis of Social Exclusion Paper 73. London: London School of Economics.

Mac an Ghaill, M. (1988) *Young, Gifted and Black: Student–Teacher Relations in the Schooling of Black Youth*. Milton Keynes: Open University Press.

MacDonald, R. and Marsh, J. (2005) *Disconnected Youth? Growing Up in Poor Britain*. Basingstoke: Palgrave.

Macey, M. (2002) Interpreting Islam: Young Muslim men's involvement in criminal activity in Bradford. In B. Spalek (ed.) *Islam, Crime and Criminal Justice*. Cullompton: Willan Publishing.

MacLeod, J. (1995) *Ain't No Makin' It: Aspirations and Attainment in a Low-Income Neighborhood*. Boulder, CO: Westview Press.

Macpherson, W. (1999) *The Stephen Lawrence Inquiry: Report of an Inquiry by Sir William Macpherson of Cluny*, Cm. 4262. London: HMSO.

Marshall, I.E. (ed.) (1997) *Minorities, Migrants, and Crime: Diversity and Similarity across Europe and the United States*. London: Sage.

Mason, D. (ed.) *Explaining Ethnic Differences: Changing Patterns of Disadvantage in Britain*. Bristol: Policy Press.

Massey, D.S. and Denton, N.A. (1993) *American Apartheid: Segregation and the Making of the Underclass*. Cambridge, MA: Harvard University Press.

Mawby, B.I. and Batta, I.D. (1980) *Asians and Crime: The Bradford Experience*. London: Scope Communications.

Maynard, W. and Read, T. (1997) *Policing Racially Motivated Incidents*, Crime Reduction and Prevention Series Paper 84, Police Research Group. London: Home Office.

McAra, L. and McVie, S. (2005) The usual suspects? Street-life, young people and the police. *Criminal Justice*, 5(1): 5–36.

McGahey, R.M. (1986) Economic conditions, neighborhood organization, and urban crime. *Crime and Justice*, 8: 231–70.

McGhee, D. (2003) Moving to 'our' common ground: a critical examination of community discourse in twenty first century Britain. *Sociological Review*, 51(3): 376–404.

McKnight, A., Glennerster, H. and Lupton, R. (2005) Education, education, education . . .: an assessment of Labour's success in tackling education inequalities. In J. Hills and K. Stewart (eds) *A More Equal Society? New Labour, Poverty, Inequality and Exclusion*. Bristol: Policy Press.

Melvern, L. (2000) *A People Betrayed: The Role of the West in Rwanda's Genocide*. London: Zed Books.

Messerschmidt, J.W. (1993) *Masculinities and Crime: Critique and Reconceptualization of Theory*. Lanham, MD: Rowman & Littlefield.

Messerschmidt, J.W. (1999) Making bodies matter: Adolescent masculinities, the body, and varieties of violence. *Theoretical Criminology*, 3(2): 197–220.

Mhlanga, B. (1997) *The Colour of English Justice: A Multivariate Analysis*. Aldershot: Avebury.

Miles, R. (1993) *Racism after 'Race Relations'*. London: Routledge.

Miles, R. and Brown, M. (2003) *Racism*, 2nd edition. London: Routledge.

Miller, J.G. (1997) *Search and Destroy: African-American Males in the Criminal Justice System*. Cambridge: Cambridge University Press.

Mizen, P. (2004) *The Changing State of Youth*. Basingstoke: Palgrave.

Modood, T. (2003) Ethnic differentials in educational performance. In D. Mason (ed.) *Explaining Ethnic Differences: Changing Patterns of Disadvantage in Britain*. Bristol: Policy Press.

MoneyWeek (2003) How the rich are getting richer: Does inequality matter? *Money Week*, December.

Montagu, A. (1997) *Man's Most Dangerous Myth: The Fallacy of Race*, 6th edition. London: AltaMira Press.

Morrison, W. (1995) *Theoretical Criminology: From Modernity to Post-modernism*. London: Cavendish.

Morrison, W. (2006) *Criminology, Civilisation and the New World Order*. Abingdon: Routledge/Cavendish.

Muncie, J. (2004) *Youth & Crime*, 2nd edition. London: Sage.

Murray, C. (1984) *Losing Ground*. New York: Basic Books.

Neuffer, E. (2000) *The Key To My Neighbour's House: Seeking Justice in Bosnia and Rwanda*. London: Bloomsbury.

Newburn, T. and Sparks, R. (eds) (2004) *Criminal Justice and Political Cultures: National and International Dimensions of Crime Control*. Cullompton: Willan Publishing.

Newman, K.S. (1999) *No Shame in My Game: The Working Poor in the Inner City*. New York: Vintage Books.

Newman, K. (2002) No shame: The view from the Left Bank. *American Journal of Sociology*, 107(6): 1577–99.

Nicholas, S. and Walker, A. (eds) (2004) *Crime in England and Wales 2002/2003: Supplementary Volume 2: Crime, Disorder and the Criminal Justice System – Public Attitudes and Perceptions*, Home Office Statistical Bulletin 2/04. London: Home Office.

Nicholas, S., Povey, D., Walker, A. and Kershaw, C. (2005) *Crime in England and Wales 2004/2005*. London: Home Office.

Nightingale, C. (1993) *On the Edge: A History of Poor Black Children and Their American Dreams*. New York: Basic Books.

Nikolic-Ristanovic, V. (2000) *Women, Violence and War*. Budapest: Central European University Press.

Norris, C., Fielding, N., Kemp, C. and Fielding, J. (1992) Black and blue: An analysis of the influence of race on being stopped by the police. *British Journal of Criminology*, 43(2): 207–24.

Office for National Statistics (2003) *Census 2001: National Report for England and Wales* (Table S101, p. 121). London: The Stationery Office. http://www.statistics.gov.uk/downloads/census2001/National_report_EW_Part1_Section2.pdf.

Office for National Statistics (2004) *Social Trends*, No. 34. London: The Stationery Office.

Olson, S. (2002) *Mapping Human History: Discovering the Past through Our Genes*. London: Bloomsbury.

Ouseley, H. (2001) *Community Pride Not Prejudice: Making Diversity Work in Bradford*. Bradford: Bradford Vision.

Overy, R. (2004) *The Dictators: Hitler's Germany, Stalin's Russia*. London: Allen Lane.

Owen, D. (2003) The demographic characteristics of people from minority ethnic groups in Britain. In D. Mason (ed.) *Explaining Ethnic Differences: Changing Patterns of Disadvantage in Britain*. Bristol: Policy Press.

Pain, R. (2003) Youth, age and the representation of fear. *Capital & Class*, 80: 151–71.

Panayi, P. (ed.) (1993) *Racial Violence in Britain 1840–1950*. Leicester: Leicester University Press.

Pantazis, C. (2006) Crime, 'disorder', insecurity and social exclusion. In C. Pantazis, D. Gordon and R. Levitas (eds) *Poverty and Social Exclusion in Britain: The Millennium Survey*. Bristol: Policy Press.

Pape, R.A. (2006) *Dying to Win: Why Suicide Terrorists Do It*. London: Gibson Square.

Parsons, C., Godfrey, R., Annan, G., Cornwall, J., Dussart, M., Hepburn, S., Howlett, K. and Wennerstrom, V. (2004) *Minority Ethnic Exclusions and the Race Relations (Amendment) Act 2000*. London: Department for Education and Skills.

Patterson, O. (1997) *The Ordeal of Integration: Progress and Resentment in America's 'Racial' Crisis*. Washington, DC: Civitas/Counterpoint.

Patterson, O. (1998) *Rituals of Blood: Consequences of Slavery in Two American Centuries*. New York: Basic Civitas.

Pawson, R. (1989) *A Measure for Measures*. London: Routledge.

Pearce, N. and Hillman, J. (1998) *Wasted Youth: Raising Achievement and Tackling Social Exclusion*. London: IPPR.

Pearson, G. (1976) 'Paki-Bashing' in a North-East Lancashire cotton town: a case study and its history. In G. Mungham and G. Pearson (eds) *Working Class Youth Culture*. London: Routledge.

Percy, A. (1998) *Ethnicity and Victimisation: Findings from the 1996 British Crime Survey*, Home Office Statistical Bulletin 6/98. London: Home Office.

Perri 6 (1997) *Escaping Poverty: From Safety Nets to Networks of Opportunity*. London: Demos.

Petersilia, J. (1985) Racial disparities in the criminal justice system: A summary. *Crime and Delinquency*, 31(1): 15–34.

Pfeifer, M.J. (2004) *Rough Justice: Lynching and American Society 1874–1947*. Chicago: University of Illinois Press.

Phillips, C. and Bowling, B. (2002) Racism, ethnicity, crime and criminal justice. In M. Maguire, R. Morgan and R. Reiner (eds) *The Oxford Handbook of Criminology*, 3rd edition. Oxford: Clarendon Press.

Phillips, C. and Bowling, B. (2003) Racism, ethnicity and criminology: Developing minority perspectives. *British Journal of Criminology*, 43(2): 269–90.

Phillips, C. and Brown, D. (1998) *Entry into the Criminal Justice System: A Survey of Police Arrests and Their Outcomes*, Home Office Research Study 185. London: Home Office.

Phillips, D. (1998) Black minority ethnic concentration, segregation and dispersal in Britain. *Urban Studies*, 35(10): 1681–1702.

Phillips, M. (1998) *All Must Have Prizes*. London: Warner.

Phillips, M. and Phillips, T. (1998) *Windrush: The Irresistible Rise of Multi-racial Britain*. London: HarperCollins.

Pilkington, A. (2003) *Racial Disadvantage and Ethnic Diversity in Britain*. Basingstoke: Palgrave Macmillan.

Piquero, A., Farrington, D. and Blumstein, A. (2003) The criminal career paradigm: Background and recent developments. In M. Tonry (ed.) *Crime and Justice: A Review of Research*, Vol. 30. Chicago: Chicago University Press.

Pitts, J. (2001) *The New Politics of Youth Crime: Discipline or Solidarity?* Lyme Regis: Russell House Publishing.

Polman, L. (2004) *We Did Nothing: Why the Truth Doesn't Always Come Out When the UN Goes In*. London: Penguin.

Power, A. and Tunstall, T. (1995) *Swimming against the Tide: Polarisation or Progress?* York: Joseph Rowntree Foundation.

Poynting, S., Noble, G., Tabar, P. and Collins, J. (2004) *Bin Laden in the Suburbs: Criminalising the Arab Other*. Sydney: Sydney Institute of Criminology.

Presdee, M. (2000) *Cultural Criminology and the Carnival of Crime*. London: Routledge.

Proctor, R.M. (1988) *Racial Hygiene: Medicine under the Nazis*. Cambridge, MA: Harvard University Press.

Prunier, G. (1997) *The Rwandan Crisis: History of a Genocide*, revised edition. London: Hurst.

Rafter, N.H. (1997) *Creating Born Criminals*. Urbana: University of Illinois Press.

Rainwater, L. (1970) *Behind Ghetto Walls: Black Families in a Federal Slum*. Chicago: Aldine Atherton.

Ramamurthy, A. (2006) The politics of Britain's Asian youth movements. *Race & Class*, 48(2): 38–60.

Ratcliffe, P. (1997) 'Race', ethnicity and housing differentials in Britain. In V. Karn (ed.) *Employment, Education and Housing among the Minority Ethnic Populations of Britain*. London: HMSO.

Ray, L. and Smith, D. (2004) Racist offending, policing and community conflict. *Sociology*, 38(4): 681–99.

Ray, L., Smith, D. and Wastell, L. (2003) Understanding racist violence. In B. Stanko (ed.) *The Meanings of Violence*. London: Routledge.

Ray, L., Smith, D. and Wastell, L. (2004) Shame, rage and racist violence. *British Journal of Criminology*, 44(3): 350–68.

Reader, J. (1998) *Africa: A Biography of the Continent*. London: Penguin.

Rees, L. (2005) *Auschwitz: The Nazis & The 'Final Solution'*. London: BBC Books.

Reiman, J. (1990) *The Rich Get Richer and the Poor Get Prison*. London: Macmillan.

Reiner, R. (1985) *The Politics of the Police*. Brighton: Wheatsheaf.

Reiner, R. (1993) Race, crime and justice: Models of interpretation. In L. Gelsthorpe (ed.) *Minority Ethnic Groups in the Criminal Justice System*. Cambridge: Cambridge Institute of Criminology.

Reiner, R. (2000) *The Politics of the Police*, 3rd edition. Oxford: Oxford University Press.

Rex, J. and Mason, D. (eds) (1986) *Theories of Race and Ethnic Relations*. Cambridge: Cambridge University Press.

Richardson, L. (2006) *What Terrorists Want: Understanding the Terrorist Threat*. London: John Murray.

Ritchie, D. (2001) *Oldham Independent Review: Panel Report*. Oldham: Oldham Metropolitan Borough Council and Greater Manchester Police.

Robinson, D. (2005) The search for community cohesion: Key themes and dominant concepts of the public policy agenda. *Urban Studies*, 42(8): 1411–27.

Rose, S., Lewontin, R.C. and Kamin, L.J. (1984) *Not in Our Genes: Biology, Ideology and Human Nature*. London: Penguin.

Roseman, M. (2002) *The Villa, the Lake, the Meeting: Wansee and the Final Solution*. London: Allen Lane.

Rowe, M. (1998) *The Racialisation of Disorder in Twentieth Century Britain*. Aldershot: Ashgate.

Rowe, M. (2004) *Policing, Race and Racism*. Cullompton: Willan.

Rushton, J.P. (1997) *Race, Evolution, and Behavior: A Life History Perspective*. New Brunswick, NJ: Transaction Publishers.

Russell, K.K. (1998) *The Color of Crime: Racial Hoaxes, White Fear, Black Protectionism, Police Harassment, and Other Macroaggressions*. New York: New York University Press.

St Clair, W. (2006) *The Grand Slave Emporium: Cape Coast Castle and the British Slave Trade*. London: Profile.

Sampson, A., and Phillips, C. (1992) *Multiple Victimisation: Racial Attacks on an East London Estate*, Police Research Group, Crime Prevention Unit Series, Paper no. 36. London: Home Office.

Sampson, R.J. and Laub, J.H. (1993) *Crime in the Making: Pathways and Turning Points through Life*. Cambridge, MA: Harvard University Press.

Sampson, R.J., Raudenbush, S.W. and Earls, F. (1997) Neighbourhoods and violent crime: A multi-level study of collective efficacy. *Science*, 277, 15 August.

Schaffer, R.T. (2006) *Racial and Ethnic Groups*, 10th edition. Upper Saddle River, NJ: Pearson/Prentice Hall.

Sewell, T. (1997) *Black Masculinities and Schooling: How Black Boys Survive Modern Schooling*. Stoke-on-Trent: Trentham Books.

Sharp, C. and Budd, T. (2005) *Minority Ethnic Groups and Crime: Findings from the Offending, Crime and Justice Survey 2003*, Online Report 33/05. London: Home Office.

Shute, S., Hood, R. and Seemungal, F. (2005) *A Fair Hearing? Ethnic Minorities in the Criminal Courts*. Cullompton: Willan Publishing.

Sibbitt, R. (1997) *The Perpetrators of Racial Harassment and Violence*, Research Study 176. London: Home Office.

Sigelman, L. and Welch, S. (1991) *Black Americans' Views of Racial Inequality: The Dream Deferred*. New York: Cambridge University Press.

Sigelman, L., Bledsoe, T., Welch, S. and Combs, M. (1996) Making contact? Black–white social interaction in an urban setting. *American Journal of Sociology*, 101(5): 1306–32.

Simms, B. (2001) *Unfinest Hour: Britain and The Destruction of Bosnia*. London: Allen Lane.

Simpson, L. (2004) Statistics of racial segregation: Measures, evidence and policy. *Urban Studies*, 41(3): 661–81.

Simpson, R. (2005) On the measurement and meaning of residential segregation: A reply to Johnston, Poulsen and Forrest. *Urban Studies*, 42(7): 1229–30.

Sims, L. and Myhill, A. (2001) *Policing and the Public: Findings from the 2000 British Crime Survey*, Home Office Research Findings No. 136. London: Home Office.

Smith, D.J. (1994) Race, crime, and criminal justice. In M. Maguire, R. Morgan and R. Reiner (eds) *The Oxford Handbook of Criminology*. Oxford: Oxford University Press.

Smith, D.J. (1997) Ethnic origins, crime, and criminal justice. In M. Maguire, R. Morgan and R. Reiner (eds) *The Oxford Handbook of Criminology*, 2nd edition. Oxford: Clarendon Press.

Smith, D.J. (2005) Ethnic differences in intergenerational crime patterns. In M. Tonry (ed.) *Crime and Justice: A Review of Research*, Vol. 32. Chicago: University of Chicago Press.

Smith, D.J. and McVie, S. (2003) Theory and method in the Edinburgh Study of Youth Transitions and Crime. *British Journal of Criminology*, 43: 169–95.

Smith, H.O.J. (2003) *The Nature of Personal Robbery*, Home Office Research Study 254. London: Home Office.

Smith, P. and Natalier, K. (2005) *Understanding Criminal Justice: Sociological Perspectives*. London: Sage.

Smith, T. (1999) *The Emerging 21st Century American Family*, General Social Survey Change Report No. 42, National Opinion Research Centre. Chicago: University of Chicago.

Social Exclusion Unit (1998) *Truancy and Social Exclusion*, Cm. 3947. London: SEU/The Stationery Office.

Social Exclusion Unit (1999) *Bridging the Gap*, Cm 4405. London: SEU/The Stationery Office.

Solomos, J. (2003) *Race and Racism in Britain*, 3rd edition. Basingstoke: Palgrave Macmillan.

Solomos, J. and Back, L. (1996) *Racism and Society*. London: Macmillan.

Spalek, B. (ed.) (2002) *Islam, Crime and Criminal Justice*. Cullompton: Willan Publishing.

Spohn, C. (2000) Thirty years of sentencing reform: The quest for a racially neutral sentencing process. *Criminal Justice*, 3: 427–501.

Steinbacher, S. (2005) *Auschwitz: A History*. London: Penguin.

Stenson, K. (1996) *Young People, Race and Crime*, Occasional Paper 1, Social Policy Research Group. High Wycombe: Buckinghamshire College.

Stephenson, M. (2007) *Young People and Offending: Education, Youth Justice and Social Inclusion*. Cullompton: Willan.

Stevenson, B. (2004) Close to death: Reflections on race and capital punishment in America. In H. Bedau and P. Cassell *Debating the Death Penalty: Should America Have Capital Punishment?* Oxford: Oxford University Press.

Stone, V., Cotton, D. and Thomas, A. (2000) *Mapping Troubled Lives: Young People Not in Education, Employment or Training*. London: Department for Education and Employment.

Sugrue, T.J. (2005) *The Origins of the Urban Crisis: Race and Inequality in Postwar Detroit*. Princeton, NJ: Princeton University Press.

Suttles, G. (1968) *The Social Order of the Slum: Ethnicity and Territory in the Inner City*. Chicago: University of Chicago Press.

Suttles, G. (1972) *The Social Construction of Communities*. Chicago: University of Chicago Press.

Taylor, G. (2005) *Buying Whiteness: Race, Culture, and Identity from Columbus To Hip-Hop*. Basingstoke: Palgrave.

Taylor, I., Evans, K. and Fraser, P. (1996) *A Tale of Two Cities: Global Change, Local Feeling and Everyday Life in the North of England. A Study of Manchester and Sheffield*. London: Routledge.

Thomas, H. (1997) *The Slave Trade: The History of the Atlantic Slave Trade 1440–1870*. London: Phoenix.

Thurston, L.L. (1947) *Multiple-Factor Analysis: A Development and Expansion of 'The Vectors of the Mind'*. Chicago: University of Chicago Press.

Tolnay, S.E. and Beck, E.M. (1995) *A Festival of Violence: An Analysis of Southern Lynchings, 1882–1930*. Chicago: University of Illinois Press.

Tonry, M (ed.) (1997) *Ethnicity, Crime and Immigration: Comparative and Cross-national Perspectives*. Chicago: University of Chicago Press.

Tonry, M. (1995) *Malign Neglect: Race, Crime, and Punishment in America*. Oxford: Oxford University Press.

Vandiver, M. (2006) *Lethal Punishment: Lynchings and Legal Executions in the South*. New Brunswick, NJ: Rutgers University Press.

Vold, G.B., Bernard, T.J. and Snipes, J.B. (2002) *Theoretical Criminology*, 5th edition. Oxford: Oxford University Press.

Wacquant, L. (2000) The new 'peculiar institution': On the prison as surrogate ghetto. *Theoretical Criminology*, 4(3): 377–89.

Wacquant, L. (2002) Scrutinizing the street: Poverty, morality, and the pitfalls of urban ethnography. *American Journal of Sociology*, 107(6): 1468–1532.

Wacquant, L. (2005) The great penal leap backward: Incarceration in America from Nixon to Clinton. In J. Pratt, D. Brown, M. Brown, S. Hallsworth and W. Morrison (eds) *The New Punitiveness: Trends, Theories, Perpectives*. Cullompton: Willan.

Waddington, P.A.J. (1999) *Policing Citizens*. London: UCL Press.

Waddington, P.A. and Braddock, Q. (1991) Guardians or bullies? Perceptions of the police among adolescent black, white and asian boys. *Policing and Society*, 2(1): 31–43.

Waddington, P.A.J., Stenson, K. and Don, D. (2004) In proportion: Race, and police stop and search. *British Journal of Criminology*, 44: 1–26.

Walker, A., Kershaw, C. and Nicholas, S. (2006) *Crime in England and Wales 2005/6*. London: Home Office.

Walker, M.A. (1988) The court disposal of young males, by race, in London in 1983. *British Journal of Criminology*, 28(4): 441–60.

Walker, M.A. (1989) The court disposal and remands of white, Afro-Caribbean, and Asian men (London, 1983). *British Journal of Criminology*, 29(4): 353–67.

Walker, S., Spohn, C. and DeLone, M. (2004) *The Color of Justice: Race, Ethnicity. and Crime in America*, 3rd edition. Belmont, CA: Wadsworth.

Wallman, S. (1982) *Living in South London: Perspectives on Battersea 1871–1981*. London: Gower.

Wallman, S. (1986) Ethnicity and the boundary process in context. In J. Rex and D. Mason (eds) *Theories of Race and Ethnic Relations*. Cambridge: Cambridge University Press.

Wardak, A. (2000) *Social Control and Deviance: A South Asian Community in Scotland*. Aldershot: Ashgate.

Watt, P. (2006) Respectability, roughness and 'race': Neighbourhood place images and the making of working-class social distinctions in London. *International Journal of Urban and Regional Research*, 30(4): 776–97.

Watt, P. and Stenson, K. (1998) The street: 'It's a bit dodgy around there': Safety, danger, ethnicity and young people's use of public space. In T. Skelton and

G. Valentine (eds) *Cool Places: Geographies of Youth Cultures*. London: Routledge.

Webster, C. (1994) Racial harassment, space and localism. *Criminal Justice Matters*, No. 16, Summer.

Webster, C. (1995) *Youth Crime, Victimisation and Racial Harassment: The Keighley Crime Survey*. Bradford: Centre for Research in Applied Community Studies, Bradford & Ilkley Community College Corporation.

Webster, C. (1996) Local heroes: Violent racism, spacism and localism among white and Asian young people. *Youth & Policy*, 53: 15–27. Reprinted in N. South (ed.) (1999) *Youth Crime, Deviance and Delinquency*. Aldershot: Ashgate.

Webster, C. (1997) The construction of British 'Asian' criminality. *International Journal of the Sociology of Law*, 25: 65–86.

Webster, C. (2001) Representing race and crime. *Criminal Justice Matters*, 43: 16–17.

Webster, C. (2003) Race, space and fear: Imagined geographies of racism, crime, violence and disorder in Northern England. *Capital & Class*, 80: 95–122.

Webster, C. (2004) Policing British Asian communities. In R. Hopkins Burke (ed.) *Hard Cop/Soft Cop: Dilemmas and Debates in Contemporary Policing*. Cullompton: Willan Publishing.

Webster, C. (2006) Race, youth crime and justice. In B. Goldson and J. Muncie (eds) *Youth Crime and Justice*, London: Sage.

Webster, C., Simpson, D., MacDonald, R., Abbas, A., Cieslik, M. and Shildrick, T. (2004) *Poor Transitions: Young Adults and Social Exclusion*. Bristol: Policy Press.

Weindling, P. (1989) *Health, Race and German Politics between National Unification and Nazism 1870–1945*. Cambridge: Cambridge University Press.

Welch, S., Sigelman, T., Bledsoe, M. and Combs, M. (2001) *Race and Place: Race Relations in an American City*. Cambridge: Cambridge University Press.

Wetzell, R.F. (2000) *Inventing the Criminal: A History of German Criminology, 1888–1945*. Chapel Hill: University of North Carolina Press.

Whitfield, J. (2004) *Unhappy Dialogue: The Metropolitan Police and Black Londoners in Post-war Britain*. Cullompton: Willan.

Wikstrom, T. and Loeber, R. (1998) Individual risk factors, neighbourhood SES and juvenile offending. In M. Tonry (ed.) *The Handbook of Crime and Punishment*. New York: Oxford University Press.

Wilbanks, W. (1987) *The Myth of a Racist Criminal Justice System*. Monterey, CA: Brooks/Cole.

Wilson, J.Q. and Herrnstein, R.J. (1985) *Crime and Human Nature*. New York: Simon and Schuster.

Wilson, W.J. (1987) *The Truly Disadvantaged: The Inner City, the Underclass, and Public Policy*. Chicago: University of Chicago Press.

Wilson, W.J. (1996) *When Work Disappears: The World of the New Urban Poor*. New York: Knopf.

Wood, M. (2004) *Perceptions and Experience of Antisocial Behaviour: Findings from the 2003/2004 British Crime Survey*. London: Home Office.

Worley, C. (2005) 'It's not about race, it's about the community': New Labour and 'community Cohesion'. *Critical Social Policy*, 25(4): 483–96.

Young, J. (1999) *The Exclusive Society: Social Exclusion, Crime and Difference in Late Modernity*. London: Sage.

Young, J. (2002) Crossing the borderline: Globalisation and social exclusion: The sociology of vindictiveness and the criminology of transgression. www.malcolmread.co.uk/JockYoung/crossing.htm, accessed 25 February 2005.

Zimring, F.E. (2003) *The Contradictions of American Capital Punishment.* Oxford: Oxford University Press.

Index